Writing a Research Paper in Political Science

A Practical Guide to Inquiry, Structure, and Methods

Second Edition

Writing a Research Paper in Political Science

A Practical Guide to Inquiry, Structure, and Methods

Second Edition

LISA A. BAGLIONE

Saint Joseph's University

Los Angeles | London | New Delhi
Singapore | Washington DC

Los Angeles | London | New Delhi
Singapore | Washington DC

FOR INFORMATION:

CQ Press
An Imprint of SAGE Publications, Inc.
2455 Teller Road
Thousand Oaks, California 91320
E-mail: order@sagepub.com

SAGE Publications Ltd.
1 Oliver's Yard
55 City Road
London, EC1Y 1SP
United Kingdom

SAGE Publications India Pvt. Ltd.
B 1/I 1 Mohan Cooperative Industrial Area
Mathura Road, New Delhi 110 044
India

SAGE Publications Asia-Pacific Pte. Ltd.
33 Pekin Street #02-01
Far East Square
Singapore 048763

Acquisitions Editor: Charisse Kiino
Production Editor: Sarah Fell
Copy Editor: Barbara Corrigan
Typesetter: C&M Digitals (P) Ltd.
Cover Designer: Paula Goldstein, Blue Bungalow Design
Marketing Manager: Chris O'Brien

Library of Congress Cataloging-in-Publication Data

Baglione, Lisa A.

Writing a research paper in political science: a practical guide to inquiry, structure, and methods/ Lisa A. Baglione. — 2nd ed.

p. cm.
Includes bibliographical references and index.

ISBN 978-1-60871-991-4 (pbk.: alk. paper)

1. Political science—Authorship. 2. Political science—Research. I. Title.

JA86.B24 2011
808'.06632—dc23   2011025074

This book is printed on acid-free paper.

12 13 14 15 10 9 8 7 6 5 4 3

About the Author

Dr. Lisa A. Baglione is professor and chair of the political science department at Saint Joseph's University. Her major fields of study are international relations and comparative politics. Dr. Baglione has published works exploring postsettlement peace building; the arms control decision-making process in the United States, the Soviet Union, and Russia; and the research paper–writing process and has coauthored articles on the transformation of the Russian polity and economy in the early postcommunist period. Currently, she is researching conflict transformation in the twenty-first century. At Saint Joseph's, Dr. Baglione teaches a course called Introduction to Political Science Research, in which she developed the ideas, advice, and techniques offered in this work.

To Steve
who makes everything better

Contents

List of Tables and Figures

Preface

The purpose of this book is to fill a major void in the literature on research and writing in political science. While there are numerous high-quality texts on research methods (and far more general social science methodology books) as well as a number of excellent writing style guides, when I wrote the first edition, there were no works that were explicitly designed to help students write a research paper, from start to finish. In filling this gap, this book seeks to accomplish some of what both of the other kinds of texts do—provide students with an understanding of and appreciation for the logic of inquiry and social science methodology and further develop written communication skills—but it also does more. Its aims are to show students what a research paper contains and how to write one well. To achieve these goals, this book has to teach research, methodological, logical, analytic, and writing skills. Perhaps no other texts currently do this because accomplishing these tasks is seemingly so difficult. Or perhaps the absence of similar books reflects the faculty's deep internalization of the norms and conventions of research paper writing.[1] Political scientists know them and have known them for so long that the process almost seems natural, one innate to everyone. But as all of us who grade student research papers bemoan, a wide proportion of our students clearly lacks the skill set required to write an excellent one.

If someone had told me when I started teaching that I would be writing this book, I would have been incredulous. Interestingly, my first significant teaching job had me mentoring about ten students a semester who were writing public policy theses at Cornell University's Washington Center. That experience was invaluable for my development as a political scientist and as a teacher. I am sure that many of the ideas that are central to this book were planted by Jack Moran and Steve Jackson, then the two intellectual forces behind the Cornell-in-Washington program. Jack originally developed an approach to teaching research methods that broke the process down and focused on writing each piece of the paper. Thus, Cornell students wrote a literature review, developed a model and argument, designed their research project, and then performed their data analysis. When I was at the Cornell Center, Steve was teaching the course in this same way. Obviously, I have taken this idea but developed it further. In addition to arriving at my own approaches to explaining these sections of a research paper, I have added detailed discussions about arriving at a question, writing an introduction, coming up with good headings and titles, presenting an effective conclusion, and editing and revising.

My interest in and desire to pursue this project has evolved as my academic career has. In many ways, it has developed in response to the huge student need for help in improving writing and research skills. I have learned that students who can write good, even excellent, essays are at a loss when they need to complete a major research paper. I shouldn't have been surprised, because this kind of writing is by no means natural and is not something that is taught in secondary school or even at the college level. Thus, my own experience has made me realize that a book that teaches how to write a research paper is vitally necessary for college students.

In addition, I have been teaching a course on research paper writing and have been encouraged by colleagues to put my ideas forth in book form. My hesitation to pursue such a project stems from my recognition that what I have to say is not news to any professional political scientist. It is common sense for someone with a PhD. But I owe an enormous debt of gratitude to Francis Graham Lee, especially, for convincing me that while these basic ideas are not necessarily groundbreaking, no one has put them forward in book form in this way, and no one has found a way to summarize and simplify the elements of the research paper as I have. Graham and I have taught a course on basic methodology and writing skills in one form or another for the past ten years at Saint Joseph's University. He has been a wonderful sounding board for my ideas, and with his help, I have pursued this project. Moreover, I know that I have included many of his ideas here (the introduction as a contract, the introduction as a first impression, and the importance of feeling proud of one's final paper, to name a few).

The first edition benefitted greatly from the advice and comments of Scott Robinson and Robert Ostergard, and I'd like to give special thanks to Michael Kanner. The efforts of these three reviewers certainly improved the final text, as did my interactions with Susan Liebell and Mary Frances Malone. Susan spent hours talking to me about this project, and then she carefully read and commented on the draft. My former student, Mary Frances Malone of the University of New Hampshire, gave me excellent advice on how to communicate and explain more effectively the elements of the research design and data analysis. I also want to thank George Dowdall, Kim Logio, and Deborah Lurie, all from Saint Joseph's University, for reminding me of some techniques of data analysis that I had long forgotten.

The second edition would not have been possible without the encouragement of Dan Caldwell and the insights of Steve McGovern. Again, Susan Liebell and Graham Lee provided me with guidance, as did Becki Scola. My students at Saint Joseph's have always been an essential part of this project, and my revisions here are the direct result of my attempts to improve the way that I explain the research process as well as to find material that contemporary students will find interesting and relevant. I extend my thanks also to Charisse Kiino at CQ Press and the nine reviewers who made suggestions on how to improve the first edition: Rachel Cobb, Suffolk University; Kimberly Cowell-Meyers, American University; Michelle Deardorff, Jackson State University; Tim LaPira, James Madison University; Christopher Marcoux,

Virginia Tech University; Laura Olson, Clemson University; David Schmitt, Northeastern University; Kirsten Taylor, Berry College; and Joseph Young, Southern Illinois University. I also want to thank the wonderful editorial staff who made my prose better and who made sure that the finished product looked beautiful. Thank you, Barbara Corrigan and Sarah Fell.

I would also like to thank Charisse Kino who reacted enthusiastically to my suggestion that we include web resources along with this book. I have assembled materials for instructors that are intended to be both helpful and useful with students. A series of tip sheets deals with the basics of writing, both at the macro and micro levels, alongside worksheets that help students progress through each of the phases of the project. I also include the checklists that are also printed at the end of most of the chapters in the book. Instructors can customize these materials to their specifications or simply make the originals available to students. Go to http://college.cqpress.com/sites/baglione to register and download materials. I am particularly grateful to Becki Scola (especially for help summarizing the topics in the American sub-field), as well as Graham Lee and Steve McGovern. Also, I appreciate my students' efforts working with these resources which helped me understand which of my own ideas worked well and which needed refining. My attempts to address students' needs have certainly helped improve the materials that are available.

Despite all this wonderful help and inspiration, I alone am responsible for any flaws that remain in the text.

I dedicate this book to my husband, Steve McGovern, who has (among other things) helped me develop as a political scientist, researcher, and writer over the past twenty years. Without him, I would have given up on academia, but both his confidence in me and our common project of learning about politics as well as how to write better, evaluate arguments with evidence, and think more clearly have helped keep me in this profession that I so dearly love. His optimism about me and about life is a wonderful gift that I cherish. I thank him for his love, support, and partnership on which I can count as a constant, even when I am grading research papers!

NOTE

1. Thomas Deans, *Writing and Community Action: A Service-Learning Rhetoric with Readings* (New York: Longman, 2003), 136.

So You Have to Write a Research Paper

Let's be honest. When many students look at a new course syllabus and view the assignments, seeing that the professor has assigned a research paper typically brings one of two reactions. A first possible response is one of horror. Many students dread the assignment because they don't know how to write a research paper. Students with this viewpoint may drop the course because of this requirement, be panicked about it all semester, or just ignore the assignment until the last moment (as if it might somehow go away) and then turn "something" in. The other typical response is, "No problem, I'll just write a *report* on something I'm interested in." Neither reaction is productive, nor are the strategies mentioned for dealing with the dreaded assignment fortunate. The goal of this book is to teach you how to write a research paper so that you (1) won't respond in this fashion and (2) will realize why the typical reactions are so problematic.

First, a research paper can be intimidating because—and this point is very important to remember—few secondary schools and institutions of higher learning bother to teach how to write one anymore.[1] Yet many faculty give research paper assignments, as if knowing how to write one were an innate ability that all college students possess. Research paper writing, however, is a set of skills that needs to be developed. These skills can be taught and learned, as well as used throughout a college career.[2]

Second, research paper writing is so daunting because the task seems unbounded. Where do you start? What is a good topic? How do you know where to look for information? What does the text of such a paper look like? How do you know when you're done? This concern with boundaries is obviously related to the general ignorance about what constitutes a research paper. But another problem here is recognizing that writing, whether for a research paper or in some other form, is discipline specific.[3] Faculty often forget to make that point explicitly, and students are used to focusing on writing skills as consisting of only grammar, usage, and paragraph construction. While those skills are certainly important, they are not the only ones that students need to develop for writing good research papers, particularly in political science.

Political science has its own conventions (which are similar to those of the other social sciences and in some instances even related to those in the natural sciences) for paper writing that students must learn. Just because you received an A in freshman English does not mean that you are ready to write and receive an A on your political science research paper. You not only must learn to speak a new language (the vocabulary of political science) but must adopt the conventions, values, and norms of the discipline.[4] Here again, faculty have so successfully internalized these norms that they forget that students need to be taught them. This book, however, will teach you to write a research paper in political science, demystifying the structure and the process. Developing this set of writing skills will be useful to you in a number of ways: not only will it help you write more effectively in this discipline, but it will allow you to see more easily the conventions that apply to other fields of study. In addition, once you know the style and format for any subject, your reading comprehension skills in that discipline improve, and understanding even the densest academic tome will become easier. Why? Because scholars use this structure themselves, and once you know what to expect from the form of an article or book, you will be more able to distinguish the argument from the evidence, the logic from the information, or the normative claim from the underlying principles.

Third, knowing how to write a research paper is something that will be useful to you throughout your life. You might find that statement funny, thinking to yourself that you are writing research papers only to get your degree, but thereafter, you intend to be working in the corporate or nonprofit world. (My apologies to those of you out there who see an academic career in your future.) Well, if you were amused, you need to stop laughing and recognize that you likely will spend much of your career writing, and a good portion of that writing will be persuasive communication that (1) surveys a number of opinions or studies on a particular problem, (2) assesses logically the strengths and weaknesses of the various approaches, and (3) uses evidence from a case or cases of particular interest to you, your boss, and/or your clients to determine what the best approach to this problem is for your purposes. In effect, then, you are going to be writing research papers for your living, no matter what you do. So why not learn how to do it now and develop the aptitude so that you will be in a better position in your future?

Knowing how to write a research paper is an acquired talent, not something with which you are born. When you master the set of skills involved, you are empowered. By learning how to write that research paper, you acquire expertise—skills of reading comprehension, writing, research, and analysis—that will enable you to do well in all of your classes. Moreover, these are all talents that you will use in your future career, whether you are an attorney, CEO, activist, public servant, politician, businessperson, or educator. Such professionals are frequently asked to evaluate information and provide recommendations. For instance, imagine you are working at the U.S. Justice

Department and are asked to determine the impact of the Patriot Act. At the outset, you are going to need to find the legislation itself and then define what *impact* means. You also will need to justify your definition and explain from where and why you selected your information. Once you have some data, you have to analyze them and then write up your findings in a form that will impress your boss. You will learn all of the skills required to do an excellent job on this project in this book.

WHAT IS A RESEARCH PAPER? A FEW HELPFUL METAPHORS

Most students think that a research paper in political science is a long, descriptive report of some event, phenomenon, or person. This is a dangerous misconception that focuses on determining facts. Numerous methodology and philosophy of science texts will explain that true facts are often elusive because researchers interpret what they see or because they report only what they deem important, knowingly or unknowingly, failing to provide a more complete picture.[5] While we will return to the topic of data collection later in the text, the problem that I am raising here is the one that characterizes so many papers: conceiving of them as "data dumps," or all the information that you can find on a particular topic. Descriptive reporting is only one part of a political science research paper. It is an important part, and having a chance to learn about politically relevant events, persons, or phenomena is probably why you are a political science major. But knowing about politics is not being a political scientist. For political scientists, details are important, but only if they are the right ones, related to either the logics or the norms that you are exploring or the precise evidence required to sustain or undermine an argument. Facts for the sake of facts are boring and distracting.

Two metaphors help to explain the balance that you should seek. The first is that of a court case. In writing your research paper, you are, in essence, presenting your case to the judge and jury (readers of the paper). While you need to acknowledge that there are other possible explanations (e.g., your opposing counsel's case), your job is to show that both your preferred logic and the evidence supporting it are stronger than any competing perspective's framework and its sustaining information. Interesting details that have nothing to do with the particular argument you are constructing can distract a jury and annoy the judge. Good lawyers lay out their cases, connecting all the dots and leaving no pieces of evidence hanging. All the information that they provide is related to convincing those in judgment that their interpretation is the correct one.

If you find the analogy of the courtroom too adversarial, think of your paper as a painting. The level and extent of the detail depends on both the size of the canvas and the subject to be painted. Too few details in a landscape can make it boring and unidentifiable, whereas too many in a portrait can make the subject unattractive or strange.[6]

One more metaphor on which I will rely throughout this book is the research paper as a marathon. In both cases, the final product—the paper or the race—is the culmination of great efforts. Just as the typical person cannot expect to get up on the morning of a marathon, go to the starting line, run for more than twenty-six miles, and finish the race, so too a student needs to go through preparatory steps before completing the research paper. While runners stretch, train, get the right nutrition and rest, and prepare mentally for years, months, and days before the big race, students need to practice their writing and develop their logic, find the right kinds of information, and work on stating their case as strongly and effectively as possible. All of these tasks require time and energy. Only with adequate preparation do the marathoner and the student finish the race and the paper, respectively.

While few of us are likely to run a marathon, everyone who reads this book will write a research paper. My point in writing is to show you that if you follow the advice spelled out here, you will not only finish your paper but turn in something of which you feel proud. Too often I have seen students rushing at the end just to get their papers done, without really caring about quality. Their feelings are at times understandable. They didn't know how to approach the project, haven't asked for or received any guidance, and are having a totally unsatisfying time working on their research papers. When this is the case, not only is the end result poor, but the exercise itself is a failure as an assignment. You can have a rewarding and satisfying learning experience if you devote time to the process and you conceive of it as consisting of smaller, definable tasks. Each piece can be accomplished on its own, and the parts can then be assembled and reworked to create a coherent and significant whole. In effect, then, the tasks are like the marathoner's efforts to prepare months and weeks before a race—stretching, running for distance, weight training, getting adequate nutrition and rest—they're then all put together on race day to finish with a respectable time (as each runner defines it).

In fact, if we continue this running analogy, I am asking you to consider the moral of the fable of the tortoise and the hare: slow and steady will win this race. While some people have natural talent (whether it is as runners or writers), individuals finish marathons and write research papers because they are determined, diligent, and skilled. The hare may be the more naturally gifted and the faster runner, but the tortoise industriously persists throughout the course to win the race. Be the tortoise![7] Work on your paper slowly but surely throughout your course, and you will produce a fine final product.

WHAT RESEARCH PAPER WRITING ENTAILS

This book seeks to teach you the basics of writing a research paper in political science. Each chapter is devoted to a particular section of the research paper and the skills that you need to develop to make that piece of your final product a good one. The research paper–writing process can be broken down into ten distinct but interrelated tasks,[8] which map into different sections of the paper as specified in Table 1.1. Because institutions use different-length terms (semesters, trimesters, and quarters) and some students using this book might even be writing theses of longer duration, I'm providing a suggested calendar in relative terms. By setting out deadlines along the way, I am underlining the notion that you cannot write a research paper in a matter of days or hours. Moreover, while I will be stressing that you frequently will be rethinking your drafts, you do need to put ideas on paper—thus the suggested deadlines. The timing here, however, is provisional, and you should look to your instructor's guidelines as you work on your project.

Each of the following chapters will identify precisely what you need to do to accomplish these tasks and write the different sections of the paper. In the text that follows you will find instructions, examples of actual student efforts, and some exercises to help you understand the concepts and develop the skills that you need to write each part of the paper effectively. At the end of each chapter, I will provide a practical summary to guide you through writing that section and remind you of the tentative calendar that keeps you on track to make slow and steady progress. Please remember, research paper writing takes time: to develop a question; find appropriate sources; read and understand them; write, think, plan, and conduct your research; reflect on its significance; and finally, revise and edit. While Table 1.1 makes the process appear to be linear—you work through one task, complete it, and then move on to another—do not be fooled: the quality of your writing improves as the clarity of your ideas does. Thus, your paper benefits from reconsideration and iteration. So get started, work steadily, follow the deadlines that your professor provides for finishing each section, and do not be ashamed to rethink and change earlier thoughts.

When I teach my course, I ask the students to write their papers in four installments, with each one building on the previous work. In the first, students turn in draft research questions, explaining why they are good ones, and annotated bibliographies as well as normal bibliographies; for the second, they sharpen their questions and write their literature reviews (based on their annotated bibliographies) and Model and Hypothesis sections; for the third, revisions of their earlier work are included along with draft titles, research designs, and the beginnings of Analysis and Assessment sections. In the fourth installment, they finish their Analysis and Assessment sections, rework the preceding parts of their papers, and develop conclusions, introductions, and titles. As an additional guide for my students, I provide them with writing checklists that they fill out before handing in each installment. I have included these for your use at the end of the appropriate chapters and in the web resources available with the book. As you will see, these checklists follow directly from the practical summaries. You should think of them as rubrics for your own papers and should consult them as you work through your sections.

Table 1.1 Research Paper: Tasks To Be Accomplished, Sections, and Suggested Calendar

Tasks	Sections/ Assignment	Suggested Calendar
(1) **Develop** a good topic or, more accurately, **a good** research **question,** and **find** excellent, related scholarly sources.	Annotated Bibliography	At the outset (refine over the first third of course)
(2) **Identify, classify, explain, and evaluate** the most important **scholarly answers** to that question, and (3) **assert a thesis.**	Annotated Bibliography Literature Review	By end of first third of course
(4) **Develop a model and hypothesis** (if necessary, given your research question).	Model and Hypothesis	By end of first half of course
(5) **Revise** and (6) **Edit.**	All sections	Throughout course, with an intense effort in last two weeks
(7) **Plan the study,** with attention to defining and selecting appropriate cases to study, operationalizing concepts, identifying data sources, creating instruments for generating data (if necessary), and explaining methodology. In addition, **justify** this plan and **recognize** its potential flaws.	Research Design	During the second two thirds of course
(8) **Evaluate the hypothesis or thesis** across the chosen cases.	Analysis and Assessment	During last half of course
(9) **Write a conclusion** that reminds the reader of the findings, discusses why these results emerged, and suggests paths for future research and (10) **an introduction,** with the thesis clearly stated, that both explains why this question is interesting and important to multiple audiences and provides an overview of the paper. In addition, develop a title that conveys the question, cases, and argument in an appealing fashion.	Conclusion Introduction Title	In the last two weeks

The design of my course and this book might be striking to some because I require my students to begin writing as soon as possible. This recommendation may seem counterintuitive. "How can I write when I am still learning about a subject?" most students ask. The response is that writing is part of the thinking process, and you cannot make adequate intellectual advances without starting to write, and therefore think, from the outset. By the end of the process, you will have a draft that looks very different from the first one that you wrote, but that final version that you put forth is a product of the thinking and learning that you did all project long. If you do not put your initial thoughts on paper, then you are not likely to remember them and will not produce the same work as you would have had you begun writing earlier. This book encourages (and in fact demands) that you write your research paper in pieces, beginning with the first substantive parts of the paper and revising as you proceed. Insisting on writing from the outset makes clear a distinction that most students don't recognize: *revising* and *editing* are different processes. Revising entails rethinking and major rewriting, whereas editing consists of fixing grammatical errors and format mistakes and varying word choice.

BLUEPRINT OF THE BOOK

In the paragraphs that follow, I will briefly explain the contents of each chapter of the book. I recommend that you read this now to gain a better general understanding of the research paper–writing process. If you like, come back to these discussions prior to reading each chapter as a way to help you focus on the main tasks to be accomplished in that section. Remember, however, that this process is a long one, akin to a marathon, and that the most successful students take the attitude of the tortoise as they work through each of the steps.

In chapter 2, we take up the challenge of determining a good research question. Posing a question that is interesting and important to you, scholars, policymakers, and the average citizen is the key to a good choice. As you will see, coming up with an interesting query is one of the hardest and most important parts of the project. It sets the stage for the whole research paper. As we consider what makes a compelling question, we will note the diversity of kinds of research in which one may be engaged as a political scientist. And you will meet six students whose interests and research topics will reappear at different points in the book. You will even see excerpts of some of these students' efforts to give you examples of how others like you have handled the distinct tasks involved in writing a research paper.

After identifying a research question, you are ready to look at how others, namely scholars, have answered similar queries.[9] In chapter 3, you begin work on the second phase of your project: determining and understanding the academic debate. At this point, you need to discover how scholars answer your research question in both its general and specific form, if possible. You will begin this process by working on the annotated bibliography. In chapter 3, you will learn about finding good, scholarly sources and using these works to lead you to others. In addition, I will introduce you to the different forms of citation and discuss the difference between paraphrasing and plagiarizing. Sources are good ones if they provide answers to your research question; your goal here is to uncover the commonalities and differences in the works of scholars. By the end, you should be grouping your books and articles into schools of thought—common answers to the research question that are united by a similar approach, such as pointing to a particular factor as the key cause or sharing a methodology.

Then, in chapter 4, you continue the process of finding, summarizing, and categorizing excellent scholarly arguments by preparing a literature review. This is the first section that you actually write; in essence the annotated bibliography provides you with the notes and framework for the literature review. This section presents the different answers to your research question and assesses their strengths and weaknesses. You conclude your literature review with a *thesis*, your preferred answer to the research question.

For certain types of empirical research, this thesis has to be developed further to guide you through the rest of the project. Chapter 5 then helps you translate this thesis into a *model* and *hypothesis*. A model is a kind of flow diagram that identifies the cause(s) and effect as concepts and asserts graphically that X → Y (where X leads to Y). While the model helps you focus on the key factors that you will need to study, it does not specify exactly how they are related. Does Y increase if X decreases? Because you cannot tell from the model, you need the hypothesis. The hypothesis identifies the ways in which these factors are related and is typically stated as, "the more of X, the less of Y," if you are positing a negative relationship between two continuous variables. (If you were expecting a positive relationship, the sentence would read, "the more of X, the more of Y.")[10]

Before proceeding further, the text acknowledges that all good writers take an enormous amount of time to revise and edit their work. You will too. At this stage, in chapter 6, you focus on how to revise and edit, as your paper is only satisfactorily done when it is polished. Producing an excellent final work requires you to check to make sure that each section accomplishes what it should; that the paper is well written and has no silly typographical, grammatical, or spelling errors; and that you have followed all of the formatting instructions that your professor has specified. Chapter 6 provides details on the revising and editing process, and to be successful, you should return to its advice every time you have drafted something and think you are about ready to turn it in.

Once you have a sense of what you want to assert and which factors are essential in your argument, you are about halfway through this project, at the equivalent of mile 12 in this marathon. Chapter 7 walks you through the research design, which provides your research plan and your reasons that it is a good one. In this section, you design your evaluation or test of your hypothesis, and this undertaking is multifaceted. Here you determine which set of cases you need to study to conduct a fair assessment. You also explicitly state how you will translate the concepts into identifiable or measurable entities. Locating sources and data is important here, too, and you will see how the kind of information that you need at this stage is very different from what you relied on earlier. Finally, you explain exactly how you will generate your information, for example, identifying how you will know which values your variables take on or providing a sample survey if you plan to administer one.

Throughout this section, you acknowledge any weaknesses and profess any compromises you had to make in designing your project because of difficulties in finding the best case, determining more precise measures for a concept, or obtaining the data you wanted. As you will see, designing a perfect project is often impossible. Thus, every researcher has to make tough choices and explain both why these decisions are warranted and what their potential effects are. If you have good reasons, you understand the possible drawbacks, and the problems are as limited as possible, your instructor will be willing to allow you to proceed.

In his classic textbook on methodology, W. Phillips Shively notes with tongue in cheek that political science is not rocket science. Natural scientists and engineers have verifiable physical laws that have been shown to hold and describe the situations in which they are interested, as well as instruments that can precisely measure the phenomena they are investigating. In political science, we have few laws, difficulty translating key concepts into measurable entities, and trouble collecting or getting access to good data. Thus, as Shively notes, political science is not rocket science—it's much harder! [11]

In chapter 8, you learn how to analyze and assess the hypothesis. Using the plan you developed in your research design, you analyze the values of your concepts across your cases to assess how well the data support your contention. Does the evidence confirm your hypothesis? This is the part of the paper about which students are most excited; it is also what most students conceive of (prior to learning what a research paper really is) as the only important part of the paper. However, as I hope to show throughout this book, the Analysis and Assessment section of the paper cannot stand alone. It makes sense and carries weight only after you have performed the other tasks. Moreover, by surveying the literature, developing a thesis and then a model and hypothesis, and carefully designing the research, you are in a better position to write a focused and convincing assessment of the evidence, principles, and/or logic that can sway a reader to hold the same view that you do.

Once you have determined how well your hypothesis reflects reality you are ready to wrap up your paper. Using the running analogy, you are at mile 22 here, done with the hard part, and now all you need is the stamina to complete the race. Chapter 9 provides instructions to help you finish the two essential bookends for your project—your introduction and conclusion—and assists in revising your title. Perhaps surprisingly, you turn to the conclusion first, since you need to know what you are concluding when you write the overview in your introduction. Just like the marathoner, you cannot simply give up in the last few miles, limp to the finish line, and feel satisfied. You need to complete the race/paper strongly with an effective conclusion that ties the whole project together, reminds the reader of what you have achieved, explains why these accomplishments are important, considers both the limits of the research and whether this project provides insights that are applicable to other situations, and poses questions for future research. This section is particularly important if you believe that the compromises you had to make in the research design had a negative impact on your findings. If appropriate, you should explain your continuing confidence in your hypothesis, as well as discuss what you have learned about the choices that you made and what might be more productive paths to pursue. Remember, regardless of whether your hypothesis was confirmed or rejected or the jury is still out, if you have proceeded in the fashion recommended, you should be pleased with your findings. The whole point is to learn something in the research process, not to be right.

Upon completing the conclusion, you turn to the introduction and then to devising an excellent title. A good introduction communicates the question and thesis of the work as well as entices people to read the paper. In addition, the introduction provides the writer and reader a road map or snapshot of the whole paper. Academic writing in political science is very different from mystery or even most fiction writing: readers don't like surprise endings. Think for yourself how difficult reading an article is when the author isn't clear about his or her question, argument, or how that contention is linked to the literature, methodology, cases, and findings. Each of these essentials should be communicated clearly and effectively, with minimal jargon. In addition, writing the introduction provides an opportunity for refining the paper's title. A good title will, in a few phrases, convey your question, argument, and cases.

So now that we have specified the tasks to be completed and the parts of the research paper that have to be written, we have begun the process of demystifying the political science research paper. Whenever you find yourself getting foggy on the process and the goals, turn back to Table 1.1 and remind yourself,

> To write this research paper, I have to accomplish ten tasks, and I have to write six distinct sections. Each of these sections has a definite purpose and a set of tasks that I can accomplish. And after I finish each one, I can check them off as a "completed draft," realizing that I will continue to think about and improve on each section as I continue.[12] Moreover, in the practical summaries and the writing checklists at the end of the chapters, I have precise recommendations regarding what I have to do to finish each section. Thus, every part of the paper becomes manageable, particularly if I work on this project over a period of time. In fact, I have a suggested calendar for completing each of the ten tasks. Thus, if I follow the directions and the advice spelled out here, I can turn in a paper that is compelling to any reader and of which I will be proud. In effect, then, if I am the tortoise and proceed slowly and steadily, I will win the race!

NOTES

1. National Commission on Writing in America's Schools and Colleges, *The Neglected R: The Need for a Writing Revolution* (New York: College Entrance Examination Board, 2003), http://www.collegeboard.com/prod_downloads/writingcom/neglectedr.pdf.

2. Marijke Breuning, Paul Parker, and John T. Ishiyama, "The Last Laugh: Skill Building through a Liberal Arts Political Science Curriculum," *PS: Political Science and Politics* 34 (September 2001): 657–661.

3. For an excellent discussion about the peculiarity of writing for each field, see chapter 4, "Writing in Academic Communities" in Thomas Deans, *Writing and Community Action: A Service-Learning Rhetoric with Readings* (New York: Longman, 2003). Deans advances the concept of a "discourse community"—"a group of people who are unified by similar patterns of language use, shared assumptions, common knowledge, and parallel habits of interpretation" (p. 136). Such a term certainly applies to academic disciplines such as political science.

4. Ibid. Throughout this chapter, Deans develops the metaphor of writing in a particular discipline as being a traveler, a visitor to "strange lands." He does so by including two interesting works: an essay by Nancy Sakamoto and an article by Lucille McCarthy. Sakamoto examines the differences in the ways Japanese and Americans conceive of and carry on conversations, while McCarthy explicitly uses the phrase "Stranger in Strange Lands" in the title of her paper examining how one particular student fared when trying to write across the curriculum during his freshman and sophomore years.

5. Some works will question whether any true facts actually exist. See, for example, Paul Rabinow and William M. Sullivan, eds., *Interpretive Social Science: A Reader* (Berkeley: University of California Press, 1979). Postmodernists will be disappointed with my discussion of the research process because much of what I ask students to do will seem consistent with "brute data approaches." For that terminology, see Charles Taylor's piece in Rabinow and Sullivan, *Interpretive Social Science,* titled "Interpretation and the Sciences of Man," (pp. 25–71, especially pp. 53–54). I would argue, however, that the process of how intersubjective understandings come about can be modeled, that we need ways of putting forth contentions about social reality that are systematic, and that one's conclusions can be evaluated by others. Thus, I ask those of you who are skeptical of social scientific methodology because of its inattention to constitutive processes to bear with me to see whether I am able to deliver a guide that works for the kinds of studies that you would like to see performed.

6. Of course, some artists have had great success with these extremes that I am calling inadequate. Yes, I am a political scientist and not an art critic.

7. In working on this book, I learned that Eviatar Zerubavel, in his well-respected work, also uses Aesop's famous fable to explain the approach one should take to writing. See his *The Clockwork Muse: A Practical Guide to Writing Theses, Dissertations, and Books* (Cambridge, MA: Harvard University Press, 1999), 12.

8. In their first presentation, these tasks are put forth in a simplified manner. I will explain and develop the complexities in the ensuing chapters.

9. Some undergraduate papers in political theory may not include a literature review of secondary sources. Look to your instructor for guidance about whether and how she or he wants you to handle the task of identifying and classifying different perspectives.

10. The alternative is if the variables are noncontinuous or discrete (also referred to as category variables, which can come in unranked versions called *nominal*—such as sex or religion—or ranked versions called *ordinal*—such as educational achievement of primary, secondary, some college, college graduate, or postgraduate). With discrete variables, the basic hypothesis would read something like the following: "If X is A, then Y is B, but if X is C, then Y is D." Please note that we will discuss types of data—nominal, ordinal, and interval—in more detail in chapters 5 and 7.

11. W. Phillips Shively, *The Craft of Political Research,* 5th ed. (Upper Saddle River, NJ: Prentice Hall, 2002), 17.

12. If you are writing these as formal drafts for your instructor to review, you will be receiving excellent feedback to help you write a great paper. Be sure to address and respond to the questions and comments that your reader makes, and don't hesitate to consult your professor during the process. In addition, whether you have a faculty reader or not, you can also benefit from the feedback of a friend, classmate, or member of your institution's writing center. Find a reader, and realize that criticism is useful; comments help you sharpen your ideas and improve your skills.

Getting Started: Finding a Research Question

Starting a research project is truly a formidable task. It is challenging because good research topics are usually very specific and, in fact, not topics but rather questions or puzzles. In this chapter, I will define the characteristics of a good research question and walk you through a variety of ways of finding one.

Some of you may wonder why you need a question at all, given that there are many interesting topics to investigate. There are three main reasons for locating a query. First, topics are too broad and contain within them many subissues. For instance, to acquaint yourself with everything related to either campaigns and elections in the United States or democratization around the world is a huge undertaking. You want a manageable challenge! Second, a question links you to a controversy and allows you to become engaged in the scholarly and/or policy debate by both interacting with the ideas being contested and examining some information to evaluate the veracity of those claims. Thus, a good question gives you focus and puts you in the thick of one controversy (not many). Moreover, it allows you the opportunity to develop your analytic skills as you weigh both theoretical perspectives and evidence that relate to the arguments. Third, a question gives you a reason to write: you must provide an answer. Having a question therefore helps propel you forward to the response and gives you a clearer indication of when you're done—when you have offered and evaluated an answer.

CHARACTERISTICS OF A GOOD QUESTION

All great research questions share five qualities, and you can use these criteria to help you generate a topic and then transform it into a question for study. Research questions are *interesting* and *important* to you, scholars, the public policy community, and ideally, ordinary citizens. A good question is also *short* and *direct:* if you need multiple lines or sentences to state your query then you still have some work to do refining it into one that captures people's attention and concisely identifies a question. Finally, your research must be *doable.* In other words, you need to pick a question that you can actually answer with the resources available to you. As we will see in chapter 7 there are many creative ways to find evidence and perform studies, but you will want to keep in mind some potential informational limits (a strange thought in our connected world) and consider adjusting your question accordingly.

There is a sixth criterion—that the question be puzzling. Political scientists love these types of queries because they investigate the counterintuitive and promote our understanding of theory. Finding a puzzling question is not always possible, although sometimes you can pick instances to study that will make your query a puzzle. Typically, however, your professor will agree that an interesting and important question that is concise, direct, and doable is fine.

FIND SOMETHING INTERESTING

OK, great, I've given you criteria, but now how do you satisfy them? You need to recognize from the outset that finding a good research topic and question takes effort. The right ones won't simply pop into your head, and often, when students hastily choose, they end up dissatisfied later on in the process. Unfortunately, then they have already committed too much time and too many resources to change. Thus, you want to work at the outset on satisfying that first criterion: start by asking what is interesting to you. Some students are really excited about a topic, and for them, picking a general area of research is relatively easy, but not effortless. For others, this task is more of a challenge, but here are some strategies to help. A first method is to write down what motivated you to become a political science major. In addition, thinking about your career aspirations and extracurricular activities can be inspirational.

Let's use the experiences of some students to illustrate these approaches. The first is Latisha, who became particularly energized because of Barack Obama's candidacy in 2008 and her experiences volunteering, which made her believe that politics was her calling and political science should be her major. Thinking that a new era was beginning, Latisha had a lot of hope in 2009, although her optimism has more recently been tempered by the polarization and seeming incivility in American politics. She can't help but wonder whether what has happened is more than a simple midterm correction. Does race have something to do with the current political discourse and the reception Obama has received? Reconsidering her career choice given the contemporary nature of American politics, Latisha is now thinking of law school.

Another student, Samantha, chose political science because she is a political news junky who is fascinated by the coverage and loves to write. Given her interests, she got involved in the school newspaper to hone her journalistic skills. Sam's become increasingly impressed with the way that politicians, activists, and celebrities use new media—social networking sites and Twitter, for instance—to frame what the public knows. Moreover, she has a hunch,

Table 2.1   Finding a Topic: Students with Clear Passions, Activities, Interests, or Aspirations

	Latisha	Samantha	Joe
Why the major	2008 election	News junky	Early geography buff 9/11
			Challenges of stability after conflict
Career aspirations	Elected official Attorney	Not sure	Bureaucrat or expert on international democratization and development
Extracurricular activities	Student government Partisan politics	School newspaper	Not related[a]
Interesting topics	Obama	Media and elections	Iraq and Afghanistan
	Polarization/ incivility	New media	Postwar democracy
	Race	Gender and media	Postwar development

a. Be careful in making this judgment. Being involved in organizations often brings political issues to the fore. Tap into any and all of your experiences to find topics of interest to you.

especially given her own experiences and observations, that gender is very important, not only affecting how the media cover someone but also influencing how people seek to portray themselves.

Then there is Joe, who came to the field because he was always interested in the world. At a very young age, he began poring over maps, examining flags of the world, and learning about different regions. Growing up outside of New York City, the tragedy of 9/11 was incredibly real to him, and he has carefully followed the conflicts in Afghanistan and Iraq and the challenges involved in creating stable and productive societies after violence. He hopes someday to be working in international affairs and promoting development and democracy.

Using academic and political passions, extracurricular activities, and interests and aspirations, our three hypothetical students might create the lists provided in Table 2.1.

A fourth way of picking a topic is to think about which courses you enjoyed or which segments of your favorite courses you liked best. Locate your books and notes from those classes; if you don't have them, you've made a mistake because you should always keep the materials from your major courses. I know the refund is tempting, but often you get relatively little money when you sell your books back, and these are excellent resources for the rest of your academic career. Hold on to your notes as well. Your faculty members use their time to provide you with the information they believe is essential for mastering a subject. Do not just throw this wisdom away at the end of the term. Remember, you are supposed to be cumulating knowledge and skills throughout your college career—expanding on what you have learned before—and your books and notes are the foundations from which you build. If you were a foreign language major, you could not survive a literature class without first achieving language proficiency. So too, you should think about your own field of study as a cumulative endeavor. Your political science courses are building on each other; you are not simply learning a set of facts about different countries, institutions, time periods, public policies, political philosophies, or interstate interactions. So keep your books to consult as you take advanced courses in the major. If you have no textbooks now, however, go to your library and check one out (or as a last resort, go to your professor and see if you can borrow one). Textbooks and readers are extremely useful sources not only for question generation but for the next stage of the research process, the phase of determining how different scholars have studied your puzzle. At this stage, use the table of contents, photos, illustrations, and tables to point you in the direction of interesting topics. After you've narrowed your interests by rereading the text in places, use the source lists and recommendations for further readings to help you find out more about your potential topic.

Imagine that Mike really enjoyed his Civil Rights and Civil Liberties class. He was especially interested in the issues that involved racial profiling and immigrants, both legal and illegal. His course readings on this topic were related to finding terrorists and stopping them before they committed

Table 2.2 Finding a Topic: Using a Favorite Course and Linking Your Interests to Contemporary Events

Interest	Mike
Favorite course	Civil Rights and Civil Liberties
Favorite part of course	Racial profiling
	Immigration
	Terrorism
Links to current events	Arizona's efforts
	Amendment to restrict automatic citizenship at birth in United States
Interesting topics	Profiling
	National security versus civil liberties?
	Immigration and federalism
	Immigration and citizenship

violence, and he found the issues involved there fascinating. More recently, profiling and immigration have been the subjects of discussion because of both Arizona's determination to catch and deport illegals and the wider drive to introduce a new amendment to the Constitution so that being born in the United States would not automatically confer American citizenship. Using these ideas, Mike can create the worksheet shown in Table 2.2.

Another way to find inspiration for a topic is thinking about something that is important to you personally; as many activists and scholars have learned, the personal is political! Andre's family has found the Great Recession very painful. He listens to the arguments between the Republicans and Democrats about what to do, cut taxes and spending or offer more government programs, and he is not sure which is correct. He does know, however, that something has to be done—and fast—because upon graduation, he needs a job. His prospects, however, are not that great, because he wants to return to his home city in the rustbelt, and the employment news has not been positive there. While this reflection on his situation might not make him happy, it could provide fodder for his research topic. Andre's concerns are related to contemporary "big" debates in the field about the role of the market as opposed to government in creating jobs. Because he is worried about the national debt, Republican arguments about decreasing spending and waste ring very true, especially given his own belt-tightening steps, but Democrats appear to make some sense too. With family members working in the auto industry, he has also followed the stories about GM's bankruptcy, government bailout, and reemergence on the stock exchange. Andre follows his hometown news and thinks there might be something to study about its local politics and economic prospects.

Sixth, recent issues of newspapers, journals of opinion, and online news coverage can be great as sources of inspiration, and they can also sharpen your focus. Kate is another student who always reads the newspaper and has observed that recently there have been more articles about women and politics

Table 2.3 Finding a Topic: Using Personal Concerns and Linking to Current Debates

Linking Concerns to Debates	Andre
Personal concerns	Recession's impact and job prospects for recent college graduates
	Economic conditions in hometown
Political debates relevant to concerns	Market versus state
	Urban development or decay
Interests/interesting topics	Deficits and debt
	Condition of General Motors
	Politics of development/decline in home city

around the world. One item that she noticed is that women appear to have had a great deal of electoral success in places where she wouldn't have expected them. She could use this insight gleaned from reading newspapers as a jumping-off point, as could you. If you have no idea what is interesting and important, high-quality media outlets will help you determine what others find compelling. From their concerns, you may be able to identify issues that you would like to study. In consulting newspapers, try to use the best. If you're interested in international or national news, then examine recent issues of the *New York Times, Washington Post, Los Angeles Times,* or *Wall Street Journal.* You will want to look at not only the main news articles but also the editorial pages, where you can see what the papers' editors think about controversial issues as well as read what outsiders (typically scholars, practitioners, and other important people) have to say in the Op-Ed ("opposite the editorials") essays. Also consult the web versions of BBC News, National Public Radio, PBS, and CNN. For exploring local issues, pick the most important relevant paper and consult its Metro section. If you're interested in San Francisco or the Bay Area, then consult the *San Francisco Chronicle;* if it's Philadelphia policy and politics, then check out the *Philadelphia Inquirer.* Look for the papers and places where local issues are most knowledgeably covered.

Other helpful sources of topics include journals of opinion. These are publications, typically in magazine format, that have a clear political bent to their articles and are not reporting the news so much as seeking to convince you of their editorial position. Some of the best ones are, on the right, *National Review* and *Weekly Standard;* in the center, *New Republic;* and on the left, *The Nation* and *American Prospect.* What seems to help students most is to read recent issues of the publication with which they are least likely to agree. That strategy tends to get students annoyed and motivated to explore the contentions advanced.

Some of you might be wondering why, in thinking about topics, I am encouraging you to reflect on and explore primarily contemporary events and controversies. I have three reasons. First, in my experience, students, particularly those who do not have a specific issue in mind, do not have that much detailed knowledge of the past. Therefore, to sift through history to find something compelling is very hard. Second, one of my goals for you is to perform some original empirical work. That means that I want you to investigate a political issue or policy as no one has done before. Now, doing an original study does not mean that you can work only on contemporary topics. In fact, excellent work is always being done in history, political science, and sociology (and other disciplines) that reexamines the past. However, I have found that when students choose a research paper topic about something in the past (typically that they know a lot about), they fall into what I call the "report trap." Students then seek to describe everything they have learned from others' research. Usually, they also split the difference between the competing explanations, arguing that the best way to understand their issue is to somehow combine the main existing views. This approach is flawed methodologically and is not a reflection or exercise of your analytic or intellectual capacity. Finally, I want your research to ask a question for which you *need* to know the answer (and you do not already have in your head your preferred explanation). Being compelled not by your professor but by some internal spark is a great motivator. Finding contemporary debates, then, and entering into them is my way of encouraging students to identify the kinds of topics that are interesting, important, and even puzzling: those good question criteria. Of course, sometimes those contemporary debates lead us to reconsider issues of the past. But now you understand that if you do reexamine an event or issue you will be doing original research and not, for instance, finding two good books and combining their arguments in some way. No, in the research paper–writing process, you are going to learn to be the scholar or policy analyst and assess your argument with information that you interpret. Don't worry; you aren't going to do this alone. In chapter 7, on research design, you will learn how and when to lean on the work of others and the conditions under which you can generate your own information. But these issues are a much later concern, and I have to ask you to trust me and your instructor that if you follow this method, your paper and study will be successful and compelling.

In sum, while there are many ways to get you started on finding a research topic, nowhere will you find a flashing neon light that says, "Here's a great topic; take it!" Instead, you need to follow any or all of the methods described here—considering (1) why you chose your major; (2) what your extracurricular activities are and how they might be related to politics and political issues; (3) your career aspirations; (4) your favorite classes; (5) your personal concerns; and (6) current events and debates.

There's one last exercise that I'm going to ask you to engage in: you should acknowledge explicitly why these topics are interesting to you. In addition, if you have reflected on current events or your old courses and performed some news research, you should also consider why this topic might be interesting to policymakers, scholars, and citizens. Each of these three groups has different priorities. Policymakers, including politicians, bureaucrats, and practitioners, are looking for solutions. They want to fix the problems they identify in society; thus, their interests tend to be practical and applied in nature. Some will also be interested in ideology and the philosophical underpinnings of policies. Scholars have similar practical and ideological concerns, but they are often also trying to explain or interpret events. Typically, they are engaged in some academic debate, trying to show that their arguments or theory is better at explaining or predicting politics or behavior than others. While citizens can also be policy professionals and scholars, we often imagine them to care about how issues directly affect their lives. So ask yourself, Why would my topics be interesting to these three groups?

As you start the research process and begin to identify a topic, I recommend that you engage in self-reflection and fill out the chart presented as Table 2.4. You don't have to fill in every space, but the more you do now, the more certain you will be of your choice. In addition, some of the work

Table 2.4   Using Multiple Techniques to Find a Topic That Is Interesting to Multiple Audiences

Technique	You
Why the major?	
Career aspirations	
Extracurricular activities	
Favorite course	
Favorite part of course	
Links to current events	
Personal concerns	
Political debates relevant to your interests, activities, career hopes, and concerns	
Newspaper research on hot and compelling issues and controversies	
Journal of opinion research on hot and compelling issues and controversies	
Interesting research topics	
Why are these topics interesting to you? Why are they interesting to scholars, policymakers, and citizens?	

here—making links to theoretical and policy debates and identifying why your topics are interesting to multiple audiences—will give you a head start on completing other parts of the paper. At this point, seek to have a few (no more than three) candidate topics. In the next stage, we'll start to translate topics into research questions and then give you criteria for choosing the best query. Because each topic can lead to multiple questions, you are OK with even one subject that you are enthusiastic about. But don't simply settle with the first idea that pops into your head, or you may regret it in the future.

DETERMINING WHY YOUR TOPIC IS IMPORTANT

Along with being interesting, your research question should be important to you and a larger community of scholars, policymakers, and citizens. You may doubt that your particular interest—Facebook as a tool for campaigning for Samantha or the plight of Detroit for Andre—could be important, but you will be pleasantly surprised to learn that many people share your curiosity. To identify the level of scholarly interest, you can look up your topic in an *online database* of academic articles. Some excellent databases for this purpose include Academic Search Premier (from EBSCOhost Research Databases); Journal Storage: The Scholarly Archive, more popularly known as JSTOR; Project

MUSE; and ProQuest Research Library. These can help you locate articles in the premier journals in political science as well as related fields such as economics, history, sociology, and various area studies. You may want to start by reading several book reviews or article abstracts to get a better sense of why academics find this subject important. Once you have found a good source in your search, note the subject terms associated with this article or book. Use these to search for more, or in several of the databases, you have the option to find "more articles like these" with a click of the mouse. Take advantage of this shortcut.

Students are too willing these days to rely exclusively on sources they can read on or print from their computers. While digital materials are wonderful, there's a wealth of knowledge that you can acquire in the library. First of all, books are extremely important repositories of knowledge, and you typically cannot get access to full-length scholarly works online for free. In addition, older and sometimes more recent issues of some journals might not be available electronically. JSTOR, in particular, can have a relatively long lag time before a publication is posted. Moreover, databases index different subsets of journals. You may have chosen a database to search that doesn't include one of the most important journals for your topic. So be sure to use your library's online catalog to find books and the major journals concerned with your topic. In addition, go to the library, and actually poke around. If you find a good book or journal, chances are that shelved near that source you will find several other interesting and useful ones. And of course, you should let the first sources that you identify lead you to other ones. Look at what the authors cite as key works and be sure to read those books and articles too.

For some help determining whether and why your topic is significant to ordinary people, you can brainstorm and come up with reasons on your own. You can also consult news articles and opinion pieces on these subjects. While scholarly sources are important later on, these popular pieces give you a useful perspective at this very early stage. Journalists write with the general reader in mind and explain the importance of the news to members of the community. Editorial writers and columnists also make the case for the larger significance of events or policies. How do you find these types of articles? Here you can search using LexisNexis (a legal resources and news database) as well as Academic Search Premier or ProQuest Research Library. Notice that in any of these databases, you can often specify the magazine, journal of opinion, newspaper or type of paper, and type of article (news, editorial, Op-Ed) along with the subject you are searching. When using these news sources be aware of both the audience for whom the authors are writing and any ideological leanings. For instance, you will find different political perspectives in the *Weekly Standard, New Republic, American Prospect*, and *The Economist*. You will also find varied coverage from newspapers that see themselves as national—that is, *New York Times, Washington Post,* or *Wall Street Journal*—versus local—*Columbus Dispatch* or *Times-Picayune*. All kinds of sources are valid for discovering the significance of your topic, but you need to be mindful of the intended audience and ideological leanings of the publication.

After you have done some research on why your issue is important, add what you have discovered to the chart that you started (see Table 2.4). If you are taking an idea from another writer, be sure that you note all the bibliographic information that you will need to cite the source of that point in case you use it in your paper.[1] Moreover, the more work you do, the more likely it is that you will be able to start narrowing in on one particular issue. While I don't want you to make that decision quickly, you also need to realize that time is limited and you need to start deciding exactly what you will study.

IF POSSIBLE, IDENTIFYING A PUZZLE

So you have found a topic that is interesting to you and that you know is important to others. At the outset, I mentioned that you also may be able to find something puzzling, and puzzles are especially good questions from the perspective of theory building. But what could be puzzling about politics, or what is a puzzle in political science? Well, I'm not talking about a jigsaw or Rubik's cube but rather an event or development that doesn't seem to make sense. A puzzling outcome is surprising *given what we know*. Another way of thinking about this kind of intellectual dilemma is that either it lacks obvious answers or the conventional wisdom appears to be incorrect. Finding a puzzle typically means linking something *empirical* (something that has occurred and is observable) with your issue or concept of interest. Sometimes, identifying a real puzzle can be very hard and is closely related to your decisions about which cases (e.g., events, years, people, and policies) you will study.

Again, locating a puzzle means that what has happened is surprising given our current theories. So perhaps for Latisha the increasing polarization and hardening of the American party system is surprising since citizens seem so evenly divided and many of them tell pollsters they hold moderate views.[2] Given this centrism, why are parties becoming more ideologically narrow? Joe wonders how anyone in the U.S. government could have thought that democracy could be built in Afghanistan after the ouster of the Taliban since the country lacked the essentials—development, institutional infrastructure, and social capital—for such a system to thrive.[3] Thus, how was this U.S. policy possible, and why would officials think that the invasion of Iraq would spark liberal democracy throughout the Muslim world?

STARTING WORDS FOR QUESTIONS

Sometimes you know enough about theory to inspire a puzzling question, but even if you don't, your current topic, while compelling, is likely too broad. You need to narrow it down further, and in this process, you will find a question. My recommendation to narrow your scope likely seems strange. Typically, students are worried about finding enough information for their papers, so they think they need an expansive subject for which they can gather lots of facts. Here again, the misconception that the paper is purely a descriptive report is misleading students. Your paper is not a story about the *who, what, where,* and *when* of politics; your paper is an analytic effort that (usually) answers *why, how, to what extent,* or *under what conditions.* What can work as long as you aren't interested in simply *what happened* but instead in something like *which policies worked* or *what does this development mean.*

Selecting the right starting word for your question is actually quite important. Sometimes if you force yourself to ask queries that you would like to answer, you can derive a good question. Students often want to pose and then respond to one that begins with "should," "ought," or "what should/ought." Questions that start this way are excellent ones as think pieces in which the foundation for what is correct has already been established. For the research paper, however, you must (1) employ some theoretical or conceptual material to develop a claim and then (2) evaluate it based on evidence. Both parts of the project—the theory, primarily the concern of the Literature Review and Model and Hypothesis sections—and the evidence—set out and evaluated in the Analysis and Assessment section but planned and justified in the Research Design section—are equally important to the success of the paper.

TYPES OF RESEARCH AND QUESTIONS

A research paper in the form I'm suggesting, then, is both theoretical and empirical (observable, factual) in nature. Your work may have *normative* implications—in other words it may provide insight into behaviors or policies that are morally superior—but this is work in political science, not ethics. For this reason, I discourage students from asking "should," "ought," or "what should/ought" questions because they tend to focus on the normative side only. Thus, I push students to use these normative queries as inspiration for formulating new ones that can fulfill the requirements of being both theoretical and empirical. For instance, if Joe were wondering, What should the U.S. and Iraqi governments do to help promote political stability and development in Iraq, he could transform this question in a number of ways. First, Joe might want to ask, To what extent have economic development programs in post-2003 Iraq been successful? Or if he thinks that the information coming out of Iraq is too spotty and/or the time frame has been too short, he could ask, In other post-conflict countries, which programs have worked to promote political stability and development? Why have they worked? Joe might even consider how peace is built in postconflict societies to see whether he thinks Iraq has a decent probability of creating stability and development.

Latisha might have started wondering whether U.S. politics should be so polarized because the incivility seems to be turning off citizens and politicians seem not to be solving the country's problems. These insights could lead her to ponder to what extent citizens are disillusioned now. For neither student are these initial questions, on the surface, puzzling, by my definition. Still, as Joe and Latisha learn more about these issues they may be able to make them puzzling. Moreover, their possible inquiries are interesting, important, direct, and researchable. So they are on the right track, in my estimation.

Undergraduate students typically perform three kinds of research: *theory advancing, public policy,* and *conceptual.*[4] Each of these types is both theoretical and empirical. Theory helped the researcher frame the answer in the first place, but the test of that theory—the ultimate judgment—results from holding up its contentions to the real world. Three factors distinguish the research: (1) whether there's a posited underlying causal relationship or correlation, (2) the extent to which the research helps solve a particular problem, and (3) what the nature of the evidence is. Theory-advancing and public policy research typically is based on an insight that asserts that some effect varies with some other factor. These elements could change simultaneously, that is, be *correlated* without any direct connection, or they could be *causally* linked, meaning changes in the first lead to modifications in the second. Theory-advancing and public policy research differ, however, according to how applied they are. Applied research is intended to solve real problems, such as how to design a good political system in a certain cultural setting or how to create a good city school system in the United States. Public policy research is applied, while theory-advancing work seeks to move our conceptual understandings forward, identifying weaknesses and strengths in existing approaches. It explores why politics is the way it is and often tries to take a stand in a debate between scholars—which answer is better or best based on logic and evidence. Similarly, conceptual research is not applied but aims to arrive at better knowledge of fundamental concepts. While there may be practical applications for theory-advancing or conceptual research, the ultimate policy spin-offs are not what motivate these inquiries. [5]

Finally, regarding evidence, theory-advancing and public policy research find their empirics in real-world phenomena, that is, election outcomes, effects of state-run health care systems, preconditions for democracy, the impact of micro-financing, or causes of war, to name a few. In contrast, conceptual papers investigate the meanings and implications of the works of great political thinkers or theoretical positions by engaging the ideas and looking to texts for clarification. Examples here might be investigating whether Thomas Hobbes is actually a forefather of liberalism or determining what peace actually means.[6] While events often inspire this work, the real-world content is neither as substantial nor as logically important to the project. Instead, ideas, clarifying concepts, and improving understandings of theories or theorists is central. The data here are the words or writings of those involved in the discussion, and claims about the meanings or definitions are evaluated based on logic and texts.

So as you work to transform your topic and your questions into doable ones, remember that your preferred type of query will vary depending on the course for which you are writing this paper or the purpose of the research. For most empirical courses, you will be encouraged to conduct theory-advancing or public policy research papers, and for theory classes, you will engage in conceptual research.[7] As you ask your question—with the appropriate starting word—remember that you need to strike a balance (depending on the type of research) between theory and evidence. Typically, you should avoid a broad theoretical question (how do we account for the nature of the international system?). Instead, you're looking for what Robert Merton dubbed "middle-range" questions:[8] in other words, questions inspired by phenomena of importance in the real world that require you to use theory and evidence to answer them. I have been guiding you toward these types of questions throughout the chapter, so if you follow the advice, you should develop appropriate ones.

USING THE ADVICE TO GENERATE QUESTIONS

Table 2.5 shows how Latisha and Joe are proceeding with their searches for a question.

As you look at Latisha's and Joe's early questions, there are a few important points to acknowledge. First, their normative instincts helped them get under way. Second, they used the appropriate starting words. Third, they did not ask questions that would require them to know what is happening in the future. While good theory helps us predict the future, we should avoid research papers that are wholly future focused. For instance, Latisha would likely not receive approval from her professor for a research paper (written in early 2011) that asked, "Will Barack Obama win a second term in 2012?" That might be an interesting think piece essay, but the empirics would not be adequate. However, often when analysts wish they could know the future, they look to other cases (see Joe's second question) to give them insight. The bulk of their work is then on another case or cases, but their research gives them some knowledge about the situation that motivated their question. Last, only one of these questions poses a puzzle.

You should also notice that Latisha and Joe have begun to justify their topics. This work is part of their insurance policy—confirming that they have picked an issue that others, especially their professor, will care about; ensuring that they will be able to find information, both theoretical and empirical, on their topic; and making a kind of down payment on a future writing assignment. As you will see, your paper's introduction will explain why your topic is interesting, important, and perhaps puzzling to multiple audiences. Doing this work now means that Latisha and Joe will have an easier time at the end of their writing projects when they need to draft the introduction.

STATING YOUR QUESTION CONCISELY AND DIRECTLY

When you can state a research question with the appropriate starting words and can justify why scholars, practitioners, and citizens would be interested in it, then you, too, are on your way to a good paper. But you're not done yet. Have

Table 2.5 Generating Questions and Identifying Their Type

Self-Consciously Transforming Topics into Different Types of Questions	Latisha	Joe
Interesting topics	Obama Polarization/incivility Race	Iraq and Afghanistan Postwar democracy Postwar development
Why interesting to multiple audiences?	Political scientists debate whether the country is polarized, how uncivil we are, and what are the impacts of polarization and incivility. Policy professionals wonder if anything can be accomplished in a time of great problems. Citizens may be disillusioned. Race remains a key issue of study and debate among scholars, policy professionals, and citizens.	Scholars wonder how to transform war-torn societies, policymakers seek to make the best decisions for our country and remove U.S. forces. Citizens worry about budgetary implications and the human cost.
Why important to multiple audiences?	Again, big scholarly debate and big issues to resolve. Many citizens are worried; many citizens are angry. If nothing is accomplished, what impact will that have on the future?	Suggests the potential limits to U.S. power and also can provide answers about what needs to be done. Unfortunately, too many societies are emerging from war-wracked past. Important to know how they should proceed.
Public policy questions	What impact is polarization having on solving key problems in the United States?	To what extent have economic development programs in post-2003 Iraq been successful? In other postconflict countries, which programs have worked to promote political stability and development?
Theory-advancing questions	Why is U.S. politics so polarized now? To what extent is U.S. politics more polarized now than it was in the past? Given polarization, how did Obama achieve some key legislative successes in his first two years?	How or under what conditions is peace built in formerly war-torn societies?
Puzzling?	The last question does reflect a puzzle. Not quite for the others; Latisha needs to know more about polarization and its alleged impacts before knowing she has a puzzle.	Not yet, but these are all good questions that Joe can pursue if his professor gives the OK.

you ever gone to a public lecture and noticed that a questioner takes too long in posing his or her query to the speaker? Are you often frustrated listening to that audience member go on about his or her issue before stating the question? If you answered yes to these two queries, then you have an instinctual understanding of the fourth characteristic of a good research question: it is short and direct. You want to identify a question and ask about it as briefly and straightforwardly as possible. For instance, notice the differing impact of two questions that Samantha could ask:

Example Question A: The media seem to have a lot of influence on politics, and candidates vary in the way that they use them. One interesting new development (and it is new as a technology as well as in its application to campaigning) is interactive media. Facebook, Twitter, and other new media give candidates new methods for engaging and attracting volunteers, donors, and voters that they never had before. These new options are in addition to traditional media coverage (wherein news organizations make a decision about whether or not to report on a candidate) and advertising, which is paid. They also are different in kind from websites and e-mail lists, which don't allow people to interact directly. Traditionally certain kinds of candidates, based on such characteristics as status (incumbent, challenger), party identification (Republican, Democratic, Independent, other), gender (male, female), and race, have had more access to media than have others. So this new media is going to be great for the previously underprivileged. Will interactive and free media give challengers, independents, and third-party candidates; females; and candidates from the nondominant racial group more of a chance to win?

Example Question B: How have different types of candidates used new media in their election campaigns? To what extent have new media helped typical underdogs get their message out?

In the first example, Samantha spends too much time explaining the background logic for her question. Yes, this information will ultimately be in her paper in some form, but she needs to get to the question and avoid showing her biases. Although she finally asks a concise question, it asks her to predict the future. Her second set of queries is preferable because it is brief, uses appropriate starting words, and is actually doable. Given resource constraints, Samantha will likely focus on only one question. Still, the lessons for you from Sam's question asking are to seek that crisp question and recognize that you will have plenty of time later in your introduction to explain why your query is interesting, important, and maybe even puzzling.

PRACTICAL SUMMARY

In this chapter, you have learned about what makes a good research question and the different kinds of research in which political scientists typically engage. Excellent research questions are interesting, important, brief, and doable.

Sometimes they are also puzzling. Consider the type of research (theory advancing, public policy, or conceptual) as you are thinking about possible research questions. The type of query that you ask is often not dependent on the topic but on the course or the purpose for which you are writing the paper. In other words, you can develop many different kinds of research questions from one topic. Use one of the beginning words, as well as your knowledge of politics and policy and your interests, to help you.

The chapter also provided several methods for generating research questions. We met six students (who will return in other chapters of this book as we work through different stages of the research process) who are learning how to discover interesting topics and transform them into actual questions. Finding such a query often takes some effort, but it is not impossible, especially if you follow the advice outlined here. Perhaps the hardest part in determining the question is uncovering a source of inspiration. I have suggested several: (1) why you are majoring in political science, (2) your extracurricular activities, (3) your career ideas, (4) topics you enjoyed in earlier classes, (5) your personal concerns and hopes, and (6) contemporary issues and controversies.

To guide you in this process, the best advice I can give you is to fill out the matrix, just as some of our students have done. Your effort in generating a research question will be very worthwhile, as getting off to a good start is essential for your future success. Once you have some good candidate questions, try to decide which one would be most fun, interesting, or possible for you to do. You should also ask which one will satisfy your professor's criteria for the assignment best. Once you think that you have the answers to those questions, focus on that one good research question. Confirm that hunch with your instructor before proceeding further. You may have to make some modifications, but I hope you will be on track.

SUGGESTED CALENDAR

In the first week or two of classes, your professor will likely want you to do the necessary work that will enable you to fill out the chart presented as Table 2.4. The goal is to identify one or more possible research questions.

EXERCISES

1. Develop research questions for students Mike and Andre. Create one theory-advancing and one public policy question for each. Be sure to identify which question is which.

2. Pick up a recent newspaper. Develop a research question based on a news article or editorial selection. Identify the type of question (theory advancing or public policy), and be sure your query starts with the appropriate words, is concise, and is doable. Explain why

others—scholars, practitioners, and citizens—would find your question compelling. Remember that they each will have different reasons for liking your question.

3. Consult one of your introductory textbooks. Develop a research question with its help. Identify the type of question (theory advancing or public policy), and be sure your query starts with the appropriate words, is concise, and is doable. Explain why others—scholars, practitioners, and citizens—would find your question compelling. Remember that they each will have different reasons for liking your question.

CHECKLIST 1: THE RESEARCH QUESTION

Below is a checklist to consult and fill out as you are developing your question. When you think you have a suitable query, state it in the first slot. See if you can check off "yes" for the next three items and answer the rest. If you can't, you know that you have more work to do to formulate a good research question. If you want to ask your professor about multiple questions, fill out a separate copy of this matrix for the other question(s) and compare your answers. Then share your work with your faculty member for feedback.

Checklist 1: The Research Question

MY RESEARCH QUESTION IS: (*type research question here*)

My question is short and direct.	Yes _____ No _____
My question is doable.	Yes _____ No _____
My question starts with one of the appropriate words (e.g., *why, how, to what extent,* or *under what conditions*) and is not purely descriptive.	Yes _____ No _____

In these ways, my question is interesting and important to scholars:

In these ways, my question is interesting and important to policymakers:

In these ways, my question is interesting and important to citizens:

In these ways, my question may be puzzling:

NOTES

1. I'll discuss citations and the importance of giving credit to sources and avoiding plagiarism in more detail in chapter 3.
2. Morris P. Fiorina with Samuel J. Abrams, *Disconnect: The Breakdown of Representation in American Politics* (Norman: University of Oklahoma Press, 2009).
3. Joe is remembering the work of Seymour Martin Lipset and Robert Putnam, among others, here. See Lipset, "Some Social Requisites of Democracy: Economic Development and Political Legitimacy." *American Political Science Review* 53, no. 1 (1959): 69–105; Putnam, *Bowling Alone: The Collapse and Revival of American Community* (New York: Simon & Schuster, 2000).
4. These terms come (with adjustments in nomenclature) from W. Phillips Shively. He identifies four kinds of research—normative philosophy, formal theory, engineering (what I call public policy), and theory oriented (here, theory advancing)—divided along two dimensions—nonempirical versus empirical and applied versus basic. For most undergraduates, formal theory papers are beyond their interest and the scope of their training, so I will not deal with them explicitly here. Discussions with political theorists and reflections on my own subfields have made me realize what political theorists share with others in the field, as all types of political scientists may write conceptual papers that make assertions about the state of the literature or engage in debates about concepts and definitions. Also, the renaming of types of research, I hope, will help reduce the confusion some students have had between Shively's terms of political theory and theory-advancing research. W. Phillips Shively, *The Craft of Political Research*, 5th ed. (Upper Saddle River, NJ: Prentice Hall, 2002), 4–6.
5. Ibid.
6. For instance, Richard Boyd, "Thomas Hobbes and the Perils of Pluralism." *Journal of Politics* 63 (2001): 392–413; Oliver P. Richmond, "Critical Research Agendas for Peace: The Missing Link in the Study of International Relations." *Alternatives* 32, no. 2 (2007): 247–274.
7. For assignments less than the full-fledged research paper in American, comparative, and international politics, you will often write conceptual papers.
8. Robert K. Merton, *Social Theory and Social Structure,* enlarged ed. (New York: Free Press, 1968). Merton was discussing the types of theories, but a middle-range question will lead to developing middle-range theory.

chapter 3

Learning Proper Citation Forms, Finding the Scholarly Debate, and Summarizing and Classifying Arguments: The Annotated Bibliography

We are like dwarfs sitting on the shoulders of giants. We see more, and things that are more distant, than they did, not because our sight is superior or because we are taller than they, but because they raise us up, and by their great stature add to ours.[1]

While the last chapter stressed that you are going to be doing original empirical work, you will be building heavily on the ideas and approaches of previous scholars and analysts. In fact, you cannot do a good job if your work is not well situated in the field's understandings of the key concepts and theories at stake in your question, events and issues, and methodologies. The annotated bibliography (AB) is the first step in finding the giants on whose shoulders you will be standing. What is crucial is to (1) uncover those authors who and sources that are the most important, (2) become satisfied not after finding one behemoth but after locating multiple *competing* arguments, and (3) understand precisely the implications of the differing claims. All of this work is an essential and critical foundation to your paper. Just as with a physical structure, if your conceptual framework is inadequate, your paper risks falling apart. The AB is where you begin the foundation on which you will base the Literature Review and Model and Hypothesis sections of the paper.

Now that you have a research question (although you will likely refine your query as you work on your first installment), your next task is to begin finding the scholarly answers to it. Before turning directly to that endeavor, you need some prior skills. I want to address the nuts-and-bolts issues of understanding the bibliography and the information you need to collect, avoiding plagiarism and properly citing sources, and learning how to take notes on materials. Providing this information first will ensure that you keep track of all the information that you need, understand the care required in using sources, and develop the skills necessary for grouping your materials. Thereafter, you will locate, understand, and classify the participants in the debate and their most significant works.

WHAT ARE BIBLIOGRAPHIES,[2] AND WHY DO WE BOTHER WITH THEM?

Each scholarly paper contains a list of works, sometimes called a *bibliography*, that provides all the sources that contributed to the work. Over the years, particular forms for displaying this information have come into being, and you are obligated to choose one style for documenting your sources and providing other information (e.g., citations and styles for headings and title pages). Proper documentation of these materials is essential in a research paper. You should be prepared from the beginning of the writing process to keep track of the sources that you use and the precise places in the text where these authors have influenced your work. That means that you must choose a particular format, such as the American Political Science Association (APSA), American Psychological Association, or Chicago (*Chicago Manual of Style*) form. In political science, any of these formats is acceptable, but your professor may have a preference for one in particular, so check before you choose. Typically, getting access to these rules is easy; many introductory writing classes assign writing manuals that contain these guides, so you may already own one. You can also consult online summaries. Please remember that you do not have to memorize the format, but you should neither make up your own style as you go along nor change the one that you use as you proceed.

Once you have chosen a format for documentation, you need to keep careful track of where and how different works influence you. First, I recommend that you open a new document and build your bibliography as soon as you start your research. That way, you won't have to type all of your sources in when you are frantically trying to finish. Also, you'll understand exactly which information you need from the outset and won't be in the position of not having a date or page numbers when you need them. Last, since you are going to be turning in an AB, amassing the source information is necessary for your first assignment.

So far, I have defined a bibliography, but my justification for writing one likely seems weak to you: you do it because it is part of the assignment and a convention on which people who write style manuals insist. Well, yes, but a bibliography is one of those ways in which we find the intellectual giants as well as communicate to others who they are. As you start your research project, you should be looking for books and articles that answer your question. Those works are not useful simply because of what the authors claim, but particularly at your early stages, their bibliographies are potential gold mines, telling you who the main scholars are whom you need to understand and what the most important works are. Bibliographies can also contain information about excellent data sources for your topic. In other words, these lists of sources help lead you to important works that you must read to do a good job on your project. And those sources will likely send you to others. Thus, the Works Cited list is a kind of treasure map, making your detective job of finding good materials much easier. Similarly, your bibliography will be a reflection of the research that you did and will show others what helped you.

PLAGIARISM VERSUS PARAPHRASING

As you write the text of your paper, you need to keep track of the precise places in your work where you benefited from both the ideas and the exact words of your sources. You do this with footnotes or in-text citations as well as bibliographic entries. The footnotes or in-text citations are how you communicate as you are proceeding through the paper which source influenced you and precisely where. Remember, you're writing a *research* paper, so your professor is looking to see that you have done *quality research*. Demonstrate your efforts in your bibliography (list of references) and your citations. Moreover, if one work helps you understand another, you need to give the author who explains the first piece credit. You might be surprised to learn that you must cite ideas, not simply quotes and figures, and that accounting has to be done at the appropriate place in the text. This point is so important that I'll repeat it: *No matter which citation form you choose, you must attribute* ideas *and* information, *and not simply quotes and data, to their original authors.* If you do not, then you are plagiarizing.

Plagiarism is an extremely serious academic offense, the equivalent of a scholarly crime. The plagiarist steals another's prized possessions—his or her thoughts and hard work—and passes them off as his or her own. Most institutions of higher learning punish plagiarists severely, putting them on academic probation or throwing them out of school. Once you have been identified as a plagiarist, you can often forget about postgraduate education, especially law school. The lesson is never to plagiarize, either intentionally or accidentally. Keep careful track of the works that have contributed to your intellectual development, and learn how to cite and paraphrase properly.

While one way to avoid plagiarism is to provide complete quotes (properly cited) from your sources throughout your paper, this approach is not the most effective. Think back to some of the works that you have read for classes or as you have been honing your question. How many of them contained a copious number of direct quotes? I am confident that none did. Instead, these authors used proper *paraphrases*, restating in their own words the sense of others' arguments and citing the original sources. Your goal, then, is to minimize direct quotes but maintain, even maximize, the footnotes. Often, mentioning the author's name in your text to associate him or her with the ideas is appropriate, but you need to find your own way of expressing those ideas. Making your version different enough from the author's can be difficult, especially if you have the work open in front of you and/or you are trying to capture the sense of a particular sentence or a small amount of text. My recommendation is that you close the book or journal and not look at it as you try to put these ideas in your own words. You will also have an easier time avoiding plagiarism if you are distilling a larger chunk of text into a smaller one. If you're trying to condense a chapter into one paragraph, you simply cannot use the precise words in the chapter. Do not consult the abstract or any summary paragraph you may find in the the book or article; you will run a grave risk of plagiarizing by not making your text significantly different from the author's. Again, do not use another writer's summary of this work without giving that person credit. Box 3.1 provides some insight into proper paraphrasing and plagiarism.[3]

The bottom line here is to use your own words but still cite the source. It was the author's idea, and your reader is likely to know that. You will impress the reader by showing that you know the literature and can express in your own words the ideas of the scholar. If you find, however, that you simply cannot effectively communicate this author's arguments in your own words, then use a direct quote. The direct quote also requires its own footnote, of course. Whether you've conveyed the ideas or used a direct quote, you need to include in the citation the page number from the text from which either came.

ANNOTATING THE BIBLIOGRAPHY

Now that we understand what a bibliography is, why it is important, how serious an offense plagiarism is, and how to avoid it, we turn to annotation—what is it and why do it? In writing an AB you are providing a list of the works (so you will have a jump on your final bibliography), but you are adding something else to it. Underneath each entry, you write a paragraph that contains a summary of the *arguments of the work,* as well as key information about the cases and the findings. Please note that to yield useful information, you must summarize the argument, not the topic. For instance, if you were like Latisha, searching for works on polarization, and you were discussing only the topic, you would be writing, "This work is about political polarization in America." Well, of course! For the AB to help you—and all of the tasks presented in this book are designed to assist you, not simply to make extra, unnecessary work—then you have to think about (and capture in your paragraph) that piece's thesis (which is likely closely connected to how it answers your research question); how the author defines concepts that are crucial to your topic; what instances, cases, or data sets the work uses to assess its argument; and what the findings (or conclusions) are.

Reading and taking good notes on your sources is essential then, and many students have trouble with this step. Box 3.2 provides some advice. Your notes

BOX 3.1 **Paraphrasing and Plagiarism: Knowing the Difference**

Immediately below is an excerpt from John Lewis Gaddis, *We Now Know: Rethinking Cold War History* (New York: Oxford University Press, 1997), 87–88. After that, I've provided examples of paraphrasing and plagiarism, documented in APSA form. Can you tell which is which?

Original Source:

> Nuclear weapons were developed in a traditional way, but in an untraditional place. The way was traditional because scientific advances—particularly the discovery of atomic fission in the late 1930s—coincided with an opportunity to use them, which was the onset of World War II; it was not the first time the prospect of a war had stimulated the development of technologies with which to fight it. The place, though, was unexpected. Despite its impressive industrial capabilities and deeply-rooted military traditions, the United States through most of its history had hardly led the world in developing new war-fighting technologies. Americans had tended to imitate rather than to originate weaponry, and during the 1920s and 1930s they barely managed to maintain functional professional forces at any level. The army he commanded was still training with horses and mules when in October 1941 the President of the United States authorized a crash program, in collaboration with British and Canadian allies, to produce an atomic bomb.

1. According to John Lewis Gaddis, nuclear weapons were developed in a typical way but in an unusual location. The way was typical because science and its applications occurred at the same time that a war started (1997, 87–88).

2. John Lewis Gaddis contends that the American development of nuclear weapons in the 1940s was in some ways usual and in others unusual. As usual, engineers and scientists in that decade found a real-world application for the theoretical discovery of fission. Atypically, however, the United States, along with Great Britain and Canada, was the site of this innovation. In the past, other countries in the world had been at the forefront of military technology, while the United States was a follower. This time, however, the United States took the lead (Gaddis 1997, 87–88).

3. Americans tended to copy rather than to invent new armaments, and during the interwar period they barely managed to keep professional forces at a functional level.

Answers:

1. **Plagiarism.** Although the author and page numbers are provided, the student uses Gaddis' first eight words verbatim. In the rest, the sentence construction and language are far too close to Gaddis'.

2. **Paraphrasing.** The student has captured the sense of the paragraph in her own words. She gives the author credit in the citation and provides the page numbers.

3. **Plagiarism.** The student uses the same sentence construction and words very similar (with some synonyms) to Gaddis'. In addition, the student fails to give the author any credit (either in the text or with a citation). (Even if the student had provided a citation here, it still would have been plagiarism because the sentence structure is too similar to Gaddis'.)

BOX 3.2 **How to Read and Take Notes on Articles and Books**

Scholarly articles and books can be very difficult to read, but you need to learn to do so in order to use these materials in your research project. As you approach this task, you should remember that scholars tend to follow the same basic outline for their research papers that you are being exposed to now. Understanding that papers or books are written in sections or chapters that typically perform the same basic tasks is a useful key to unlocking part of the meaning of these works. The rest you will have to discern for yourself. Below, I have some advice for reading and taking notes so that you will more quickly and accurately understand academic authors. Please note that this advice can help you with any reading you have to do for your courses, not just your reading for your research paper.

Step 1—CHECK IT OUT:[a] First, look at the piece and try to determine its logical structure by reading and thinking about the *headings* in the text. These titles are the author's outline, so they give you a key to the plan of the essay. Can you identify the introduction, literature review, methods section, analysis section, and conclusion? After you finish reading and thinking about the headings, read the introductory and concluding sections. DO NOT TAKE NOTES UNTIL AFTER YOU HAVE READ BOTH. When you finish, you should be able to write down the author's argument (also called a thesis). If the thesis is not clear, reread the conclusion until you can identify it. Now, you are ready to begin reading the text. The rest of the work will provide the logic and evidence that led the author to conclude with that thesis.

Step 2—MARK IT UP/LOOK IT UP: Go back to the beginning and read the text carefully, with the goal of identifying the argument and the evidence that the author provides to support the thesis. As you read, mark the text and make brief notes in the margins near any important, interesting, or confusing items. Try to mark where the author provides the argument and gives evidence to support the thesis. Also, have a dictionary handy so that you can look up words that are unfamiliar to you. DO NOT simply skip over words that you do not know. If you do not know the meaning of the words the author uses, can you really expect to understand the argument? In your notes, write down the definitions of the words that you look up, and learn them. If the dictionary doesn't seem to provide a good definition (perhaps because the term is one specific to political science), look up this word in the glossary of the appropriate textbook.

Step 3—WRITE IT DOWN: After you have finished reading the article, you can go back and take notes. Your job is to identify the author's argument (double-check your work in step 1 above) as well as to determine the logic and evidence that the author provides to sustain his or her reasoning. Go back to the marks in the text, and write down material that provides insight into the author's reasoning and the facts that he or she cites to support the thesis. Also, be sure to look again at the passages about which you were unsure initially. Do you understand them now? If not, write down in your notes exactly what is not clear to you.

Step 4—CRITIQUE IT: Now think critically about what you have read and recorded. Is the author's argument logical? For instance, is it plausible that the identified cause could lead to the particular phenomenon in question? Then look at the evidence that the author supplies. Does that evidence really support his or her claim? Is the author using the facts properly, or has he or she slanted them to help make the case? In addition, can you think of other facts that the author does not include that will discredit the argument? Can you think of a similar instance that will not fit? Jot down any problems that you can see with the author's argument, the use of evidence, or the application of this approach to a comparable case. Or, more positively, does the author's argument seem to apply to other similar cases? Has the evidence been used carefully? Why is this piece so good?

Step 5—RELATE IT: Finally, relate this piece to other works that you have read. In which school of thought or family of theories would this piece belong? To which works is this piece similar? From which is it different? Why?

If you follow the guidelines specified here, your notes on your readings will look like the following list. (Please note that you may not always be able to fill in something for each part. For instance, you might not find any logical or evidentiary problems, or the author might not use any terms with which you are not familiar. But you should always identify the thesis, logic, and evidence and the work's links to other things you have read.)

- Thesis:
- Logic:
- Evidence:
- Cases other than the ones you want to study for which this argument makes sense:
- Vocabulary:
- Critique:
- Logical problems:
- Evidentiary problems:
- Other cases for which this argument does not make sense:
- Relationship to other works you have read:
- In which school of thought or theoretical family does this piece belong?
- To which works does it seem most similar? Why?
- To which works does it seem most opposed? Why?

These notes should form the basis for writing the summary that will annotate your bibliography.

NOTE

a. This step is especially important if your source is a book. At the point of the annotated bibliography, you likely won't have the time to read the whole book and get through other sources too. So use the introductory and concluding chapters to help you find out what you need for this project. Realize that you will likely have to go back to the book and read more as you proceed.

become the basis for the paragraph summary that will follow your biblio-graphic entry.

In reading these sources, remember that a scholar will write his or her book or article in a form similar to the one you are learning about here for research papers. So you should be able to find the literature review section and discover how an author divides the field into schools of thought.[4] An author will also tell you who are the most important proponents of each view and what the essential works to read are. Thus, once you read a literature review, you are on your way to unlocking the scholarly debate on your question and finding other excellent sources to consult for your own paper. You still must use care, how-ever, not to accept someone else's assessment of the field on face value. Each author has a particular argument that he or she is making, and while you may agree with it, you cannot be sure until after you have read other principal works too. Thus, you should read a few scholarly works or literature review sections carefully to help you have an idea of the debate and the major players in it.

IDENTIFYING THE KEY CONCEPTUAL ISSUES

Now you know what you need to do and why, but how should you get started on the AB? Your first job is to find good sources, and the best place to start is your question and the concepts that you identify in it. Those concepts will lead you to the issues that political scientists are debating. Because you need to uncover the scholarly answers to your question, you will be looking for scholarly sources, that is, the work of academics. While journalists and commentators may provide interesting answers and insights into your question, they should not be the authors that you are searching for at this stage. Who are scholars, and where can you find their work? Scholars tend to be professors (working at uni-versities or colleges) or people employed by think tanks and public policy and governmental institutes. These people usually publish their work in books (often, but not exclusively, ones that are published at university presses, text-book publishers, think tanks, and under certain imprints of large publishing houses) and in what are called peer-reviewed journals, periodicals with a policy of sending any piece that comes in for consideration out to other experts to review and approve. Academic journals publish a varying number of issues a year but aren't weekly like *The Economist*, for instance. Scholarly journals tend to have footnotes and bibliographies. More policy-oriented journals (e.g., *Social Policy, Foreign Affairs,* or *Current History*) may lack the list of sources, but the articles that appear in them can be extremely relevant and are peer reviewed.

With the need for scholarly sources in mind, we will turn to the task of finding some. Let's start, as mentioned, with an examination of some of the questions that our first three students suggested:

Latisha: Why is U.S. politics so polarized now, and what are the consequences of polarization?

| Samantha: | To what extent and in which ways have different types of candidates used new media in their election campaigns? |
| Joe: | How or under which conditions is peace built in formerly war-torn societies? |

Conceptually, Latisha is concerned with political polarization, Samantha wants to understand more about campaigns and new media, and Joe is interested in peace after internal war. Often, the terms we use in our questions tap us into different variants of the literature, with different priorities; for instance, here Joe is asking about what happens after *internal* war, and while how states recover from *interstate* and *civil* conflict might be similar, Joe should try very hard to focus his search on peace after *internal* conflict. He will also find that although he identifies the phenomenon as *peace,* some scholars make an important distinction between that term and *stability.*[5] He will need to consider both concepts and potentially adjust his question if he finds that he is actually more interested in one than the other.

SEARCHING FOR SOURCES

Once you have identified the key concepts at issue, go back to your materials from related courses (textbooks, *anthologies*—edited volumes that contain a collection of articles written by different authors—and course packs). Notice what I have not suggested: I have not recommended that you perform a Google (or other Internet search-engine) search. Your goal is to find scholarly sources that answer your research question. While the web is a fabulous source of information and you could ultimately find many of the same materials that you will uncover using the methods I suggest, you need a certain degree of knowledge to use the Internet wisely for scholarly research. You cannot trust that every article posted on the web is important or accurate. This is also not the time to search for facts or turn to encyclopedia-type sources. An encyclopedia can provide important basic information as you are starting your process, and it is fine for primary and secondary school reports, but report writing is behind you. Now, you are to engage in the scholarly debate and process.

Back to our search of course materials, use the tables of contents and indices to find the sources on your subject. Reread and take notes on (1) the key concerns, arguments, and issues involved with this concept and (2) the authors and sources (sometimes in the text and footnotes and usually at the end of the chapter in the For Further Reading section). The materials mentioned should be the next place to look for information, and if you find important substantive material in that chapter—for instance, definitions of the concepts and characterizations about the debate in the field—then you should make your first bibliographic entry, taking care to note the source and other relevant information.

Perhaps, however, your issues are too recent or too specific for your course texts. What should you do then? (Actually, you should proceed through this step even if your search through course materials helped you find some good sources.) Take those words that you identified from thinking hard about your question and perform a search using the online Library of Congress (LoC) catalog, or if you are a student at a research university—one that trains graduate students in our field and thus is likely to have an excellent scholarly book collection—you can search your own library catalog.

Latisha followed this method, went to the LoC site, and typed in "polarization and American politics" as a keyword search. Box 3.3 contains some of what she saw.

Notice six things about these results. First, the dots in front of the author's name (if there is a name supplied) indicate how relevant the search results are likely to be given the terms used. In Latisha's case, the results I've shown you are all highly relevant (receiving the top number possible). Second, if the book has authors (not editors) the first author's name appears first and again after the title. The book, then, is not an anthology, an edited volume that collects the works of many writers. This also signifies that this author should be listed first. Do not change the order of the authors listed (even if they are not in alphabetical order). The sequence is intentional and often reflects the level of contribution to the work. Third, the titles are hypertext, and you can click on them for more information. Fourth, the publication date is provided, and often when you're starting your search you want to look at the most recent publications because they will give you the newest perspectives while also citing (and often summarizing) the arguments of the old. Thus, they help you do some of your work. Fifth, while the information that you will need for your bibliography is here in the citation (after you click the hypertext), please realize that depending on the format you are using, you might have to change capitalization and the order of the information. The listing also may provide extraneous material that you don't need. So have your style guide near you when you are doing your work so you can write your citation properly the first time. Sixth, Latisha received a "Goldilocks" number of hits on her search, not too many, not too few (more than 10, but fewer than 50). Actually, Latisha first searched for "polarization and politics" and got more than 100. Then, she added the adjective *American* and returned a more manageable and more relevant set of books given her research interests.

Remember that the search process takes careful thought, sometimes a little luck, and always perseverance. If your search terms are not leading you to other sources, you likely need to do a better job in generating these terms. So go back to your course materials or those articles that aided the generation and refinement of your question. Ask yourself again, What are the key concepts at stake? Who does my textbook identify as important? If you can locate new authors, titles, or search terms, use them to lead you to new ones. If you still haven't had success, then consult a reference librarian for help. That person will be well

BOX 3.3   **Results from a Library of Congress Online Catalog Search**

DATABASE: Library of Congress Online Catalog
YOU SEARCHED: Keyword (match all words) = Polarization and American Politics

●●●●● Baumer, Donald C., 1950- Parties, polarization, and democracy in the United States / Donald C. Baumer, Howard J. Gold. 2010

●●●●● Abramowitz, Alan. Disappearing center : engaged citizens, polarization, and American democracy / Alan I. Abramowitz. 2010

●●●●● Beyond the boundaries : a new structure of ambition in African American politics / Georgia A. Persons, editor. 2009

●●●●● Abramowitz McCarty, Nolan M. Polarized America : the dance of ideology and unequal riches / Nolan McCarty, Keith T. Poole, and Howard Rosenthal. 2006

versed with subject searching and will be able to identify new terms. The librarian, however, can only help you. You need to do the primary thinking about your question and what you're really interested in. The important points, however, are not to give up and to use the resources you have to your advantage. Also, finding sources takes time. Be sure to allot yourself enough.

Now let's return to Latisha and her search for sources. She decided to click on the first two titles to find out more. Clicking on the hyperlinks not only will give her all the publication information she needs and the numbers she will need to find the books in the library but also will provide great information to help her assess the potential value of the books and will lead to more sources (see Box 3.4).

What's interesting here are the two publishers: Paradigm Publishers and Yale University Press. These are different kinds of publishing houses, both of which have value in Latisha's search. Paradigm Publishers typically publishes specialty textbooks, to be used in upper-division classes for undergraduates. Thus, this work will have lots of relevant information, citations, and arguments and will be presented in a style that is highly accessible to college students. This kind of book can offer a great start. Other similar presses are CQ Press, W. W. Norton, Rowman & Littlefield, Routledge, and Lynne Rienner, among others. The second book's publisher is Yale University Press. As Yale University is a major research university, its press publishes what it considers to be the best of contemporary scholarship. This book (also called a *monograph*, a scholarly work on a relatively narrow topic) by Abramowitz, then, is an essential part of the debate you are likely to enter (unless you transform your question away from its concerns) and is a must for you to understand. Moreover, as a good scholar, Abramowitz has included a discussion of the scholarly disagreements

BOX 3.4 **Learning More from the Library Record**

◄ Previous Next ►

| Brief Record | Subjects/Content | Full Record | MARC Tags |

Parties, polarization, and democracy in the United States / Donald C. . . .

Relevance:	●●●●●
LC Control No.:	2009036149
LCCN Permalink:	http://lccn.loc.gov/2009036149
Type of Material:	Book (Print, Microform, Electronic, etc.)
Personal Name:	Baumer, Donald C., 1950-
Main Title:	Parties, polarization, and democracy in the United States / Donald C. Baumer, Howard J. Gold.
Published/Created:	Boulder : Paradigm Publishers, c2010.
Description:	xi, 243 p. : ill. ; 24 cm.
ISBN:	9781594516672 (hardcover : alk. paper)
	1594516677 (hardcover : alk. paper)
CALL NUMBER:	JK2265 .B38 2010
	Copy 1
— Request in:	Jefferson or Adams Building Reading Rooms
— Status:	Not Charged

in a conceptual, or literature review, chapter. This work will also help you identify the key issues, though from Abramowitz's perspective. Because you know you need to examine the debate, you have to be sure that you don't allow the first work that you read to sway your opinion too much. Realize that authors will portray their approach in the best light and will be stressing the weaknesses of others. You, on the other hand, have to look to those others and see how they justify their positions.

The records also tell you where to find the books. If you were at the LoC or a research library, you could use both the call numbers and the locations to physically get the books. You can use this information (as well as the title and author) to search for the books in your own college library; however, if your

◀ Previous Next ▶

| Brief Record | Subjects/Content | Full Record | MARC Tags |

The disappearing center: engaged citizens, polarization, and American. . .

Relevance:	●●●●●
LC Control No.:	2009033737
LCCN Permalink:	http://lccn.loc.gov/2009033737
Type of Material:	Book (Print, Microform, Electronic, etc.)
Personal Name:	Abramowitz, Alan.
Main Title:	The disappearing center : engaged citizens, polarization, and American democracy / Alan I. Abramowitz.
Published/Created:	New Haven : Yale University Press, c2010.
Description:	xi, 194 p. : ill. ; 25 cm.
ISBN:	9700300141027 (cloth : alk. paper)
	0300141629 (cloth : alk. paper)
CALL NUMBER:	JK2261 .A28 2010
	Copy 1
— Request in:	Jefferson or Adams Building Reading Rooms
— Status:	Not Charged
CALL NUMBER:	JK2261 .A28 2010 FT MEADE
	Copy 2
— Request in:	Jefferson or Adams Building Reading Rooms - STORED OFFSITE
— Status:	Not Charged

institution doesn't own them, don't fret. If you've started your work early enough, then you can request the books through interlibrary loan. In many cases, you can receive what you need in a week. Thus, starting early and choosing what you need is very important, particularly when you don't have a large library at your own school.

There's still more useful information to glean from the records. One of the key values of sources is in helping you find additional ones. For this, not only do you need the physical books and their bibliographies, but you can also use the records to help you find better searching terms and similar sources. If you click on the hypertext that follows "LCCN Permalink," you will find the records shown in Box 3.5.

BOX 3.5 **Learning from the Permalink**

Parties, polarization, and democracy in the United States

LC Control No.:	2009036149
Type of Material:	Book (Print, Microform, Electronic, etc.)
Personal Name:	Baumer, Donald C., 1950- » <u>More like this</u>
Main Title:	Parties, polarization, and democracy in the United States / Donald C. Baumer, Howard J. Gold.
Published/Created:	Boulder : Paradigm Publishers, c2010.
Related Names:	Gold, Howard J., 1958- » <u>More like this</u>
Description:	xi, 243 p. : ill. ; 24 cm.
ISBN:	9781594516672 (hardcover : alk. paper)
	1594516677 (hardcover : alk. paper)
Contents:	1. Political parties in the twenty-first century — 2. Parties and the electorate I : images of the parties — 3. Parties and the electorate II : the dynamics of party polarization — 4. The mid-term elections of 1994 and 2006 — 5. Parties in power : Congress, presidents, partisanship, and gridlock — 6. Political parties in Anglo-America — 7. Looking backward and forward : the election of 2008 and the future of American politics.
Notes:	Includes bibliographical references and index.
Subjects:	Political parties—United States. » <u>More like this</u>
	Elections—United States. » <u>More like this</u>
	Polarization (Social sciences)—United States. » <u>More like this</u>
	United States—Politics and government—1989- » <u>More like this</u>
LC Classification:	JK2265 .B38 2010
Dewey Class No.:	324.273 22
Other System No.:	(OCoLC)ocn320191831
Geographic Area Code:	n-us---

What is great about these matrices is that for the first source you learn the chapter titles, providing you a greater sense of what the book concentrates on and how it proceeds. In the record for both this book and the scholarly monograph by Abramowitz, you see new search terms to try (under "Subjects") as well as a link to books about those related subjects. In addition, you can find more works by the authors by clicking on the hypertext after their names. Thus, you are on your way to finding many useful works, and you've been looking at only two sources! How many books you need depends on

The disappearing center : engaged citizens, polarization, and American . . .

LC Control No.:	2009033737
Type of Material:	Book (Print, Microform, Electronic, etc.)
Personal Name:	Abramowitz, Alan. » More like this
Main Title:	The disappearing center : engaged citizens, polarization, and American democracy / Alan I. Abramowitz.
Published/Created:	New Haven : Yale University Press, c2010.
Description:	xi, 194 p. : ill. ; 25 cm.
ISBN:	9780300141627 (cloth : alk. paper) 0300141629 (cloth : alk. paper)
Notes:	Includes bibliographical references and index.
Subjects:	Political parties—United States. » More like this Party affiliation—United States. » More like this Polarization (Social sciences) » More like this United States—Politics and government—2009-» More like this
LC Classification:	JK2261 .A28 2010
Dewey Class No.:	324.273 22
National Bibliography No.:	GBB056649 bnb
National Bibliographic Agency No.:	015542056 Uk
Other System No.:	(OCoLC)ocn434744479
Geographic Area Code:	n-us—

your assignment, how easy your access to these books is, and the nature of your topic.

After you find some important books (important because they are relevant given your topic and they are either very recent or what everyone tells you are the classics, i.e., older and essential works in the field), then it is time for you to turn to database searching to find important articles. Scholars write both books and articles (actually, some tend to write books, some write articles, and some write both). They publish their books with scholarly, textbook, and some trade presses, and they publish their articles in multiple kinds of journals, too. For the AB, you're trying to uncover the most important arguments or answers to your question, so you want to find scholarly journals. Sometimes the journals of opinion, news articles, and/or editorials that helped you formulate your question are also relevant, and you can summarize them, but remember these alone are not sufficient. You must rely most heavily on scholarly sources.

To find these, begin searching databases that index journals to help you find important articles about your topic, or if your search through books has already helped you identify some key articles, use the databases to find them. We've already become acquainted with some of these library databases from our work developing the research question. I frequently suggest that my students start in Academic Search Premier and ProQuest (under "Research Libraries"). I like these because they index a number of scholarly journals and they usually have very recent issues online. Other useful databases include Project MUSE and JSTOR, but be careful with JSTOR because there is a delay in bringing materials online.

When you search, you will want to use all that you have learned before to help you find appropriate sources. Search using your key concept (from your question), the names of the authors you found (in your texts or from the LoC search), and the additional subject terms that you turned up in your earlier search. Then, use those terms and similar techniques to return just the right number of good sources. What's nice about database searching is that you can also read an abstract of an article and get a sense of the argument and the article's utility before you read the whole work. Use the abstracts to help you choose the best articles (as well as to help you a bit with your summary, but be very careful not to plagiarize here!). Once you have picked a manageable number of good sources, you will have to read them as I have outlined above and write original summaries for the AB, summaries that help you understand not only what the authors are arguing but whom they are arguing against, whom they agree with, and how they came to their conclusions. Then you are ready for the last phase.

IDENTIFYING SIMILAR ARGUMENTS AND GROUPING YOUR SOURCES

When you are working on your AB, I recommend that you have two bibliography files to work from. One contains only the list of sources in alphabetical order, properly written according to the format you have chosen. This file will become the one that you build on all semester long and submit with your later installments. The other includes both the bibliographic entry and the summary paragraphs appropriate for your AB assignment. The second, annotated one you are going to play around with, in violation of the bibliographic conventions, moving sources so that they are grouped with other sources that make similar arguments, not arranged alphabetically. My logic here is to get you to see whether you actually have multiple, different answers to your research question and to identify what the essentials to those answers are. If you know you have two or more answers then you are going to be in a good position to write about the debate in your literature review. (You can't have a debate with just one argument with which all your authors agree!) In addition, if you can articulate what those answers have in common, then they are likely to be similar, and you are likely to have found what academics refer to as a school of thought, a similar approach to answering the question.

So as you are working on the AB, consciously group your works. Now, if you've found an important scholarly work—like Abramowitz for Latisha—you will also know the way that the author divides the field. You will want to be aware of his or her categories, but not necessarily committed to them. Maybe you'll like the author's labels, maybe the categories are the standard ones for everyone who studies polarization in the United States, or maybe you will think that his or her perspective is misguided. Keep in mind all of those possibilities. If you end up liking his or her approach, you can borrow the terms (giving proper credit in a citation, of course) and use that scheme (and the citations) to help you make sure that you have the most important sources in your bibliography. If you don't like it, you can look for others that better match your ideas and needs or even make up your own set of labels.

The main points, however, are to be sure that (1) you are able to identify what the source is arguing in response to your question and (2) you are finding different types of answers. If all your sources agree, then you have to go back and search for more works. Use the works you have to find out with whom these authors disagree. Realize that no matter how much advice I give you, neither your professor nor I can provide the magic formula for looking only at the works that you will use in your research. Everyone doing this type of project reads and thinks about some works that he or she won't use. Some of that inefficiency results from your being at an initial phase of your project and not always sure of your direction. Still, your efforts are all worthwhile, as perfect efficiency in searching is impossible. If you use these techniques you will minimize the time that you perceive as unproductive; however, most of us need to go down a few alleys as we learn more about our questions and topics. Just try to be as focused as you can, and stay clear about your goal of finding the most important scholarly answers to your question,—answers that should not all agree.

ONE LAST WORD OF ADVICE: GENERIC SCHOOLS OF THOUGHT

When you're in the midst of locating sources, finding only the most recent ones or the arguments with which you agree can be really tempting. You can also sometimes have a hard time thinking about what else might be relevant or how some previous readings (e.g., from other courses) might be helpful. That's when you should remember that in political science there are (arguably) four broad schools of thought.[6] For ease of remembering them, I refer to the group as IIIE or "Triple I E"—*Interests*, *Institutions*, *Ideas*, and *Economics*. Thinking through these factors and their possible impact on your subject of interest can be very helpful, and I guarantee that you have all seen explanations that use these elements.

Interest-based approaches assert that actors make decisions that maximize their priorities. In American and comparative politics, these are often called rational-choice theories; in international politics, some refer to these as rational-actor approaches. From this viewpoint, agents take the steps that best serve their interests, whether the actors are voters deciding whether turning out to cast a ballot is worth the effort, protestors thinking about coming out for a demonstration when the threat of violent regime retaliation is looming, or a country determining whether an intervention will serve its power position. *Institutional* perspectives focus on the rules or structures of institutions and show that these established routines or patterns have an impact on outcomes. For instance, in studying elections, political scientists know that the type of electoral system—whether it is first past the post or some form of proportional representation scheme—affects how candidates and voters behave and the outcome of the contest.[7] The third *I* here—*ideas*—is actually a catchall term for ideas, identities, and cultures. These types of explanations contend that what actors think, who they are (or who they think they are), and what they value determine results. Some of the factors involved might be called psychological, whether these are the schemas and scripts that actors use to make sense of the world or one's orientation (e.g., positive and outgoing) toward society or sociological, that is, elements of an identity such as race, gender, ethnicity, or socioeconomic status. Culture could mean a particular world culture as well as those sets of values and practices specific to an organization or group. Last, a final group of explanations stresses the role of *economic* (or sometimes socioeconomic) factors. Typical assertions of the primacy of economics include those that argue that recessions cause the party in power to lose in midterm elections and that wealth produces democracies around the world.[8]

This discussion about the generic schools, I hope, helps you focus on the driving forces in politics, reminds you of perspectives that you have learned about in your classes, and links you to the debates in the field and even the broader culture. How do different people account for your phenomenon? The value of remembering these generic schools is that they can keep your mind open to multiple, possible understandings as well as link you to other scholarship and perspectives. Using the generic schools of thought to spin out possible explanations is a kind of mental exercise to help warm you up as you conduct your research to find the actual scholarly explanations out there; moreover, this activity helps you avoid missing an obvious answer. It provides you with the stamina to keep looking for different approaches when you are searching for books and articles as well as gives you some ideas for creative ways to link your research to other strands of inquiry that you have seen in your academic career.

WRITING THE ANNOTATED BIBLIOGRAPHY

As we have seen, your goal is to identify the scholars who have made the biggest contributions to answering your question and use them to help you move forward on your paper. Those great works enhance your own understandings and help build a solid theoretical foundation for your project. After you have located some excellent sources and begun summarizing them as suggested above, you can classify your answers and write your AB. I suggest that your AB contain four distinct and important elements, stated here in the order in which you should work on them. First is your research question. You want to be sure that you have a clear one and that ultimately your sources are answering it. You need to state the query in the AB not only for your benefit but also for your instructor's. This way you both will be able to evaluate whether your question and your sources are well suited to each other and whether you are finding alternative answers. Second is your sources, listed as bibliographic entries and written in a consistent form. This should be the easiest part of your AB. Third, you should work on the summaries of your sources, with special attention to the arguments and the points of contention between authors. Fourth, and last, is the job of trying to characterize the school, stating what is essential to the argument and perhaps even giving the approach a label.

Latisha started working on her AB. At the outset, she read her assignment and noted that her professor wanted her paper written in American Psychological Association form. Latisha began using the works from the journals of opinion that she consulted as she was mulling over her topic and trying to identify a question. Through interlibrary loan, she received the Abramowitz book first, which then led her immediately to some other important authors and works. She is not yet finished, but a draft of her AB follows below. Notice that she was able to link her research to works that she had read or learned about in her classes (see Putnam, Yglesias, and Robinson and Ellis), and she still might decide to add something on wedge issues[9] to her first school. Latisha knows that she still needs to find other adherents of each school and look for some scholarly articles, but she is on her way to developing a good understanding of the scholarly debate around her research question.

The Beginnings of Latisha's AB

<u>Research Question:</u> Why is U.S. politics so polarized now, and what are the consequences of polarization?[10]

School 1: Elites are highly polarized, and their vitriol alienates many citizens and leads to a breakdown in representation.

Fiorina, M. P., with S. J. Abrams. (2009). *Disconnect: The breakdown of representation in American politics.* Norman: University of Oklahoma Press.

Fiorina, M. P., with S. J. Abrams & J. C. Pope. (2006). *Culture war? The myth of a polarized America* (3rd ed.). New York: Pearson Longman.

Responding to both media characterizations and what they see as incorrect academic readings of the data, Morris P. Fiorina contends that citizens tend to be comfortably situated in the middle of the ideological spectrum (2006, 11–12; 2009, 12–20). Elites, on the other hand, occupy the ideological extremes. Thus, the polarized debate in politics is simply a product of elite and media manipulations. Citizens are not always very well informed because they don't pay close attention to politics, and when they are they do not necessarily have very strong likes or dislikes. They are often forced to make choices (especially at election time), but those selections do not capture accurately their political views, which are usually moderate (2006, 27–28). This risk of elite polarization is that citizens become further turned off by politics. Politicians, then, increasingly do not adequately represent the views of their constituents (2009, 24–48).

Robinson, M., & Ellis, S. (2004, August). Purple America. *The Weekly Standard, 9*(46), 27–29. Retrieved September 1, 2011, from Social Science Module (Document ID: 678149531).

Although they differ with Fiorina and his coauthors on the emphasis on elites' being disconnected from their constituents, Robinson and Ellis stress that there are no "blue" or "red" states. Instead, citizens from all states elect people from both parties (p. 27). While the Pew Research Study finds significant evidence of polarization, these authors claim that a closer look at the data shows something else. Citizens are, for the most part, in the middle, and "purple" reflects their partisanship more than blue or red (p. 29).

School 2: Citizens are highly polarized; this polarization has positive and negative consequences.

Abramowitz, A. I. (2010). *The disappearing center: Engaged citizens, polarization, and American democracy.* New Haven, CT: Yale University Press.

In direct opposition to Fiorina, Alan I. Abramowitz (2010) argues that most citizens are politically engaged, and they are taking increasingly polarized views. He concedes that a segment of the portion of Americans has little interest, but this portion is a minority and is shrinking. This polarized majority, then, does not follow politicians but leads elected officials and candidates to more partisan and ideological positions. More citizens than ever are highly engaged in politics, as recent voter turnout, activism, and political contributions show. These behaviors are very positive because they reflect the democratic ideal, the rule of an informed and involved citizenry. In fact, American political parties are now approaching the once-thought-of ideal: ideologically consistent, responsive, and responsible groupings of representatives (pp. 4–5). Engaged citizens have strong ideological views, and they tend to seek out people like themselves. Unlike in the past, people tend to live, go to school or work, and worship with people who share their own positions. Given the changes in the media, citizens can also block out sources of information that don't correspond to their views (Chapters 3–5). Thus, not everything about this polarized America is positive for politics, as U.S. institutions were not designed for ideologically consistent and responsive parties. Given U.S. institutions, as well as the almost even ideological split among the public, polarization means gridlock and the increasing frustration and alienation of the remaining part of the public, which is not as interested in politics (pp. 111–138).

Yglesias, M. (2007, April). The great divider. *The American Prospect, 18*(4), 47–49. Retrieved September 1, 2011, from ABI/INFORM Global (Document ID: 1252185511).

Partisanship and ideology are increasingly aligning. Geography, religion, gender, and of course race are now more than ever correlated with citizens' political views (p. 47). While events may drive popularity of presidents and enhance their ability to govern, this support can be fleeting, particularly among those who aren't strong partisans, when the relevance of a crisis fades (p. 49).

School 3: Polarization results from a society with dense social networks among those who agree and very little contact among those who don't. The consequences, however, are negative for encouraging deliberation and considered choice.

Mutz, D. C. (2006). *Hearing the other side: Deliberative versus participatory democracy.* New York: Cambridge University Press.

According to Diana C. Mutz (2006), dense social networks are great for creating an enthusiastic and engaged citizenry but not good for engendering a tolerant society (pp. 7–10). Characteristics we have tended to idealize in a citizen—informed, engaged, opinionated, and involved—are actually contrary to the flexible and open society our national narrative and our democratic theory praise (pp. 34–44). Polarization has come about because people who are actively engaged are increasingly inclined to shut themselves off from ideas that and others who they neither like (perhaps seeing those others as "liberals," "rednecks," or "extremists") nor want to know. The consequences for democracy are significant. People are less exposed to opposing viewpoints and policies and less willing to consider seriously alternative perspectives. Mutz claims this loss threatens tolerance as well as the quality of the political process and political outcomes (Chapter 3). We may have a good deal of participation, but not enough deliberation—thoughtful and comprehensive consideration of issues. Both factors—participation and deliberation—are equally important and essential to the good health of the American polity; deliberation must be revived today without losing participation (pp. 128–135, 147–151).

Putnam, R., with R. Leonardi & R. Y. Nanetti. (1994). *Making democracy work: Civil traditions in modern Italy.* Princeton, NJ: Princeton University Press.

Putnam, R. (1995). Bowling alone. *Journal of Democracy, 6*(1), 65–78.

Mutz's argument builds on a line of reasoning most associated with Robert Putnam. In the first work here, *Making Democracy Work,* Putnam and his colleagues seek to understand whether regional variation in the quality of democracy in Italy has continued since the 1970s institutional reforms that put in place common structures throughout the land (pp. 8–13). In particular, he contrasts the impact of socioeconomic modernity and civic community on institutional performance (his proxy for democracy) and finds that civic community—how engaged citizens are in associations—is a far better predictor of the quality of democracy than is modernization (see Chapter 4, especially). In the second work, "Bowling Alone," Putnam changes the name of that key factor from civic community to social capital and contends that the decline in social capital—the links that citizens have with others, particularly others with whom they wouldn't ordinarily associate—in the United States has led to a decrease in social trust and has dangerous consequences for democracy.

Like Latisha, you should try as soon as you can (even when you haven't finished identifying all your key sources yet) to begin your AB. Better to know sooner rather than later whether you have different approaches, whether you understand the arguments, and what you are lacking. And don't be surprised if you find that you have to jettison some of your sources because they stray from your ultimate focus. This is a stage to refine your research question, cull sources, and find new ones to enhance your understanding of the debate.

PRACTICAL SUMMARY

The steps to follow when you need to write the AB are the following:

1. Determine which citation form—Chicago, American Psychological Association, or Modern Language Association—you will be using; your professor might have a preferred form. Make sure you have access to a guide.

2. Find the most important scholarly answers to your research question by

   a. interrogating your question to identify the central concepts;

   b. consulting materials from related classes to find key authors, sources, and concepts;

   c. using the LoC catalog online or that of a research library to find materials and, potentially, better search terms—order or go get these works as appropriate; and

    d. searching article databases for scholarly articles using what you have learned about search terms, good authors, and important journal articles.

3. Read the sources, and

    a. take careful notes that summarize the source's answer to the research question,—focus on the arguments offered and be sure to pay attention to with whom this author agrees and disagrees;

    b. be careful not to plagiarize,—take careful notes and write down page numbers for the exact places where you find material; and

    c. keep track of all the essential bibliographic information and start your paper's source list, using the proper form.

4. Place your sources into schools of thought by characterizing the answers offered. Sometimes a one-word label will suffice; other times you will need more information to distinguish between them.

SUGGESTED CALENDAR

Follow your professor's instructions, but typically you will want to complete the AB at a relatively early stage of the course. Pay careful attention to format, understanding the argument, paraphrasing, and carefully noting page numbers. Realize, too, that even after you have handed in this assignment, you will continue reading relevant materials and you will engage in a similar thinking and analytic process to be able to integrate your new sources effectively into your paper. Recognize that you will likely come back to your classification scheme, rethink some elements of it, and include more sources. Still, work to identify and label the key schools and highlight the most important factor(s) at this early time.

EXERCISES

1. Take Samantha's question and key concepts. Search for them on the LoC website and find three scholarly books. Also identify other important search terms.

2. Take Joe's question and key concepts. Search for them on one of the online databases available at your institution. Pick three excellent (scholarly and from prestigious authors) and recent articles. Identify new search terms for Joe.

3. Take the sources listed in Latisha's example AB, convert them, and place them in the correct order for a bibliography for a paper written in Chicago style.

CHECKLIST 2: ANNOTATED BIBLIOGRAPHY

In your first installment, you will turn in your question and your AB. Back in chapter 2 you saw what was essential for developing a good question. This rubric identifies the key requirements for the AB. Pay close attention to these elements through the writing process, not simply when you think you are done, because at that point, you may not have enough time to fix any problems or weaknesses.

Checklist 2: Annotated Bibliography

I have used an approved citation form for my bibliographic entries.	Yes _____ No _____
I have provided summaries of the arguments of these works and have not simply summarized the topic. (Thus, my summaries are relatively long and contain footnotes or in-text documentation, depending on the format I am using.)	Yes _____ No _____
I am "sitting on the shoulders of giants" and have found the most important sources, ones that several people cite as the key works.	Yes _____ No _____
I have found at least two schools.	Yes _____ No _____
I have grouped my sources into schools. This means that I typically have more than one source in each group and each of the works in a school asserts a common answer to the research question.	Yes _____ No _____
I have come up with a way to label or characterize my school; I understand how the works within the group are similar.	Yes _____ No _____
I have found a variety of sources—some books, some journal articles—but the vast majority of them are scholarly.	Yes _____ No _____
I am keeping open another bibliography file that includes all of the works (without the summaries) formatted appropriately and in alphabetical order.	Yes _____ No _____

NOTES

1. While the fundamental ideas of this quote are typically attributed to Sir Isaac Newton, many believe the original source is John of Salisbury and his work *Metalogicon* of 1159. This quote reflects his precise words. For discussion, see http://www.phrases.org.uk/meanings/268025.html.

2. This book (in its footnotes and its bibliography) uses Chicago style, and I am using its term here (and will continue to do so throughout) for the list of works consulted in a project. The Modern Language Association calls this the "Works Cited," and for the American Psychological Association it's "References." In all styles, the works are listed in alphabetical order by author last name. They are not numbered. Each approach treats the entries slightly differently, so consult a manual for the precise format.

3. See Diana Hacker, *A Pocket Manual of Style,* 4th ed. (Boston: Bedford/St. Martin's, 2004), 115–126, 157–164, 185–192.

4. Sometimes, you can find an article that is solely a literature review. This will be very helpful in understanding the different approaches to your research question. Still, you should not copy or reiterate all of that author's analysis. You must think through the literature on your own. A great place for finding articles that summarize a field of inquiry is Ira Katznelson and Helen V. Milner, eds., *Political Science: State of the Discipline*, Centennial ed. (New York: Norton, 2005).

5. Oliver P. Richmond, "Critical Research Agendas for Peace: The Missing Link in the Study of International Relations." *Alternatives* 32, no. 2 (2007): 247–274.

6. Not all political scientists are satisfied with this division of the field. Some prefer a focus on levels of analysis, and others would say that the subfields are too different for commonalities. I remain committed, however, to getting students to think in terms of causal or key factors as they search for answers to their questions, and thus I think that this scheme works well.

7. Note, of course, that institutionalist explanations can also be rational-choice perspectives as the rules within institutions establish the incentives and guidelines for gains-seeking behavior.

8. Students of international politics will know these perspectives by different names. Triple I E maps into realism, liberalism, constructivism, and Marxism, too, although not all explanations that focus on economics are Marxist in international politics or other fields.

9. See Daniel A. Smith and Caroline J. Tolbert, *Educated by Initiative: The Effects of Direct Democracy on Citizens and Political Organizations in the American States* (Ann Arbor: University of Michigan Press, 2004); Peter Shrag, *Paradise Lost: California's Experience, America's Future* (New York: New Press, 1998).

10. Notice that Latisha actually has two questions here. At this stage, I typically allow students to proceed with two questions because they are still learning and trying to understand what they want to study. Other faculty might have a different opinion, and students themselves should acknowledge that asking multiple questions typically means more complexity and work.

Making Sense of the Scholarly Answers to Your Research Question: Writing the Literature Review

The next phase of the project is when you start writing actual parts of the paper. The work that you have done so far is extremely important for laying the proper foundation, and now is the time to begin the aboveground construction. I can't stress enough how essential a high-quality framework—a good question, excellent sources, detailed summaries of the arguments, and schools of thought—is. If you don't have this foundation, please do what you need to do now: spend more time and/or get some help from your instructor or a reference librarian. If you do not, you will be frustrated trying to complete the literature review (LR).

The LR is typically the first section of the paper after the introduction. It explains to the reader how scholars have answered the research question, both in its generic and in its specific forms. In laying out the scholarly responses, it groups the answers into schools of thought, replies that share common elements, and labels each group. The LR also assesses the strengths and weaknesses of each school, examining the quality of the logic and how well each approach accounts for cases other than the ones being addressed directly in the paper. Sometimes, the LR concludes by choosing one approach as the most compelling. Later, you will use that best perspective to develop a model and hypothesis for your paper.

As you write the LR (and all the other sections), you should strive to make it a coherent essay that could stand on its own, although it also is linked to the rest of the paper and performs a precise function (or set of tasks) for your project. Each part, then, should have an interesting and appropriate title or heading that captures its argument and purpose. Notice, similar to the tasks involved in annotating the sources in your bibliography, I have asked you to identify the *argument* and not simply the topic when you come up with a heading. Great titles communicate a contention and force you to answer (and therefore help you focus on), What am I really doing here? In addition, longer paper sections (like the LR) will also have their own introductory and concluding paragraphs, as any proper essay should. So in this section, we will also be learning a bit about some fundamentals for structuring an essay—coming up with a good title and writing appropriate introductions and conclusions.

PREPARING FOR AND UNDERSTANDING THE LITERATURE REVIEW

In your annotated bibliography (AB), you have done much of the heavy lifting for the LR. However, even after you have turned in your AB, you likely will hear from your professor that you need to adjust or narrow your question in some way or that there were some important authors that you forgot to include or some arguments that you didn't understand precisely. You may even want to rethink the names of your schools. Thus, at the outset of this next phase, you inevitably will continue the work of refining your question, finding additional sources, capturing their arguments, and thinking about how to characterize and label the schools. Taking the work of the AB a step further, the LR is a coherent essay that identifies, explains, names, and assesses the answers to your research question in an interesting way.

The first time you heard *literature review,* you may have been somewhat confused. You may be used to thinking of literature as fiction, works that you read for pleasure or in an English or foreign language class. Academics, however, use the term *literature* to refer to a scholarly body of work. In your search so far, you have been identifying the essential books and articles (I have been referring to them as "sources") for answering your question. Some of these works are classics, older ones that "everyone" working on this topic cites; others may represent the newest phases of the debate. Still, no empirical research paper goes forward without this section, as you must literally demonstrate that your work "sit[s] on the shoulders of giants." In fact, as you read LRs (embedded in your sources) you will often notice that scholars find ways of linking their writing to classic works as well as the books and articles that everyone seems to be talking about at a particular moment in (intellectual) history. You should try to do that too.[1] If you haven't spent sufficient time in preparation of your AB mulling over your relevant introductory textbooks (for Latisha and Samantha that would be American government; for Joe it would be the introductions to both international and comparative politics), as well as any specialized courses (for Latisha and Samantha, again, any number of classes related to parties, campaigns, and elections; for Samantha a class on the media and politics; and for Joe a course on international security, internal conflict, democracy and democratization, or theories of international politics), do it now. These fundamental debates and schools can help you both interpret and organize the relevant literature.

There is no magic formula for answering your question and dividing the field. In the last chapter, I told you about "Triple I E"—interests, institutions, ideas, and economics—which are often key factors in explanations. Have those in mind, but also read and think carefully about what the scholars in your AB have said. What is essential for writing the LR is finding good works that answer *your* question. These authors, who are concerned with the same issues that you are, will lay out the debate for you, particularly in their own LRs and their characterization of their own contentions and those of the scholars against whom they are arguing. Thus, working hard to find excellent sources is essential, and thinking carefully about how participants in the debate about your question frame their answers is crucially important.

Our student examples here can be instructive. In answering the question, Why is U.S. politics so polarized now, and what are the consequences of polarization? Latisha found three answers: first, scholars arguing that elites were to blame and their behavior imperiled representation, a school she might call the "Elites Are at Fault and Imperiling Representation" approach; second, observers who argue that citizens have become more engaged and partisan and that these developments have positive connotations too, the "Citizens Are Energized and Acting Appropriately for Democracy" school; and last, those who agree that people are involved but worry that a new kind of intolerance is pervading politics and undermining careful deliberation, the "Activist yet Intolerant Citizens Endanger Democracy" group. While Latisha found the first two schools very easily once she started reading Abramowitz (and his points sounded familiar, given what she had read in her American government text), continued digging led her to the third school. Then, she had to sit and think for a while about how to capture the essence of all these arguments (the answers to her questions) in coming up with labels. She succeeded, and now she is ready to write an LR.

THE FUNDAMENTALS OF THE LITERATURE REVIEW

In this first substantive section of the research paper, your goal is to write a coherent essay that typically answers these four fundamental sets of questions:

1. What are the different schools of thought that have developed in response to your research question, in both its general and its specific (if possible) form? Who are the most important authors identified with each school, and how have they influenced subsequent scholarship?

2. How would each school answer your question? (The label for the school should be associated with the essence of its response.)

3. What are the strengths and weaknesses of the answers of each school?

4. Which school's argument is the best for your purposes and why, or which school would you like to continue to pursue and why?

Let's take some time to understand each of these questions better. The first one assumes that you will communicate your research question in your section. It acknowledges that you have found schools that provide relatively coherent answers to your question. While you need to identify the authors who are central to each school, you typically don't organize the LR around them, as in "Smith argues X, but Johnson states Y, and Black says Z matters." You need to find a group that coheres around an argument, an answer to the research question. With some work, you can use those key reasons or justifications to come up with a label for the school.

Please note, also, that question 1 recognizes that you need to consider what scholars say about the general concept at stake in your question as well as some of the details of the specific instances you are interested in studying. For instance, you may remember that Samantha posed a question about the effect of new media on campaigning in the United States. Well, because Twitter and Facebook are relatively new political tools, she might not be able to find many scholarly works that discuss their impact. She likely will find, however, a good deal of scholarship on how candidates use the media in their campaigns. Sam, then, needs to be sure to consult this more general literature (on media and elections) along with the specific (new media)—if it is possible—in her LR. Samantha, though, has to be prepared for the instance in which she can't find much scholarly work on the use of new media. In that case she will be blazing a new trail but still be grounded in the literature because she will be using the insights of those who have studied older media forms to influence volunteers, donors, and voters.

As you lay out your different schools, you should also provide their answers to your research question. Stay focused on characterizing the answers and using the replies to group your sources. Being able to state the basic answer and see how scholars differ in replying is key here. Sometimes, students think that if they just keep reading more on their topic they will be OK. Please remember that you have moved beyond a large topic now. You want answers to your question, and if you haven't found any (or if they all seem to agree), then you have a problem. Predicting exactly what is wrong is difficult, but typically the lack of any or a variety of answers means you need to find other (perhaps more or wholly different) sources and maybe adjust your question. It could also indicate that you need to read more carefully and that you need some help understanding the materials. Still, you should not ignore your inability to find answers and group them into schools and assume it will somehow get better. Take some action now. Any combination of the strategies of spending more time (using the various methods suggested in chapter 3) and getting assistance from your professor or reference librarian will help. Please, however, do not assume that others will do the work for you. Faculty and librarians will guide you, but it is neither their jobs nor their goal to tell you what to do. They want to give you tools to enable you to move forward. Thus, before you seek help, you must have questions and you must have put in significant effort.

Returning to our set of objectives for the LR, the third one is to evaluate the quality of each of these answers. This one is tricky because students often make up their minds about an approach too early and try to skew their discussion of it when they first introduce it. My goal is for you to introduce and explain the school with as little bias as possible. In fact, when you present the school you should have no words of judgment in your discussion, and you should explain it as one of its adherents would. Try to get inside the heads of those scholars and see why this group of very smart people finds this approach compelling. After you have approached each school with an open mind and given its adherents their chance to convince you, you must take on the task of evaluating the schools. Does each response make sense logically? If not, explain why. Also, does an answer seem to be empirically correct, at least when applied to other cases? (This is not the place for evaluating how well your argument fits the specific reality you are interested in, although if an approach is clearly not applicable to your favored situation, then you should note its inadequacy.)

Last, one of the goals of the LR is to use reason to limit what you will study. Remember our quote about the giants? Well, if each school is analogous to a behemoth, you need to pick only one to sit on. Typically, you don't have the capacity to work in multiple, different theoretical traditions (just as you physically can't sit on more than one giant), and so you have to choose. Sometimes, this choice will be relatively easy. You will likely perceive one school to be best, given the analysis that you did in response to the third question.[2] Other times, however, you won't be sure that one answer is superior, yet you will still need to make a choice. Then, you have to state the criteria that you are using for pursuing one approach and not the others. One way of choosing is deciding that one approach is new and understudied; another reason for selecting may be that a certain argument is currently getting the most attention in the popular media or from policymakers and you would like to subject it to scholarly attention. Whatever your reasons, you need to explain them and use them to help you choose. Typically, though, authors proceed by concluding that one school is logically and empirically best.

In the end, remember that this type of essay—one that evaluates conceptual or theoretical approaches—is probably familiar to you. You have likely taken essay exams in which you were asked to explain the different answers to a certain question or different interpretations of a key concept, assess them, and make a final judgment in which you state which one you prefer. Thus, you have already had practice in this type of writing and thinking.

WRITING THE LITERATURE REVIEW

As was already mentioned, when you write this section (and any other) you are trying to write some text that could serve as a stand-alone essay—with a purpose all its own—but that also performs an essential part of the greater whole: to communicate the conceptual basis of your research. Since this is the first section that you are writing for the paper, we will discuss not only what is specific to this section (see the previous examination and explanation of the four key questions above) but also what is common to any essay: the LR needs its own title, introduction, and conclusion. While you will find an extended discussion of how to write each of these important parts of the whole paper in chapter 9, consider this an important preview.

When you write longer papers you use headings to set off sections (making the work easier to write, read, and understand), communicate the structure of the essay, and keep your focus. What is a good title for an LR? You may think, "'Literature Review,' that's perfect." Well, as you were reading the scholarly works, did you see many published authors who used that title in their papers? Typically, authors use more informative headings, just like you would use a more specific title than simply "Essay 1" for the first essay that you wrote for one of your classes. Good titles (just like good research papers) do not simply describe the contents; they communicate the purpose and usually the argument. The objective of the LR is to lay out and explain the scholarly answers to your research question, assess their quality, and come to some conclusion about which one you will pursue further. Because of the emphasis here on understanding the literature, classifying it, and explaining the multiple arguments, I suggest that LR headings revolve around the various approaches and not your conclusion or favorite school.

Latisha, the student whose draft AB we've read, could offer the following titles for the LR section: "Polarization and Its Effects: Three Views" or "Why American Politics Is Polarized and What It Means for Politics." Both of these headings are far better than the purely descriptive "Polarization in America and Its Effects." Can you see why? This third title does not capture what the section is really about. This part of the paper is looking at explanations for polarization and assessing its implications; it is not simply describing each. Something to notice from Latisha's exercise in title writing is that she doesn't have just one research question but two—why polarization occurs and what its effects are. Latisha wants to think before she proceeds further: does she want to have two, and can she handle both? These are questions about her desired focus (is she interested in both questions, or should she simply concentrate on one?) and the scope of the paper (how much time does she have, and how long should the paper be?). She may be able to choose herself, or perhaps when her professor assesses her research question and her AB, the feedback will steer Latisha in one direction. Typically, in the writing of the LR students have to choose what exactly their question(s) will be and whether they will answer more than one.

After the title, you need to provide an introduction, which serves as an overview to this section. For the LR, then, the introduction explains (1) there is a scholarly debate on your research question, and there are roughly X number of schools; (2) each school offers a specific answer to your question (and be sure to convey precisely what that response is); (3) the approaches have various strengths and weaknesses; but (4) one school seems to be the best one or is the most compelling to investigate. Notice how closely the introduction mirrors what your purpose is. Of course, the introduction expresses these points in brief. You develop them further in the rest of the paper, and the last element (4) is the main focus of your concluding section, although your conclusion also reminds the reader a bit of what the section's goals were.

I can't stress enough that an LR is not simply a set of paragraphs that summarize books and articles. Instead, an LR captures and explains the different answers to the question and explains the underlying reasons for the disagreements between scholars. This section also assesses the logical strengths and weaknesses of the answers and then ultimately settles on (concludes with) one approach that the author finds particularly compelling. Why that approach is so interesting and should be pursued further is justified and explained.

There are several ways of organizing an LR. One is to present the approaches in chronological order, as a means of showing the historical development of an area of inquiry. Another is to mention and discuss the schools from the least to the most preferred. If your instructor has not identified a way to proceed, choose the order that best works to highlight the debate and makes your tasks (of introducing the schools, the various arguments, their strengths and weaknesses, and your preferred position) easiest for you.

As I noted earlier, when you are first setting out a perspective, you should present a school in its most favorable light. To give each school a fair chance, I recommend that you present all of them before you begin the evaluation. Moreover, as I noted above, you should try to think like a member of that school. Thereafter, when you have thought of all the strengths of each approach, you can assess them critically, particularly with respect to their logic and explanatory power (for cases other than the ones you want to study). If you wait, then you will reduce the risk of mixing the analysis with the exposition, in other words the explanation of the school's argument. In addition, if you try really hard to respect each perspective, I am hoping that you will move beyond your initial intellectual prejudices.[3]

In addition to knowing what it should contain, the best way to understand how to write an LR is to look at good examples and model your work on them. In preparing your AB, you have surely found sources that have LR sections (for articles) or chapters (in monographs) that are organized as I have suggested and accomplish the goals that I have laid out for you.

Because matching a scholarly example might seem intimidating, I offer you here some excerpts from Joe's LR. Remember his interest in the challenge of creating stability and development in Afghanistan and Iraq? Well, as he began researching his topic, Joe became increasingly intrigued by the challenge of creating postwar stability. One article, in fact, discussed whether El Salvador was an appropriate model for transforming war-torn societies, and after a bit more investigation, Joe decided to focus his efforts on understanding the extent to which El Salvador has succeeded in developing a stable and successful polity since its civil war of the 1980s.[4] Here is the opening of his LR section, complete with the heading and introductory paragraph, written in Chicago style. After the introduction, I have edited out the discussion of three of his schools but have included here his exposition of the fourth one followed by the section's conclusion. Can you see Joe doing what I have recommended?

How to Account for Postconflict Stability: Four Perspectives[5]

Almost twenty years after the Chapultepec Peace Accords brought an end to the Salvadoran civil war, El Salvador has still not fully recovered. Scholars have offered several theories to account for how a country can overcome lingering hostilities, economic hindrances, and political unrest and create a multifaceted peace. In particular, four schools of thought warrant closer examination and analysis: Separate and Balance, Reconciliationism, Political Populism, and Institutionalism. Proponents of Separate and Balance contend that states that have experienced civil war, especially ethnic conflict, cannot return to normal, with people living together peacefully. Therefore, the international community must take drastic measures to separate the populations into distinct territories, maintain defensible borders, and ensure a balance of power between them.[a] Second, Reconciliationism maintains that in a postconflict society, past transgressions and inequalities must be discussed to reduce the likelihood of a return to conflict.[b] Third, Political Populism focuses on political participation and opening avenues for civic engagement for all members of society.[c] Last, instead of focusing on the grass roots, Institutionalism emphasizes the roles of governmental and nongovernmental organizations in providing society's basic needs.[d]

For the case of El Salvador, Separate and Balance is not applicable. While there were ethnic overtones to this civil war, it was not primarily about social identity. In addition, neither the international community nor national participants have had the desire to divide the country. Similarly, Reconciliationism is shortsighted in its aspirations and offers no real road map for state building and peace building. Political Populism is also unwieldy; it presupposes that the avenues for civic engagement are easy to install and that political participation is sought by every level of society. Institutionalism, on the other hand, focuses on arguably the largest scale, on building up the structures by which a state can properly function. Thus, this fourth school can best explain how El Salvador has recovered since the 1992 Chapultepec Peace Accords as well as how it can continue to develop its economy and state of political stability. . . .

Let's skip to Joe's discussion of the fourth school of thought and the section's conclusion.

The final school of thought is Institutionalism. Institutionalist scholars hold that a society undergoing a postconflict transition process faces a very real threat of instability and even violence. Unlike Reconciliationism, which places a heavier emphasis on truth telling and atonement along religious or ethnic lines, Institutionalism focuses more on political tensions and designing the appropriate institutions both to channel political differences and to serve ordinary people. The logic here is that to support peace, citizens need security, a decent living standard, and a government that seems at least somewhat fair. Scholars Edward D. Mansfield and Jack Snyder explain that especially in countries that are democratizing, political instability is a very real threat. They point out that liberalizing states are hardly ever peaceful, and conditions are ripe for political extremism and fierce nationalism. As they explain, "the early stages of democratization unleash intense competition among myriad social groups and interests. Many transitional democracies lack state institutions that are sufficiently strong and coherent to effectively regulate this mass political competition."[e] To prevent actors from fostering this intense competition, Institutionalists acknowledge the fundamental role of powerful governmental institutions such as political parties, court systems, and the news media. Creating these foundations of the political system can take some time to accomplish, but their role is essential in preventing both intense nationalism, or jingoism, and the adoption of expedients such as "logrolled overcommitments and nationalist outbidding strategies, [which] heighten the risk of external conflict"[f] at a time when the state cannot afford to do so.

Institutionalist scholars will admit that political stability cannot be accomplished solely through building structures and proper governing bodies. They do hold, however, that order is a necessary condition for long-term peace and prosperity. According to political scientists Roland Paris and Timothy D. Sisk, "without adequate attention to the statebuilding requirements of peacebuilding, war-torn states would be less likely to escape the multiple and mutually reinforcing 'traps' of violence and underdevelopment."[g] Charles T. Call and Elizabeth M. Cousens also elaborate on this need to properly strengthen the state via its institutions: "state building . . . enhances mechanisms for security and conflict resolution at the national level that should carry legitimacy in the eyes of the populace and the outside world. Such mechanisms—be they justice systems, policing systems, or service delivery agencies—provide a credible arena and framework . . . for social groups to express preferences and resolve conflicts nonviolently."[h]

A key way that a governing body can assert authority and appear stable is its creation of necessary and fair institutions. In a war-torn society, the victors are wary of sharing power with their former opponents, and their adversaries fear turning in their arms. This trust, however, is essential for forward movement, and making sure that institutions are procedurally fair and deliver just outcomes is essential for continued progress. Obviously, the independent development of political structures may not be possible in some cases, and an outside party might be necessary to assist in the installation of those institutions, including, for example, political parties, a strong financial sector, or an apolitical military. What makes this challenging is the potential for "such missions [to] represent a new form of colonial control over the territory of the war-torn state."[i] Colonialism may not sound too likely in the twenty-first century. However, if an outside actor plays a significant role in creating a country's government and other major institutions, the government's authority might be undermined. Institutionalists hold that a society should try to build up its own order if at all possible.

Doing so can ensure that radical political actors are held in check and that the governing bodies can be perceived as effective and efficient.

Political scientist Michael T. Klare adds that people, if they become disenchanted with their governing bodies, will look to other sources of authority. He writes, "Greatly contributing to the intensity of recent ethnic and religious strife is the erosion . . . of central state authority in poor third world countries experiencing extreme economic, political, and environmental stress. In such countries . . . people lose all confidence in the state's ability to meet their basic needs and turn instead to more traditional, kinship-based forms of association."[j] While popular sentiment could arguably be the driving force behind these state mechanisms, state institutions perform one of two functions. They can serve as an outlet for civic engagement (e.g., in the electoral process), or they can function as a sort of gauge of popular sentiment. For example, a country's central bank might adjust its monetary policy based on consumer confidence or economic forecasting. Thus, the strength of these mechanisms is crucial to maintaining order and building peace.

In conclusion, Institutionalism presents the strongest case for creating stability in war-torn societies. Separate and Balance is both impractical, based on the desire and ability of the world community to remain involved, and not applicable to the particulars of the Salvadoran case. While the Reconciliationist and Political Populist schools are useful for analyzing how a society can begin to recover from a period of intense conflict, both approaches paint an incomplete picture. Reconciliationists place heavy emphasis on making previous aggression and wrongdoing widely known. In this sense, this school can be criticized as backward looking. It does not offer any real guidance for improving the society or establishing institutions or laws that would prevent continued transgressions. It is also too optimistic in that it supposes that citizens can reconcile with their oppressors and that violent and/or hate-filled individuals can change their ways. Scholars of Political Populism focus almost solely on ensuring that citizens' ability to interact with their government is not only possible but easy. This grassroots approach is, unfortunately, rather idealistic. This school does not offer any clear means for promoting this interaction. Additionally, it does not account for the possibility that certain popular groups could prove to be socially destabilizing forces in their quest for participation (e.g., if a populist group uses violence as a means of political expression).

Institutionalism succeeds where the other three do not. It accounts for the actual structures and mechanisms by which a state can function properly. This school provides an arena for outside actors to assist in strengthening the state. Furthermore, since governing institutions can interact with every level of a nation's society, Institutionalism is best placed as a school of thought for explaining how ordinary people can actually voice their opinions and concerns. What also makes this such a viable school is its breadth. Because it encompasses institutions for several purposes (e.g., economics, voting, security), this focus can cover any policy area that needs attention.

NOTES

a.   Separate and Balance is my [Joe's] name for this school. Its adherents note its links to the Realist tradition in international politics because it accepts the rationality of actors, the importance of power in deterring aggression, and the inescapability of the security dilemma. See especially Chaim Kaufmann, "Possible and Impossible Solutions to Ethnic Civil Wars," *International Security* 29, no. 4 (1996): 136–174, www.jstor.com; John J. Mearsheimer and Stephen Van Evera, "When Peace Means War," *New Republic,* December 18, 1995, 16–21, www.ebscohost.com.

b.   Important Reconciliationists include John Paul Lederach, *Building Peace: Sustainable Reconciliation in Divided Societies* (Washington, DC: USIP Press, 1998); R. Scott Appleby, *Ambivalence of the Sacred: Religion, Violence and Reconciliation* (Lanham, MD: Rowman & Littlefield, 1999); Daniel Philpott and the contributors to his anthology, *The Politics of Past Evil: Religion, Reconciliation and Transitional Justice* (Notre Dame, IN: University of Notre Dame Press, 2006).

c.   Paula M. Pickering is an important voice here. See *Peacebuilding in the Balkans: The View from the Ground Floor* (Ithaca, NY: Cornell University Press, 2007).

d.   Major Institutionalists include Roland Paris and Charles Call. See, for instance, Roland Paris, *At War's End: Building Peace after Civil Conflict* (New York: Cambridge University Press, 2004); Roland Paris, "Bringing the Leviathan Back In: Classical versus Contemporary Studies of the Liberal Peace," *International Studies Review* 8, no. 3 (2006): 425–440, www .jstor.com; Roland Paris and Timothy D. Sisk, eds., *The Dilemmas of Statebuilding: Confronting the Contradictions of Postwar Peace Operations* (New York: Routledge, 2009). Call's major works include Charles T. Call and E. M. Cousens, "Ending Wars and Building Peace: International Responses to War-torn Societies," *International Studies Perspectives* 9, no. 1 (2008): 1–21; Charles T. Call, "Democratisation, War and State-building: Constructing the Rule of Law in El Salvador," *Journal of Latin American Studies* 35, no. 4 (2003): 827–862, www.jstor.com; Charles T. Call and Vanessa Hawkins Wyeth, eds., *Building States to Build Peace* (Boulder, CO: Lynne Reinner, 2008).

e.   Edward D. Mansfield and Jack Snyder, "Democratic Transitions, Institutional Strength, and War," *International Organization* 56, no. 2 (2002): 299.

f.   Ibid., 304.

g.   Roland Paris and Timothy D. Sisk, "Introduction: Understanding the Contradictions of Postwar Statebuilding," in *The Dilemmas of Statebuilding: Confronting the Contradictions of Postwar Peace Operations*, ed. Roland Paris and Timothy D. Sisk (New York: Routledge, 2009), 3.

h.   Call and Cousens, "Ending Wars and Building Peace," 9–10.

i.   Paris and Sisk, *The Dilemmas of Statebuilding*, 11.

j.   Michael T. Klare, "Redefining Security: The New Global Schisms," *Current History* 95, no. 206 (1996): 356.

Notice the many strengths of Joe's LR. First, Joe starts with a great title; this heading communicates effectively his purpose in this section. Thus, we know immediately what his general research question is and how many schools there are. Then, in his introduction, he gives us both more insight into that query and an outstanding preview of the whole LR. Readers are not left wondering what his schools are, what he's going to call them, what they contend, what their strengths and weaknesses are, and which one he prefers and why. Joe's use of footnotes to communicate the major scholars associated with a line of thinking is also a plus. Finally, notice that he proceeded from his least preferred to his most favored school, and he kept that order consistent throughout the essay.

In discussing the fourth school, Joe again excels. He explains why what this school contends is necessary for stability and identifies the key exponents. Also recognize what Joe doesn't do: he doesn't simply summarize each book and article and then string the summaries together. He has thought about what the most important scholars are saying. Because they all stress the role of institutions in creating stability, he settles on the "Institutionalist" label. For each of these authors, institutions are essential for transforming war-torn societies into nonconflictual ones. Joe's efforts, both in locating these works and then in reading them, were no doubt extensive. He probably had to obtain some books through interlibrary loan, but because he got an early start and had identified good sources to work on while he waited, ordering the books was not a problem. Similarly, many of his sources are from major journals and scholarly presses, so understanding them took time and concentration. Still, Joe used LRs embedded in his authors' works[6] to help him comprehend parts of the field. Then, additional reading—supplemented by his syllabus from an earlier course on contemporary peace and security issues—was helpful.

In the concluding paragraph, Joe explains why he believes that Institutionalism both is logically the best approach and is most appropriate for studying El Salvador's progress since 1992. The paragraph is short but clear. Joe provides real reasons—and doesn't simply assert that Institutionalism is better—for making his judgment.

On the whole, this is an excellent LR. Joe has accurately captured the debate in the field; he has clearly laid out the arguments, the major scholars involved, and what he finds compelling and not useful. Moreover, the whole section is extremely well written and argued. Note also the quality of Joe's sources—they come from top-notch journals or from important presses and authors—and what a nice job he has done documenting them, integrating the names of authors into his text, and giving them credit for their ideas. My one criticism is that I would like to see him use fewer direct quotes, but still, I am extremely impressed. No wonder I would ask him to allow me to share his paper with you. Fabulous work, Joe!

PRACTICAL SUMMARY

In this chapter, you have learned how to write an LR. This task is highly dependent on the work that you have done so far, designing a good research question, finding appropriate literature, and summarizing the answers to this question. If you haven't had success in the previous stages, then you will have difficulties in the process of writing the LR as well as in putting forth a good one. So if you have doubts about your question, your literature, or your summaries, speak to your professor and/or a reference librarian early in the process, and keep in mind that refining the question, finding literature, and understanding it is an ongoing process.

Central to writing the LR is finding excellent (i.e., appropriate and important) works, identifying the most important scholars involved in the debate, understanding the different answers to the research question that these authors posit, and placing these scholars into schools of thought by determining the key factors or underlying points that unite and divide them. You now know how and where to find academic authors and how to make sense of debates. In addition, the chapter gave you the four objectives you need to satisfy (and the questions that will help you accomplish that goal), showed how Latisha's AB work would prepare her for writing an LR, and included an excerpt of Joe's LR, an excellent student example. You also learned that all sections will have substantive headings (not simply named after the function of the part, such as "Literature Review") and that longer ones will also have their own introductions and conclusions, and we gave special attention to the writing of these fundamentals here. The steps to follow when you write the LR are laid out in the four questions above (and are included in the checklist below).

SUGGESTED CALENDAR

Follow your professor's instructions, but typically you will want to complete the first draft of your LR at a relatively early stage of the research process, often before the halfway point. Recognize that you may have to come back to it and rethink some elements or include more sources, but work hard now to identify and label the key schools, dividing the literature into groups that share a common answer to your research question. In writing the LR, pay special attention to developing your heading, and be sure to write an introduction and conclusion to the section.

EXERCISES

1. Think of two additional titles for Latisha's and Joe's LR sections. Why are they appropriate?

2. If you were Latisha, would you choose one question or the two she poses to proceed? Why? (And if you picked one, which would you choose and why?)

3. Consider the draft of Latisha's AB and your answers to exercises 1 and 2 above. Based on her work, write a section heading, an introductory paragraph, and the exposition of one school of thought for Latisha's LR. Use the APSA form.

CHECKLIST 3: LITERATURE REVIEW

Use this rubric to guide you as you write your LR. It summarizes exactly what you need to do to finish a successful one. In chapter 6, you will see a complementary checklist that will give attention to stylistic and formatting concerns.

Checklist 3: Literature Review

Does your literature review (LR) have an appropriate title that communicates the purpose of the section and is not simply "Literature Review"? Yes _____ No _____

Does the LR have an introductory paragraph that provides an overview of the whole paper? In other words, it names the schools, explains very briefly what they argue (with footnotes to the most important scholars included), provides a quick assessment of the strengths and weaknesses of each school, and concludes by telling the reader which approach you will continue to pursue and why. Yes _____ No _____

Would a reader of your LR know what your research question is? Why? (Write the precise text in your LR that communicates your research question, but not in question form.) Yes _____ No _____

Text:

Have you have found at least two schools? Yes _____ No _____

Have you provided different scholarly answers to your research question and grouped these answers into schools of thought, each with its own label? Yes _____ No _____

Have you named the adherents to the school and explained the school's logic as fairly as possible? Yes _____ No _____

Have you explained the weaknesses and strengths of the different schools? Yes _____ No _____

Have you written a concluding paragraph for your LR that explains (and doesn't simply assert) which school you prefer and why?

Yes _____ No _____

Have you added any new sources that you found while working on the LR to your bibliography file?

Yes _____ No _____

NOTES

1. Notice that Latisha does this by bringing Putnam's works into her annotated bibliography and showing how Mutz's book derives from Putnam's research.
2. Under some conditions, faculty may not want you to combine two or more schools. Be clear about whether your instructor expects you to pick one alone or would be satisfied with some integrated approach.
3. Certainly, this is not an easy task. Social psychologists tell us that our first impressions are hard to move beyond. Still, the best that you can do is to proceed with respect and give each approach its best chance to make its case. You may want to imagine that you are the attorney for each school, its advocate, laying out its explanation. Thereafter, you can serve as jury when all the evidence is available. Be mindful, however, that juries are supposed to leave their biases behind them and make their decisions based on the information presented.
4. David Holiday, "El Salvador's Model Democracy," *Current History* 104, no. 279 (2005): 77–82, www.proquest.com.
5. Notice that Joe's heading stresses the purpose—laying out the field, not his ultimate conclusion. If it communicated his conclusion, after the colon he would have written something like, "The Role of Governing Institutions." He can take that idea—the link between institutions—and link it to stability to name his next section.
6. For instance, Roland Paris, "Bringing the Leviathan Back In: Classical versus Contemporary Studies of the Liberal Peace," *International Studies Review* 8, no. 3 (2006): 425–440, www.jstor.com; and Edward D. Mansfield and Jack Snyder, "Democratic Transitions, Institutional Strength, and War," *International Organization* 56, no. 2 (2002), clearly explain against which approaches they are arguing.

Effectively Distilling Your Argument: The Thesis, Model, and Hypothesis

As we proceed in this paper-writing marathon, finishing the literature review is like running the first eight miles. You've completed a little less than a third of the race, and you can see a long, slightly upward-sloping stretch in front of you. But you are well trained and ready for this challenge. You will persevere by proceeding steadily and remembering that the parts of the paper are interrelated in ways that help you move from one phase to the next. The conclusion of the literature review leads the writer to a bottom line: one answer to the research question appears best. In effect, that conclusion is the fundamental *argument* or *thesis* that you will be sustaining, evaluating, or testing in your research paper.[1] Stating this conclusion in the literature review is often sufficient for guiding experienced writers through the rest of the process. For less experienced authors or for particularly complex arguments, the Model and Hypothesis (M&H) section is brief but important. It forces the author to state precisely what he or she expects to find. In an empirical paper, that statement will come in two forms—in a picture or flow diagram (*model*) and in words (*hypothesis*).

THE THESIS

Almost all of the writing (except creative writing, i.e., fiction) that you do in college will have a *thesis* or an *argument*, two terms used interchangeably in this book.[2] A thesis is a *contentious statement*, that is, a declaration or description with which reasonable people could disagree. A thesis can be either a normative claim or an empirically verifiable contention. For our purposes, a hypothesis is a special type of thesis that explores the connections between the key factors that it names. If you are investigating a hypothesis, you will try to determine whether these elements are correlated or causally related.

You are used to reading works with theses as you are exposed to them in the essays that you read for classes, Op-Ed pieces in newspapers, journals of opinion, or even some journals, particularly ones that minimize footnotes, may lack bibliographies and are written for more general audiences (such as *Social Policy, Foreign Affairs, Current History,* or *Foreign Policy*).[3] Political scientists, too, develop these types of arguments; however, we will see that to be published in the most prestigious journals, typically, authors in American, comparative, and international politics must assert hypotheses.

When writing your research paper, your thesis is your answer to the research question.[4] You have examined potential replies in the literature review and concluded that one is most compelling. You made that judgment based on your assessment of the quality of the argument's logic and its ability to account for similar occurrences of the phenomenon in question. Because there is debate about what is the best reply, you know that this thesis is contentious. Some of the students whom we met in chapter 2 have begun developing theses. Mike, who is interested in civil rights and civil liberties, has been doing some research on the intersection of that field with immigration. When he started, he went back to his class notes and remembered one of the fundamental arguments his class explored: in the United States, the courts are not an effective instrument of social change.[5] Again, many reasonable people could take issue with this assertion because the courts, particularly in the second half of the twentieth century, have played an important role in transforming American society.[6] Civil rights, women's, environmental, and gay groups, for example, have all turned to the legal system to bring about political changes. Because of the civil rights movement's litigation campaign, culminating in *Brown v. Board of Education,* many have categorically accepted the importance of using the courts for social change. This thesis calls the conventional wisdom into question.

Similarly, Latisha could assert that today, politics is more polarized than it has been in the past. Samantha might insist that female candidates use the new media in different ways than male candidates do, and Andre could argue that government support for GM and Chrysler was smart policy. All of these assertions are contentious; citizens, practitioners, and scholars could disagree. Moreover, all of these theses result from the students' knowledge of the arguments in the literature as well as their observations of the world around them. The goal of the research of each of these students would be to evaluate whether a systematic look at the evidence supports their claim or appears better at sustaining another argument.

THE MODEL

While *thesis* or *argument* is the broad term for the contention that you are investigating throughout your research, I will use another set of terms for work that is explicitly and self-consciously empirical. Theory-advancing and public policy research explore correlations (the simultaneous varying of factors) and causations (when changes in one phenomenon lead to variations in another) and seek to chart carefully the relationships between variables. Frequently, they use the language of science when engaging in their research and explaining it to others. In chapter 2, we noted that your research should seek to explain a particular phenomenon or solve some puzzle. In its most basic form, an empirical argument can be reduced to relationships between *variables*, where a variable is anything that can vary or change in value. What you are trying to explain is the effect or the *dependent variable.* This effect depends on some other factors (the causes), and it is a variable because if the value of the causes change, so too will the effect. The cause is referred to as the *independent variable.*[7]

Upon first consideration, thinking of concepts in political science as variables with values can be quite strange for students. Probably, you are used to conceiving of variables as something that you find only in math class—x or y—and values bring up the idea of numbers. Most political science majors are attracted to this subject because they believe, among other things, that this discipline will be about words, not manipulating equations with numbers. But concepts in political science can be variables and take on values. In saying that they can be variables I am simply noting that they can change. Take, for instance, the concept of party identification. In the United States, there is more than one party, and people identify with different ones or have no attachment to parties at all. Thus, the values that the variable party identification in the United States can be are Republican, Democrat, Independent, other, or none. While a large number of variables in political science cannot be measured in numbers, there are also many that can be quantified. Voter turnout, presidential popularity, educational outcomes, Supreme Court voting patterns, election results, and budget deficits are just a few examples. Other important concepts can vary by degree, for instance, partisanship (strong to weak) or level of violence (high to low). Given a particular time and place, these variables may take on different values.

In empirical research, literature reviews often divide the field into schools that identify one or more independent variables (causal factors) as more important than others. Moreover, the research question asks about the dependent variable (effect). Thus, as a result of your literature review, you should be able to generate a number of independent variables that potentially have an impact on the phenomenon in which you are interested. In effect, by performing a review of the literature you have identified the information that you need to develop a number of competing models. A model is the pictorial representation of your argument or thesis, reducing it to its bare bones, the basic elements that are related to each other.

You may wonder why you must develop a model if it follows so nicely from the literature review. Well, in one sense, the model is a check on your work; it makes sure that you have done a good job on your literature review.

Unfortunately, students sometimes use the literature review to discuss in very abstract terms the ways that different schools of thought conceive of politics instead of focusing on how each perspective answers the research question at hand. If you have done your literature review correctly and your question is seeking to explore the relationship between concepts, coming up with the variables will be easy. If you have improperly written this section, developing models will be very difficult. So if you're stuck on the model, then you know that you need to go back and redo your literature review before proceeding with your research.

Let's think back to Kate from chapter 2 and use her interests to look at the relationship between the literature review, variable identification, and models. Kate started out with a general interest in women, gender, and politics but began zeroing in on the question of why women are more likely to be elected in some countries than in others. In writing her literature review, Kate decided that this issue of whether women are in national legislatures was really related to the level of democracy that prevails in any society, reasoning that greater participation of women reflected a more open, democratic system. So to answer her question about levels of female political empowerment, she turned to the literature that seeks to explain the levels of democracy in any society. She found that there were three basic explanations: (1) an institutional argument that claims that women are more likely to be elected if they are running in a parliamentary system with proportional representation, (2) an economic development approach that asserts that higher levels of economic development lead to higher levels of political participation and empowerment of all citizens, and (3) a cultural explanation that contends that women will not fare well politically if they come from a culture that devalues women and expects them to play traditional domestic roles.[8]

Kate has done a fine job in her literature review in identifying possible key factors: institutions, economic development, and culture. If she concluded that economic development was the best predictor, she would generate the following model:

$$\text{Level of Economic Development} \quad \rightarrow \quad \text{Proportion of Women Elected to National Legislatures}$$

Please notice that in formulating the model, Kate transformed the factors into variables, things that can change. Thus, in the model section, she added the words *level of*. While some models investigate correlations, this one asserts that causation flows in a particular direction. To find that the arrow is reversed would not substantiate this model but compel the student to make a different argument.[9]

Looking at an example of a model from American politics, we could try to explain popular attitudes toward health care reform and the specific bill passed in 2010 and posit that an individual's ideology affects attitudes. We make that assertion because the health care bill replaces elements of the insurance market with government programs. Obviously, both attitudes and ideology can vary, and we would expect that the more conservative a person is, the less supportive she or he would be of health care reform. Thus, a researcher trying to understand popular attitudes could advance the following model:

Extent of   →   Strength of Support for

"Conservative-ness"   Health Care Reform

The model implies that a person's ideology affects how that person feels about a particular policy. The literature review that would have led to the creation of such a model would have explored the determinants of popular attitudes toward national (domestic) policies. The model, then, contends that ideology is the best explanation.

While the model is important for guiding your research, it is still incomplete. The model does not provide explicit information about the direction or the extent of the independent variable's effect on the dependent variable. With Kate's model, you don't know from the flow diagram what exactly will happen to female electoral success levels when economic development levels change. In fact, you may have no idea what the possible levels of economic development are. In the second example, a model accounting for support of health care reform, the way in which conservatism exerts its impact is not explicitly identified. In both cases, you need something additional to communicate the nature of the relationship and the range of values the variables can take on—that is the hypothesis.

THE HYPOTHESIS

As noted before, the hypothesis is a particular type of thesis, one that asserts that a particular cause (or causes) either is correlated with or leads to certain effects. As a thesis, the hypothesis also provides an answer to the research question based on what you learned in your literature review.

Hypotheses[10] are often stated in the following terms:

For Positive Relationships: The more of X (the independent variable), the more of Y (the dependent variable)

For Negative Relationships: The more of X (the independent variable), the less of Y (the dependent variable)

So in Kate's model, the hypothesis would be the following:

The greater the level of economic development in a state, the higher will be the proportion of women serving in the national legislature.

For the second example about ideology and attitudes, the hypothesis would be the following:

> The more conservative the person, the weaker will be the individual's support for health care reform.

In sum, the literature review often defines the variables and helps you put forth a model; it also tells you how the variables should relate to each other. You are not plucking these relationships from thin air, as you have uncovered them in your previous research. Still, explicitly writing this relationship out helps to keep you focused on your precise argument and, again, allows you to verify that your literature review accomplishes what it should. In Kate's case, the hypothesis reminds you that you are trying to determine whether increases in levels of economic development actually lead to increases in the levels of female elected officials. Note that in making this contention you are also saying the converse: decreases in development levels mean decreases in the number of women relative to men in public office. Similarly, with the second hypothesis, you are investigating whether ideological conservatives are more strongly opposed to health care reform. You expect more conservative people to be, in fact, strongly opposed to health care reform. In the first case (development and female national legislators), the variables are positively linked (higher levels of economic development lead to more women elected), and in the second, the relationship is negative (more conservative means negative support, i.e., stronger opposition).[11]

For both of our hypotheses, we can think of the values—levels of economic development, female legislators, "conservative-ness," and support—as occurring on a continuum, and thus we call these *continuous* (also called *interval*) *variables*.[12] There are values for each that span a continuous spectrum and include all the gradations in between. But not all variables can be measured in this way; instead, some reflect *categories* in which we might be interested. For instance, we might wonder whether one type of institutional arrangement aids democratic consolidation better than another. The question is not simply academic, as constitution writers in states emerging from authoritarianism are likely to be searching for a system that will work. If those would-be authors read Juan J. Linz, then they are likely to be interested in the following hypothesis: parliamentary systems are more likely to lead to democratic consolidation than are presidential ones.[13] In this case, a governmental system is not more or less parliamentary; parliamentary and presidential systems do not fall on a continuum of some factor. Instead, a governmental system either does or does not fit into the discrete category parliamentary; thus, we call this a *discrete variable*.[14]

Similarly, we could think of the independent variable in our health care reform model as type of ideology, where we imagine that respondents are, for instance, strong conservatives, mild conservatives (they lean right), moderates (in the middle of the spectrum), mild liberals (they lean left), or strong liberals.

Then our hypothesis states that strong conservatives are most likely to oppose health care reform, while strong liberals are most likely to support it. Mild conservatives would be more likely to oppose health care reform than mild liberals, but we would expect the mild variants of both conservatism and liberalism to be less intense in their sentiments than their strong partisans.

We have already seen some arguments that rely on discrete variables. Two theses that I mentioned at the outset of the chapter—regarding the utility of the court and the difference in the ways that female versus male candidates use social media—posit correlations between discrete (or category) variables. While researchers may neither be sure nor care particularly why these occurrences happen, they are very interested in showing empirically that they have found an accurate description of reality. Thus, the following contentions are hypotheses:

- In the United States, the courts are not effective instruments of social change.
- Candidates' gender affects their use of new media.

But because the variables are not continuous, they cannot be accurately stated in the form, "The more of X, the more (or less, if the relationship is negative) of Y." We still want to provide a hypothesis, however, to map out the precise direction of the relationships we expect to find. Thus, we can state, "American courts are less effective than legislatures as instruments of social change" and "Female candidates use new media to create an impression of their professionalism and receptivity, while male candidates are less likely to seek to bolster their professionalism and less interested in demonstrating receptivity to consumers of their web and social media sites." Or as we saw in our examples regarding governmental systems and democratic consolidation, "Parliamentary systems are more likely than presidential ones to lead to the consolidation of democracy," and our alternative concerning health care reform, "Conservatives are more likely than liberals to oppose health care reform."

Note one last and interesting point about hypotheses: when you state one you always give a hint as to which values of the independent variable are associated with which particular values of the dependent variables. For instance, see Table 5.1.

For the first two models, where the variables are continuous, the hypotheses give you an idea of the types of quantities you will see (e.g., high levels of development associated with high levels of women elected). Later on, when you are actually evaluating these claims empirically, you will have both a sense of what *high* (as well as *economic development*) means, and you will determine actual numbers as you find data. You might learn, for instance, that high-income countries, which you decide (or you consult the World Bank to find) means those with a per capita GDP of $35,000, are more likely to have high proportions of elected women, which based on contemporary

Table 5.1 Models and Variable Values

Model	Possible Independent Variable Values	Corresponding Dependent Variable Values
Level of Economic Development → Proportion of Women in National Legislature	High levels of development; low levels of development	High percentage of women elected; low percentage of women elected
Level of "Conservative-ness" → Strength of Support for Health Care Reform	Strongly conservative; strongly liberal	Strong opposition; strong support
Type of Institution Enacting Change → Level of Success of Change	Courts Legislatures	Lower success Higher success
Gender of Candidate → Use of New Media	Women Men	More professional image and receptive Less professional image and receptive
Type of Governmental System → Likelihood of Democratic Consolidation[a]	Parliamentary system Presidential system	Higher likelihood Lower likelihood

a. Notice this last example links a discrete independent variable with a continuous dependent one.

data you determine is more than 30 percent of women in the legislature. For a hypothesis involving discrete variables, some of the possible values are explicitly named: parliamentary systems are more likely to consolidate. *Parliamentary systems* and *more likely* are the values here.

Each paper, then, will make a contentious statement. If that argument is a causal or correlational one, the student should also (1) posit a model that isolates the variables (or key factors) and (2) state a hypothesis that explains the nature of the relationship between them.

APPLYING THESE INSIGHTS

As a result of your work in this chapter, you should be able to develop a thesis or M&H section of your paper. The conclusion of your literature review should contain the kernel of your thesis, and with a little work for an empirical paper, it can be developed into an M&H. Why should this information already be in the conclusion of your literature review? Because in that section you put forth a preferred response to your research question. Thus, in asserting that a specific answer is best (for some reasons), you are making a contentious statement with which others can disagree. Notice that you do not have to tell the reader explicitly, "The thesis is …." By concluding that one answer appears best and defending that choice, you have effectively communicated that you have a thesis.

But what if you need to put forth a model and a hypothesis because you are investigating a correlation or causation? In that case, you have a little extra work to do and need an additional section to express these ideas. As with the literature review, you should develop a specific title that fits your purposes and your paper. Because this part is short, however, you do not need introductory and concluding sections. Still, you want to develop an engaging opening, an appropriate transition sentence to link the section with what came before. Similarly, write a strong concluding sentence at the end to wrap up this section. Here is how Joe, whose literature review we read at the end of chapter 4, wrote his M&H:

Linking Institutions with Stability

Institutionalism gives the best explanation of what must happen for El Salvador to regain political and socioeconomic stability. In simple terms, this argument can be understood like so:

<table>
<tr><td align="center">Strength of Governing
Institutions</td><td align="center">→</td><td align="center">Level of Democratic
Stability</td></tr>
</table>

In essence, a state must have all the necessary mechanisms in place to address what will amount to a number of different political and socioeconomic issues. Especially for a country that is recovering from a major crisis, these issues will be particularly pressing. The state must be prepared to fix, or at the very least mitigate, the problems threatening its stability. If these institutions are well grounded and relatively nonpartisan, then the country can stabilize in a democratic fashion. If these mechanisms, however, are corrupt or rife with partisanship where there should be very little (e.g., in the military), then the country cannot and will not properly stabilize. In other words, *the stronger the governing institutions, the greater is the level of democratic stability* [emphasis added]. If these institutions are weak or underdeveloped, the fate of the current system would be in jeopardy, as instability would result.

The term democratic stability is not synonymous with peace. Democratic stability can best be defined as the ability of a democratic country to ensure security for its citizens. This includes security against violence, obviously. But it also includes financial security, the ability to maintain fiscal solvency, and the ability to participate in political processes.[a] These characteristics are, by their very nature, peaceable ones. In postconflict El Salvador, the presence of stabilizing forces like these is crucial for building and maintaining peace. By doing so, the incentives to devolve into violence and unrest should be lessened. For purposes of this analysis, then, the creation of democratic stability in El Salvador will ultimately lead to a stable, lasting peace in the country.

NOTE

a. Roland Paris and Timothy D. Sisk, "Introduction: Understanding the Contradictions of Postwar Statebuilding," in *The Dilemmas of Statebuilding: Confronting the Contradictions of Postwar Peace Operations*, ed. Roland Paris and Timothy D. Sisk (New York: Routledge, 2009), 12–14.

Joe has again done an exceptional job. First, he came up with a great heading for this section (and frankly, the M&H is the hardest one to name in an interesting fashion). His title also shows that he has easily performed an additional, crucial step. In his literature review, he concludes that the Institutionalist argument is best. But what does that mean in terms of concepts? Joe realized that each of his schools is positing an alternative factor as essential for creating democratic stability. In other words, he was able to sort through the language—all the words—to arrive at the dependent variable—democratic stability. His analysis of Institutionalism (and his naming of the school) led him to understand that this approach asserts that the strength of state institutions is most important in postconflict situations. Stronger state institutions create more democratic stability. Thus, he has found his variables, with institutions affecting stability.

As suggested, Joe writes a great first sentence, which reminds the reader of the conclusion to the literature review and moves him forward to the tasks at hand. Joe explicitly states his variables in both his section title and model—the strength of governing institutions and the level of democratic stability. Joe succeeds in identifying the key variables as well as the words that indicate that they can take on values. I put this text in italics in Joe's excerpt to stress that you must include your hypothesis, using the variables stated in your model and showing how you expect them to be related. Notice, too, how Joe's model appears on the page: a reader easily sees the model (it is in bold, is indented, and has blank lines above and below), and there is a clear left side (for the independent variable) and right side (for the dependent variable).

After he presents his model, Joe explains the logic and begins to define stability for his readers. Because he will address these concepts and their connections more in the next section, the Research Design, he moves then to his actual hypothesis so that there are absolutely no doubts about the ways in which changes in the strength of institutions affect the level of democratic stability. While that first paragraph could have been the end of Joe's M&H section, he decides to elaborate more on one of his key concepts—his dependent variable—here. His final paragraph could also fit in the Research Design section; his placement is discretionary.

As you can see, although the M&H section may be brief, do not shortchange the amount of thinking that is required in writing a good one and the importance of paying close attention to the details. You have to be able to perform that step, as Joe did, to identify the underlying factors. You are asking yourself, What do all those words in the literature review really mean is fundamentally at stake? What are authors signifying as crucial for explaining the phenomenon—the political issue or policy—that you are interested in? The phenomenon is the dependent variable, and the key factor(s) is the independent one(s). You also need to make your model look good and use the proper terminology, including a value kind of term as well as the actual variables.

As you read this section and the previous excerpt you may think that Joe has repeated himself a bit. That may be true, but some repetition—of the main points—is good. While you never want to duplicate your words precisely, you will see that in this paper you are often previewing what is to come or reminding readers of what you've done. In a longer paper that is concerned with complex issues, both you and the reader need a certain amount of reiteration to grasp all your ideas and understand their significance to the larger purpose.

PRACTICAL SUMMARY

Before proceeding with the rest of the paper, you need to be able to state your argument precisely. That succinct formulation of your argument is the thesis; it is a contentious statement that can be upheld based on normative or logical principles or verified by data. If you are performing empirical causal or correlational research, your thesis will identify variables, and you will be interested in showing exactly why and how these factors are related. Thus, you will need a separate section in your paper that provides both your model (isolating the variables that you will investigate and showing the direction in which causality operates) and your hypothesis (indicating the ways in which variables are related). If you are not making a causal or correlational argument, you still want to be sure to refine your thesis so it is extremely clear. You will state that thesis at the end of your literature review if you do not need an M&H section. No matter which kind of research you are pursuing, however, you will also include your thesis or hypothesis in your paper's introduction, which we learn about in chapter 9.

The steps I suggest that you follow when writing the M&H section are the following:

1. Return to the conclusion of your literature review, and look carefully at which school of thought you believed was the most important. By choosing one approach, you are asserting a thesis.

2. If you are working on empirical research, you would be well served to create an additional section to state what is the underlying argument of this school—which factors affect the phenomenon at stake? If these causes and the effect are not apparent after working on your literature review, then you need to go back to it and rework that section so that it focuses on the factors that explain (possible independent variables) the development you are interested in studying (dependent variable). If you cannot, then you need help from your instructor.

3. You will present your argument in both its bare-bones (model) and its relational (hypothesis) forms. The model should appear on the page in a prominent way, with the independent variables on the left and the dependent on the right, separated by an arrow. Be sure to use a value word—*level, type, strength,* and so forth—that is linked to the actual factor, for example, "level of partisanship," "type of governmental system," "strength of state institutions."

4. Be sure that you know which kind of values (discrete or continuous) your variables will take on if you are performing empirical research.

5. When you write your hypothesis, use the precise words from your model to express the hypothesis. If these terms don't capture what you wanted in your hypothesis, then you know that you have a problem and have to rework one, either the model or the hypothesis. Also remember, your hypothesis should give you an idea of how relative values (for continuous variables) or actual values (for discrete variables) will be linked. For continuous variables, your hypothesis will typically be, "The more of X, the more of Y" (for positive relationships). For discrete variables, the hypothesis will be in the form, "When X takes on one value, then Y takes on another value." (For one of our examples, "Strong conservatives will be strongly opposed to health care reform, strong liberals will be strongly in favor of health care reform, and those who lean in one direction will be less intense in their feelings than their partisans.")

6. Use a heading to separate the M&H section from the previous one. Try to pick a title that communicates what the section is about as well as what you are arguing. Remember, the section is short. It consists of

   a. a transitional sentence to link this discussion with the literature review;

   b. some additional text to remind the reader of the thesis;

   c. the actual model;

   d. some text to explain the relationship that you expect between the independent and the dependent variables—here, you are also reminding the reader of what you learned in the literature review; and

   e. the actual hypothesis, stated in basic form.

SUGGESTED CALENDAR

If you're engaging in theory-advancing or public policy research, I suggest that you complete a draft of both these first two sections at the same time because the M&H follows so directly from the literature review and they are closely connected. The work on one directly affects the quality of the other. I recommend that these be finished by the end of the first third of your course, although your instructor may have a different timetable in mind. If you cannot identify a model and/or express a hypothesis, then you know that you have not properly done your literature review and you need some help. That's a great time to go see your professor. When you do, bring your work so your instructor can see exactly what you have been thinking and can better help you.

EXERCISES

1. Read the Op-Ed page in a recent *New York Times, Washington Post,* or *Wall Street Journal.* Identify the thesis of at least one of the authors. Can you also develop a corresponding hypothesis and model for that argument? Why or why not?

2. Read the front page of a recent *New York Times, Washington Post,* or *Wall Street Journal.* Develop at least one model and a corresponding hypothesis from one of the articles that you read. What would you call the M&H section of a paper that explored one of the relationships you have identified?

3. Using the excerpt of Joe's literature review in chapter 4, develop three additional and distinct models for explaining democratic stability in postwar El Salvador. What would be their corresponding hypotheses?

4. Using Latisha's draft annotated bibliography in chapter 3, develop two models and their corresponding hypotheses.

5. Imagine that you wrote a literature review that contained these sentences in its conclusion:

   The "Money Talks" approach appears to be the best one for explaining why congressional representatives in competitive districts vote the way they do. Lobbyists who and businesses that give enormous amounts of money receive access and sympathetic action on issues important to them from elected officials who are worried about staying in office. Constituent concerns, on the other hand, have less of an impact on these representatives when it is time to vote on legislation.

   Develop a model and a hypothesis for this argument. What would you call the M&H section of this paper?

CHECKLIST 4: MODEL AND HYPOTHESIS

Below is a checklist to consult while you are writing your M&H section. Any time you cannot answer "yes," you need to go back and address the problem.

Checklist 4: Model and Hypothesis

Does your Model and Hypothesis (M&H) section have an appropriate title that communicates the purpose of the section and is not simply "Model and Hypothesis"?

Yes _____ No _____

Does the M&H section begin with at least one transitional sentence linking it with the work that you did in the literature review?

Yes _____ No _____

If you are writing an empirical paper, is the model stated in a flow diagram, similar to the student example?

Yes _____ No _____

Does it have (1) a value word or phrase and (2) a concept/variable?

Yes _____ No _____

Is it placed appropriately on the page?

Yes _____ No _____

Is the hypothesis explicitly stated, and is it in the proper form ("The more of X, the more/less of Y"—depending on whether the relationship is positive or negative—for continuous variables or "If X is A, then Y is B, but if X is C, then Y is D" for discrete ones)?

Yes _____ No _____

Have you properly cited the sources of your ideas and kept direct quotes to a minimum?

Yes _____ No _____

Remember, appearance, format, and style are important too. You'll learn more in chapter 6.

NOTES

1. The thesis will also appear prominently in your introduction, as you will see in Chapter 9.
2. Two exceptions to the universal claim at the opening of this sentence include some types of journals and journalism.
3. Please note that textbooks frequently do not have theses, instead describing the state of a field without taking a position that one approach is best. Of course, some

texts do have embedded theses. Most famously, Hans Morgenthau's *Politics among Nations* is a text in international politics that puts forth a realist view of the field.

4. Janet Buttolph Johnson and Richard A. Joslyn, *Political Science Research Methods*, 3rd ed. (Washington, DC: Congressional Quarterly Press, 1995), 53–54.

5. Gerald Rosenberg, *The Hollow Hope: Can Courts Bring about Social Change?* (Chicago: University of Chicago Press, 1991).

6. Michael McCann, *Rights at Work: Pay Equity and the Politics of Legal Mobilization* (Chicago: University of Chicago Press, 1994).

7. Certainly, there can be multiple causes or several independent variables. For simplicity's sake, I will be talking about a single cause here. Also, technically, when first stated these are concepts, and through operationalization they become variables. See chapter 6 for more about operationalization.

8. For the general explanation of the factors posited to lead to democracy, see Robert D. Putnam with Robert Leonardi and Raffaella Y. Nanetti, *Making Democracy Work: Civic Traditions in Modern Italy* (Princeton, NJ: Princeton University Press, 1993), 9–12. For discussions of what effects female electoral success, see Pippa Norris and Ronald Inglehart, "Cultural Obstacles to Equal Representation," *Journal of Democracy* 12, no. 3 (2001): 126–140; Gwynn Thomas and Melinda Adams, "Breaking the Final Glass Ceiling: The Influence of Gender in the Elections of Ellen Johnson-Sirleaf and Michelle Bachelet," *Journal of Women, Politics & Policy* 31 (2010): 109–111.

9. Theodore J. Lowi made a mark early in his career by reversing the causal arrow and claiming "policies cause politics" and not the other way around. That politics caused policy had been the conventional wisdom before Lowi came along. See his "American Business, Public Policy, Case Studies and Political Theory," *World Politics* 16 (1964): 677–715 and *The End of Liberalism: The Second Republic of the United States*, 2nd ed. (New York: Norton, 1979).

10. This form applies to variables that take on continuous or interval values. The generic statement for hypotheses for data that are expressed as categories (nominal or ordinal data) will be discussed later in this chapter as well as in chapter 8 regarding performing the analysis and assessment of the thesis.

11. We could, however, generate a hypothesis that has the same meaning but that posits a positive relationship: the more conservative an individual, the more likely he or she will be to support the market-based changes in health care.

12. Please see W. Phillips Shively, *The Craft of Political Research*, 5th ed. (Upper Saddle River, NJ: Prentice Hall, 2002), 61–62, for a discussion of continuous and discrete variables and the way these are linked to types of data—nominal, ordinal, and interval.

13. Juan J. Linz, "The Perils of Presidentialism," *Journal of Democracy* 1, no. 1 (1990): 51–69. Linz updated this article and replied to criticisms in a version published as the first chapter in Juan J. Linz and Arturo Valenzuela, eds., *The Limits of Presidential Democracy* (Baltimore: Johns Hopkins University Press, 1994). Please note that some have criticized Linz for not recognizing that there are at least three categories

of governmental systems, the two mentioned and mixed or semipresidential ones. See Anthony Mughan, "Review of *Presidentialism, Parliamentarism and Stable Democracy: The Failure of Presidential Democracy,*" ed. Juan J. Linz and Arturo Valenzuela. *Mershon International Studies Review* 39 (1995): 123–125.

14. Discrete variables can be ranked/ordinal (such as strength of ideology) or unranked/nominal (such as party affiliation) forms. In addition to continuous and discrete variables, mathematicians also identify dichotomous variables—variables that can take on only one of two variables, for example, yes/no and on/off. In social science, we typically call these *dummy variables,* and they measure the presence or absence of a characteristic. For instance, we might be looking at female or not (i.e., male), Caucasian or not, Catholic or not.

chapter 6

Revising and Editing Your Work: It Ain't Over 'til It's Over!

To emphasize the iterative nature of the writing process and the link between writing and thinking, you will begin revising and editing after you have written first drafts of the sections of your paper. Throughout the research paper–writing process, you will be returning to these tasks. If you revise and edit constantly, however, you will never move forward with the parts that you still have to write. That is why I'm asking you to strike a balance: write a few sections, revise and edit them along with what came before (usually your work on the new sections will give you insight on ways to improve the old), hand in your work for comments (if possible) or pass them along to a trusted reader, and then write some more.[1] At the end—when you have a completed draft— you can give the whole text another dose of significant attention so that you are very pleased with what you hand in to your professor.

In addition to stressing iteration and the writing-thinking connection, another important purpose of this book is to banish some misconceptions about writing. Many students believe that the world is divided into good writers and not-so-good writers: some people are born knowing how to craft great arguments, sentences, paragraphs, and essays, and the rest of us are condemned to poor prose for eternity. This idea is nonsense! Writing, just like any talent— from sports to the arts, from cooking to calculus—is part inspiration but primarily skill. And you need to practice and hone skills to improve them. Thus, you should see your draft (whether you have completed your first installment or the whole paper) as a huge accomplishment because you have put your ideas on paper. In subsequent iterations, as you work through more of the elements of the research, as your understanding of the issues involved increases, and as your writing abilities improve, your work will take on its polished shape. The vast majority of authors write numerous drafts, and scholars produce many versions of their work before the pieces actually land in a journal or with a publishing house. All authors, then, revise and edit before handing in a final draft.

Revising and editing are two distinct though interrelated tasks. *Revising* entails making what we might call the macro-level changes to your text, any significant modifications in your ideas or the structure of your paper. *Editing* refers to the micro-level changes. When you edit, you make sure that sentences flow well and are grammatically correct and that all your citations are provided and typed in the proper form, according to your professor's specifications. You also ensure that you have followed the proper formatting and other presentation instructions. Did your instructor insist on a certain font, a particular size for margins, or a minimum word count? Did he or she say you must turn in two hard copies and that no electronic copies would be accepted? Pay attention to the details!

A polished paper is carefully revised and edited, and it conforms to all the various requirements. While you may view revising and editing as tedious, think again about the metaphor of a race for your paper. Imagine if athletes could rerun their events to correct for mental and physical mistakes made or mishaps incurred. Revising and editing give you a chance to fix any of the problems that remain so that you can submit the best possible paper (or, metaphorically, run that great race). What a fantastic opportunity! In addition, you can think of the presentation—conforming to the instructions—as a great chance to make a good impression. Just as you shouldn't and wouldn't arrive in shorts and flip-flops for your interview for a summer job as a paralegal in a large corporate law firm in the city, make sure your paper looks right—as your professor and the style manual you are using define this—when you turn it in.

To revise effectively, you need to do several things. First, if you have previously handed in drafts, be sure to respond to every one of your reader's suggestions. If you don't understand them, go talk to your instructor. If you disagree with them, also discuss this with your reader. If you are unable to have this discussion with your professor, explain your reasoning for rejecting the advice in a footnote. That way your reader can see that you took his or her comments seriously. The worst mistake you can make is to ignore the suggestions of someone who has read your work carefully (and who is going to grade it).

Second, go back to the Practical Summaries and the Writing Checklists at the end of this book's chapters as a way of double-checking that each section accomplishes what it should. Third, make sure that the pieces of your paper fit together nicely. In other words, see that the transitions between sections work well, that introductions properly introduce and conclusions effectively conclude. Fourth, you will likely have new ideas about the significance of some information or concepts that you have developed during the writing process. You want to integrate these new thoughts throughout the relevant parts of your paper. In other words, ensure that there is consistency throughout your work. You shouldn't feel disappointed about either adjusting or reconsidering what you have written before. Imagine that three years ago you provided a friend a map to your house, and that person was to return today. If you failed to update your directions, the person might become lost, as exits on highways get renumbered (as do highways themselves), streets are renamed, and landmarks change or are eliminated. Think of the conceptual modifications that you have made over the course of writing your draft as infrastructure improvements to your paper.

In general, when you revise you will be changing, deleting, or adding major sections to your text. While the first draft is an excellent beginning, do not be afraid to throw away or significantly change parts of the paper that no longer work, that do not help you to achieve your goals or make your precise argument. When you are in this taking-apart stage, I would highly recommend that you keep an electronic file of the original draft under a separate name. You never know when some text that you thought was expendable will turn out to be useful in another part of the paper or even where it was originally placed. For anyone, but especially for first-time authors, the idea of cutting or altering big sections of text can be very painful. You feel that all the work you have done must show in explicit ways. Here again, remember the marathoner. We cannot see all of the six- and ten-mile training runs, nor the weightlifting, yet this person would not be the runner he or she is without having trained in this manner. All we see is the runner's race on the day of the marathon. A pared-down paper—with irrelevant words, sentences, paragraphs, and even sections cut—will demonstrate the quality that you desire. An experienced reader knows that a well-crafted text reflects a great understanding of the research process, the question, and the findings. So do not be afraid to make changes and lose some of the work that you did before. You would not have arrived at your (higher) level of understanding of the problem if you had not written these now extraneous sections. Cut them, recognizing that this information was valuable to the process but is not needed for your paper anymore.

In addition to making sure that the logic and structure of the paper are coherent and that every sentence and paragraph is essential to your overall argument, you want to pay close attention to micro-level issues. In many ways, editing is about presentation. So at the outset, you should consult your syllabus and any special instructions that your professor has given you about this paper. Be sure that your final product conforms to all of the specifications. Second, run the spelling and grammar check program that is standard on your word processor. As I am sure you know, these programs cannot find all problems—they sometimes identify specialized terms as misspellings, or they may cause you some problems identifying fragments when you are trying to summarize qualitative information in a chart—but on balance, these programs are enormously useful, and I am amazed that more students haven't made a habit of using them. The spelling and grammar check will allow you to avoid silly errors, for instance, checking subject-verb and pronoun-antecedent agreement—singular subjects take singular verbs, and singular pronouns replace singular nouns. This computer function may even teach you a bit about grammar, helping you to identify mistakes that you tend to make so that you can correct them in future writing, without the help of the program.

Third, you should take great care with your word choice, and there are three dimensions involved here. One goal throughout your paper is to express your ideas succinctly and precisely. You do not need to worry about using an impressive vocabulary, and you especially want to avoid using multisyllable words that you can't define. You undermine your argument and overall credibility when you use language imprecisely and incorrectly. So don't worry about including enough big words. Instead, seek precision. Also, make sure that you vary your language sufficiently throughout your paper. You might have found a great adjective, but if you use it five times in one paragraph the word becomes far less interesting and effective. Find another term—use a thesaurus. Other problems with word choice come when, because of the topic or concept that you are researching, you need to write about a particular event or term many times. Here again, you need to come up with synonyms for this fundamentally important issue, occurrence, or idea and should consult a thesaurus.

While you are thinking about word choice, use pronouns with great care. Not only should you limit their use, but you must make sure that the antecedent for any pronoun is clear and matches your term in number and gender. In addition, remember that *this, these,* and *that* are indefinite pronouns that you could use to refer to complicated ideas or developments, but these words are called "indefinite" for a reason. Instead of using them, find synonymous phrases for concepts or events; if you do use them, be sure their antecedents are clear.

As you edit your paper, you also want to pay close attention to your citations and any quotes or paraphrases that you have used. Make sure that your footnotes are complete and accurate. If you say that the idea was on page 117 or the journal volume number was 36, you had better be right. Be certain that you have included enough citations, and check that your bibliography is in good shape. Is every footnoted work or piece noted in an in-text citation also in the bibliography? If you're using footnotes, use the short form where appropriate. When looking at quotes, make sure that they are accurate and that the quotation marks are properly placed (unless you're using a long, indented quote, which does not require this form of punctuation). In American English, commas and periods go within the quotation marks, even if they are not the original author's. For paraphrases, go back and double check that the material is significantly different from the original text. Be certain you have not plagiarized. Also, whether paraphrasing or quoting, verify that you have included the correct page number or other identifying information for books, articles, and sources from databases and websites so that an interested person could find your source if he or she wanted. In addition, confirm that your headings and your overall title accurately convey the meanings and purposes of the sections and the paper as a whole.

To be really happy with your paper and its flow, you would be well served to get someone you respect and trust to read the paper too. You should not expect your instructor to give you a preread before the assignment is due! Having another pair of eyes and another brain thinking about your text is a great idea, as that person might see things that you miss because you are, by now, so close to the text. If you do not have a friend whom you would like as a reader, consider taking your paper to your institution's writing center to get the perspective of a fresh pair of trained eyes and some advice. You can also read your paper out loud. That recommendation might seem funny and sound painful—oh no, I have to listen to my own words! To listen carefully to the sound is precisely the point—you want to rely on your ears now to help you find any problems that your eyes may have overlooked. Your ears will tell you what sounds funny, and you should make the necessary adjustments on the basis of what the text sounds like.

You may think that your ears are unreliable, and maybe you are right. But please realize that you can improve your use of language (maybe not today, but over the next few months and years) if you pay attention to it. To improve your ability to identify good usage, I suggest that you read—fiction or nonfiction books, newspapers, magazines, and anything that you find interesting. Make a habit of reading for pleasure every day, even if only for fifteen minutes. Surely you can find that time! And when you read, pay attention to the language; don't just zoom across the page. You might even consider reading some things out loud so that you can hear what good, clear writing sounds like. Then, start to be aware of how you talk and how you can communicate verbally in a clearer and more effective manner. You will be amazed at how much you can change your mode of expression if you put your mind to it.

Before handing in your paper, you may also want to consult one of the many pocket-style manuals to help you with problems that you may have with punctuation or *homonym confusion*.[2] If you learn the rules of punctuation, or become familiar with any words that are giving you trouble, you should be able to cure this difficulty for the future. Also, you should try to transform *passive constructions*—places in the text where the subject is not performing the action of the verb—into active ones. Again, a good style manual can help you both identify and change these. Generally, English speakers consider active constructions to be clearer and better style than passive ones.

One last piece of micro-level advice—avoid using *colloquialisms* and personal pronouns, especially the second-person (either plural or singular) pronoun *you* in formal writing. I know that I have violated this rule throughout this book; I have purposely written it in a conversational style. You should write your research paper in a formal style, like a journal article or a scholarly book. Thus, you want neither to use colloquialisms (unless you are quoting an important source directly) nor to have a conversation with the reader.

Obviously, if you want to benefit from any comments you receive, you have to finish with time for both someone to read the essay and you to react to any remarks. Thus, plan ahead! You are wise to finish a draft at least twenty-four hours before the due date, with the idea that you will take a little break from the work and then return to it for final polishing. Having some time away provides you with a bit of necessary distance that enables you to be a better critic of your own work.

After you have performed that last set of revisions and edits, you are almost ready to print the relevant sections of your paper; you still have a few more steps to perform. First, make sure you have black ink in your printer! (Actually, check that the day before, and get any supplies you need then.) Second, run the spelling and grammar check again. Third, read over the text one last time (you probably have made additional changes; even after the machine has confirmed that the section is fine, sometimes in making small corrections you can introduce some silly errors.) Fourth, confirm that you have included page numbers in your text. Fifth, view each printed page on your screen. If you need to, change the page breaks so any chart, graph, or table fits fully on one page (unless it is too long) and headings are not left "widowed" or "orphaned" from their sections. (In other words, you want to be sure that a section heading or one line from a table is not found on one page while the rest is on another.) Why do all this seemingly additional work? You are making sure that your presentation is as good as possible; again think of the interview analogy: you want to look just right. Now you are finally ready to print or, if your professor has asked for the work electronically, to send it. If you are printing, look at what comes out of the printer to verify that the pages are in the proper order, and staple (some professors prefer paper clips) your paper in the top left corner. (You have double-checked all the relevant instructions, so you know how to present this work to please your professor.) Great! You are finished with this stage of your project.

I want to stress here that you should be proud of finishing each phase and also realize that you will be rethinking what you have done and adding new sections. Still, that you will continue to revise and edit does not take away from having made this forward progress.

PRACTICAL SUMMARY

After you have finished your draft—whether we are talking about a part of the paper or the whole text, you still are not done. You need to revise and edit. To accomplish these tasks, I suggest that you do the following:

TO REVISE

1. Respond to every comment that your reader made (if you had one). If you don't understand or disagree with some of them, discuss your questions with your instructor. (You are wise to clarify comments with your instructor as soon as you get them. Don't wait until you're writing the next draft to ask. That might slow you down, or it even might be too late.)

2. Treat each section of your paper as a stand-alone essay. For each section, go back and read the Practical Summary from the relevant chapter in this book to determine what the goals were for that section,

and use the Checklists to guide you. Then read that part of your research paper, making any changes necessary so that your section accomplishes all that it should.

3. After you are satisfied that each piece of the paper is in excellent shape, make sure that the transitions between sections are good. Be sure that the parts logically flow into each other, titles and subtitles are adequate, and introductory and concluding paragraphs do their jobs well.

4. Verify that any new ideas that you developed as you proceeded with your paper are effectively integrated.

5. Do not be afraid to make necessary deletions and additions of text.

TO EDIT

1. Run the spelling and grammar check function on your computer. Make the changes recommended if they make sense to you. Assume that the program is right, but remember, the program can find problems that might not actually be mistakes, such as special terms that it identifies as misspellings or fragments that are purposely included in your text.

2. Pay close attention to word choice. Make sure that your language is precise (e.g., get rid of big words that you cannot define), avoid using the same word or term over and over again, watch out for overusing pronouns, and try to eliminate indefinite pronouns.

3. Make sure your citations (both within the text and at the end of the paper) are complete and accurate. Take great care that any quotes or paraphrases are correctly included.

4. Double-check your syllabus and any assignment sheets to make sure that you have abided by any special instructions that your professor has given you.

5. Check the overall quality of your paper by consulting an outside reader and/or by reading it out loud. Change the text if it doesn't sound good.

6. Fix other grammar or usage mistakes such as punctuation, homonym confusion, passive constructions, colloquialisms, and the use of second-person pronouns.

7. Run the spelling and grammar check again. Make necessary changes.

8. Read again. Correct any remaining errors.

9. Before printing, look at how the printed pages will appear. Make sure that you have included numbers on each page. Adjust page breaks to keep key parts of the text together on the same page.

10. Print your paper, and staple or paper clip it (depending on your professor's instructions), being sure that the pages are in the proper order.

11. You are done with this stage. Celebrate and feel proud!

SUGGESTED CALENDAR

In the last several days (notice that I did not say the last night or hours) before you need to hand in some sections of the paper or, if you can, a week before the completed draft is due, you must finish the tasks of editing and revising. In general, after you think you have finished your final draft, you should put your paper down for a while to give yourself perspective. Follow the steps spelled out here, and you will be in fine shape. Then, you can more effectively revise and edit your work one last time. When you are satisfied with your text, print out your paper. Hooray! You've written a high-quality portion of the research paper. What a great accomplishment!

CHECKLIST 5: APPEARANCE, FORMAT, AND STYLE

When you are revising, the best way to consider what you need to do is to go back to the specific requirements of the particular section. So consult the earlier rubrics and make sure you have satisfied all their criteria if you want to submit a good draft. This checklist, then, should be an *addendum to all the others,* and it stresses presentation issues—editing the paper so that it avoids grammatical and silly mistakes and checking to see that you have conformed to the requirements that your faculty member spelled out. Remember, making a good impression is extremely important in helping you get a job (when we're thinking about an interview) and in getting the grade you want (on your paper).

Checklist 5: Appearance, Format, and Style

Have you properly cited the sources of your ideas and kept direct quotes to a minimum?	Yes _____ No _____
Have you avoided plagiarism? Do all these citations appear in the form your professor has specified?	Yes _____ No _____ Yes _____ No _____
If you have used a long quote, have you indented it and not included quotation marks unless you have a quote within a quote? (See a style manual for how to handle long quotes.)	Yes _____ No _____

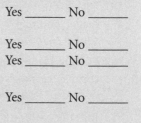

Have you numbered your pages?	Yes _____ No _____
Have you run the spelling and grammar check, recognizing that it is imperfect?	Yes _____ No _____
Recognizing the limits of spelling and grammar check, have you edited your paper?	Yes _____ No _____
Did you include a bibliography or source list that conforms to the style format your professor chose?	Yes _____ No _____
Did you ask an outsider to read your paper?	Yes _____ No _____
Did you take that person's advice in editing/ revising?	Yes _____ No _____

Add your own personal writing concerns, for example,

- subject-verb agreement,
- sentence fragments,
- run-on sentences,
- good transitions,
- word choice/overuse of words,
- homonym confusion,
- overuse of pronouns,
- passive voice, and
- appropriate length of paragraphs (more than one sentence, less than a page).

Note: You will be well served if you fill out this checklist after you finish a draft of each section of your paper.

NOTES

1. You would likely benefit from rereading this chapter after you finish every two or so sections of your paper and certainly when you have completed a full rough draft.
2. One of my favorites is Diana Hacker, *A Pocket Style Manual*, 5th ed. (Boston: Bedford/St. Martin's, 2009).

chapter 7

Making Your Plan and Protecting Yourself from Criticism: The Research Design

With the conceptual framework of your paper completed, you have one more step to undertake before proceeding with your analysis: the research design. By now you're at mile 12 in the paper-writing marathon.[1] You're almost halfway done, but you're starting to hurt. How are you going to make it? This is a difficult point, but if you can just keep going, the excitement and adrenaline rush that will come from being ever closer to the end will propel you on. Just hang in there and keep working.

The research design is where you plan what you will do to determine whether your thesis can be sustained.[2] It is also the section in your paper where you explicitly defend the choices you make regarding which instances of the phenomenon you are going to study, how to translate your concepts into knowable entities, and which sources or information you will use to determine their value. In addition, you explain exactly how you will perform your analysis. In effect, the research design is a first line of defense against criticism of your follow-through in the project: you present the logic for your decisions so that readers can see that you have made the best choices about how to proceed, given the limitations that face social scientists (i.e., not rocket scientists!)[3] regarding concept formation and translation, case selection, data availability, and general design issues.

Typically, the Research Design section completes four and sometimes five tasks. While I am presenting them in a certain order, you will later see that often you have to consider several factors simultaneously. Your to-do list includes the following:

1. select cases for study;

2. define the key concepts and establish a strategy for knowing their values (recognizing that values do not have to be quantitative);

3. identify sources of information for your analysis;

4. if necessary, write instruments, such as surveys or interview questionnaires, for generating information; and

5. discuss methodology, explaining exactly what you will do and how.

Try to work through each step and then move on to the next; however, recognize that sometimes you may need to reconsider an earlier decision. In addition to setting out your plan here, you also justify your choices and strategies as the best for evaluating your thesis given the constraints (including resources and time) under which you are operating.

RESEARCH DESIGN: THE MEDICAL SCIENCE ANALOGY

While these five steps might be clear enough, why and for what purpose you undertake them might be fuzzy. So let's turn to research that is, I hope, familiar so that you can see an analogy to your tasks. If you watch, listen to, or read the news on a regular basis, you will hear reports about the latest medical or drug tests. One of the first things to notice about these results is that doctors are often finding that what they thought earlier is now wrong or at least open to question. Going back in history, we may remember that doctors once used leeches to bleed patients in the hopes that they would suck out all the bad elements and speed the recovery. While medicine has come a long way from bloodletting, remember that negative findings (that the hypothesis is not upheld) are just as important as positive ones (that the information seems to sustain the argument). A researcher is proud of following the appropriate process and doing a good job in the evaluation, not in being right, that is, confirming a hypothesis.

Second, our medical analogy reminds us that evaluating a claim involves determining whether what we think is important really is. The medical community may know, for instance, that being physically active is essential for maintaining cardiovascular health, especially for those who are likely (because of family history or other behaviors, such as smoking, for instance) to have heart attacks. I might want to know, however, whether vigorous exercise three times a week is more useful than moderate exercise every day in combating heart attacks among those at risk for them. If I pursue this research, I am investigating a model:

Type   →   Likelihood of a Heart
of Exercise   Attack for Those at Risk

Its corresponding hypothesis is, "Vigorous exercise three times a week is more likely to reduce the risk of heart attack than is daily moderate exercise, although both are better than being primarily sedentary."[4] Here, I have a discrete variable (type of exercise) for my independent variable and a continuous one for my dependent variable (likelihood of heart attack). I am asserting that exercise—of a certain form and regularity—matters for cardiovascular health. Is my factor—vigorous exercise, three times a week—really better? Will it keep people from having heart attacks?

This medical hypothesis highlights nicely the ideas of cause and effect and the contingency of the claim. Here, I am saying that vigorous but less frequent exercise will have clearer positive outcomes (avoiding heart attacks) than will moderate daily exercise. Similarly, back in chapter 5, Joe was asserting that stronger governing institutions result in greater democratic stability. In each case, does the factor posited—vigorous exercise almost every other day or strong governing institutions—actually lead to the desired outcome—fewer heart attacks among people at risk or greater democratic stability?

To answer that question, we have to design a study that determines whether our factor is what is really responsible for the difference. That simple statement has many important points packed into it. Returning to the medical example alone, to figure out whether vigorous three-times-a-week exercise is the better form of activity, we have to also be sure that

a. we can isolate a group of people that is at risk of a heart attack;

b. we can be sure that all or even some of the people aren't doing something else that could either increase (such as smoking) or decrease (such as becoming vegetarians) their risk of recurrent heart attacks;

c. we know what the typical risk level is for this group; and

d. we can put these people into subgroups, one that exercises vigorously three times a week and one that exercises moderately every day.

In thinking about what has to be done to evaluate our hypothesis about exercise and heart attacks, we gain insight into political science research. Each of the points above (a through d) corresponds to the following methodological considerations in our research project:

a. We can identify a group of common incidents or cases. For medical research, this might be people. But in political science, our cases can be many things. If we wondered, as Kate does, why electoral success of women in parliamentary contests varies across countries, the cases are the legislative election outcomes in those countries. If we were inquiring, as Samantha is, about how different types of candidates employ new media in American national legislative campaigns, the cases could be each campaign that uses these media. When we consider cases, we also need to ask ourselves, To do a good job on our research, do we need to study all the cases (the *universe*), or can we evaluate a *sample* (a subset)? Medical research rarely looks at the universe; it is virtually impossible to control the behavior of all people who are at risk for something doctors are trying to understand. However, when we sample, we have to choose very carefully.

b. As we isolate the issues involved in sampling, we need to know the factors that others think affect the phenomenon in which we're interested, and we must try to minimize their impact. This second point recognizes that we have done our literature review. You might wonder why you need to include a discussion of the literature in the paper if you move on with simply one school. The reason is that these other approaches identify additional potential factors that could exert influence on the outcome. In our study, we have to try to isolate the importance of our preferred cause. The literature told us that smoking promotes the risk of heart attacks while being a vegetarian reduces it. Even though our goal is dampening the risk, we don't want our patients to stop eating meat. Why? If they become vegetarians, then we can't tell which factor—exercise or diet—affects their heart attack risk. So in the medical study, everyone would be prevented from smoking and from becoming a vegetarian (or doing any other things we know affect the potential for another heart attack) so that we could be sure that exercise is responsible for the medical outcomes we see.

c. Embedded into the third point are a few insights. When selecting incidents to study, each case must be similar on the most important issues. (For the medical example, that means all participants are at risk of heart attack and, as we saw in point b, that they are behaving similarly to manage their conditions.) In addition, we have to know what heart attack risk we would expect from this group. Thus, when we put our cases into a group, we would have some knowledge that all people with these characteristics exhibit the risk of having a heart attack and more precisely, for instance, that 25 percent of people with their characteristics will have another incident within three years. That "25 percent in three years" gives us a benchmark against which to measure the effects of different forms of exercise. If we didn't know what was typical, then when we designed the experiment, we would have to divide the participants into three: a first group doing nothing (the *control*), a second exercising moderately every day, and a third exercising vigorously three times a week. This dispersal allows us to know whether (1) exercise makes a difference at all and (2) vigorous exercise (less often) is better.

d. Finally, in this example, we make people do something, or we create the change in the value of the independent variable that we think will have an impact on the dependent variable. In addition to stressing that we are looking here to see exactly what different values of our key factor do to our outcome, the last point highlights a key difference between medical and political science research. People choose to be involved in medical trials, and they then typically do what doctors ask of them.[5] In political science, a true experiment—wherein the researcher can affect how much of the cause the experimental group receives—is unusual.

Thus, this familiar scientific process—that of medical trials—highlights what you seek in evaluating your thesis. Your job is not to find out that you are right. You choose a set of cases that are appropriately similar and try to isolate the factor in which you're interested. In particular, you want to keep other potential causes, those that other scholars have said are important, from having an impact. You also need to see what different values of your key factor lead to. Do they result in changes in the value of the dependent variable as hypothesized? For Kate, then, do higher levels of economic development lead to more women being elected in national parliaments? Now that we have a better understanding of the overall idea here—that we're trying to figure out whether our preferred factors are really most important in affecting outcomes— let us leave the analogy behind and turn to the challenge of designing a project in political science.

WRITING THE RESEARCH DESIGN

When you approach the research design, realize that even though you have multiple tasks to accomplish, the actual text will be relatively short. The thinking and the time involved, however, are significant, particularly if you are developing surveys or interview questionnaires. So be sure that you devote the effort required and handle this section in its parts and in sequence. A poorly designed study can lead to worthless results. In the earlier medical example, if you allow some people to smoke or you're not sure that everyone is exercising as he or she should, then you cannot tell whether vigorous exercise is better.

CHOOSING CASES

For some students, the research question identifies cases, and these instances are likely related to a person's enthusiasm for the project as well as to the puzzling nature of the query. Such questions might include the following:

- Why is U.S. politics apparently so much more polarized now than it was in the early 1980s when similar big questions about the budget, role of government, and foreign policy were at stake and government was also divided?
- Or, a variant on Kate's interest in female electoral success, Why have women been elected president recently in states such as Liberia and Chile but not in wealthier and long-standing democracies such as the United States?[6]

Both of these questions include their respective cases: in the first instance, the cases are periods of time—the early 1980s versus now—and in the second they include countries—Liberia, Chile, and the United States. For students with these questions, case selection is therefore easy. However, when the students write their research designs, they will want to think about and justify why these are good instances to study, in that they exhibit variation (in at least one case you see a large amount or the presence of your item of concern, here either polarization currently or the election of female presidents in Liberia and Chile, and in another you see discernibly different results, less polarization thirty years ago and no female president in the United States by 2010). The second one, in particular, contains a puzzle. Given the conventional wisdom, women do not usually win democratic presidential elections, especially in poorer countries that are newer democracies when they are not related to some previously powerful male figure.[7] So why would Liberia and Chile have success electing female executives before the United States, a historical leader in women's political activism and empowerment?

In addition, you hope to find cases that provide some type of control, in other words, they allow you to minimize the effects of other factors. Regarding polarization, please notice that Latisha started out reflecting on contemporary polarization. In talking to her instructor, however, she learned investigating more than one case would give her greater understanding of this phenomenon. She decided to find some reasonable case or cases for comparison. As her instructor explained, we learn not only from seeing what causes the presence or the high levels of our item of interest (polarization) but also from what causes its absence or insignificant presence.[8] So this concern with research design pushed Latisha to come up with a question that helped her pair two cases, one in which she thinks there is relatively more polarization (today) with another in which there is relatively less (thirty years ago). An important lesson from Latisha's experience, then, is that identifying at least one comparative case—conceiving of what we thought was unique as actually something that has similar instances—may not be that hard. We may be able to consider another time period, or we may be able to break up our particular case into subperiods.

Even though Latisha has found a good comparative case, she still has a challenge. She might find that isolating causal factors is difficult; a lot has changed in the past thirty years that could have contributed to polarization. In her literature review, however, she learned that contentious issues, particularly when electoral races seemed tight, have an impact on polarization.[9] Latisha's choice of cases allows her to control for these two variables since economic and security issues were pressing in the 1980s and today, and citizens were closely divided during both time periods. So presumably neither of those factors accounts for changes in polarization. Instead, Latisha hypothesizes that other developments have contributed to higher levels of polarization—the increased isolation of people from those who don't think as they do and the rise of differentiated and shock media. Note that these factors have varied over time. Her case selection will allow her to examine whether these particular changes are responsible for greater polarization.

Not all questions, however, have built-in cases, and if you have chosen such a question, you then need to take special care either to decide to examine the universe or to choose your sample so that you are including both variation and control. Regardless of whether your contentious statements are causal, correlational, or assertions of fact, you need to plan your project carefully.

Suppose you wanted to evaluate a thesis that you came across in your political theory class. You sought to investigate Richard Boyd's argument that Hobbes is an opponent of liberal associationalism because he defends and supports royal rule. He is, therefore, not a forefather of liberalism as some have contended.[10] Selecting instances to assess these contentions highlights the notion that cases encompass many factors. For this paper about Hobbes, you must decide which of his works you are going to study to evaluate your thesis. To be the most convincing, you would like to examine all of his writings so that you could see whether he consistently favored royal, absolutist rule. If you saw some variation in Hobbes' assertions, you would want to note them. Did his opinion change over time or with respect to certain issues or geographic or cultural factors? Thus, if you looked at the complete body of Hobbes' work— that is, the universe—then you could be convinced that you had a complete basis from which to make your conclusion.

Oftentimes it is not possible to study the entire universe of cases (every instance of a phenomenon) as you may lack the time or resources. So you must select a subset or a sample. Again, the goal in sampling is to choose cases that reflect the whole population (as we have already discussed) as well as to introduce as little sampling bias as possible. In other words, we do not want to pick cases that we know will confirm our hypothesis and/or discredit challengers. We need a fair evaluation of the contention. A simple example from polling may help illuminate the bias problem in case selection and why we must be careful to avoid it.

Imagine that you were a strong Republican and you were unhappy with some of the poll data reported in the news in late October 2008. You decided to determine on your own who was going to win the upcoming presidential election. To figure that out, you went to your home state, Oklahoma, and traveled around asking the following question of likely voters: "For whom are you going to vote on election day, John McCain, Barack Obama, or someone else?" You would have concluded from your research that John McCain was going to win the election in a landslide, and your research would have been terribly flawed. Why? You made a major sampling error. By questioning people in a state that is strongly Republican you skewed your results. Your literature review that examined American voting behavior should have made you aware that geography, region, and party affiliation are important predictors of votes. Thus, your sample needed to include cases (voters) in the proportion in which you would expect to find them in the likely voting population as a whole. To survey Oklahomans would have a poor effect on your findings because they are far more Republican than the national average. If you were interested, on the other hand, in understanding who was going to win this state's electoral votes in November 2008, your sample would have been a good one.[11]

This example underlines a point we saw in the medical example: the literature review (with both your conclusion and the arguments that you left behind) explicitly assists you in deciding which are good cases. Through your analysis of the scholarly answers to your question, you know which other items could affect the outcome. You think they are wrong, but you want to be sure (as in the exercise–heart attack example) that these other factors don't exert too much influence on your results. Therefore, you try to isolate the effect of your preferred cause—your independent variable—and limit or preferably eliminate the impacts of the others (e.g., smoking or a dietary change in our medical example). To do that, you typically need to *control* for other factors. When you control, you are holding these other elements constant or reducing their impact on the outcome as much as possible.

In addition, this idea of control means that you should not choose only cases that you know are good for proving your contention. In fact, expunge the words *proof* and *prove* from your vocabulary for the duration of the research project. The point in any investigation is not to prove but to learn. Would we be well served if medical researchers always found that their insights were correct? No. We want to know under which conditions their proposed solutions, be they exercise, drugs, or other procedures, appear to work; when they are ineffective or are harmful; and when the researchers aren't sure. The goal of your work, like that of medical researchers, is to design a reasonable test of your argument and to report accurately what you find. Your initial ideas do not have to be right; your job here is to evaluate and investigate fairly. In this way, you learn more about the phenomenon in which you're interested.

So in the preceding example about voting behavior, you can see that you have not controlled for party affiliation, region, race, and ethnicity (as Oklahoma is whiter than America is, on average). To do so, you would need to talk to a *representative sample* of likely voters: in other words, a subset that accurately reflects the universe of cases. Professional pollsters take great pains to define their samples and have found ways to choose only about 3,000 American voters and arrive at a good estimate of voting behavior. Note, however, that even those professionals typically identify a sampling error of plus or minus 3 percent. With a sample, it is impossible to predict perfectly, but with care you can get very close.

For other kinds of questions, you might need to control for some larger background factor that reflects changes occurring over historical periods. For instance, if you were looking at the effectiveness of courts in bringing about social change, selecting cases prior to 1930 would not make sense. The court's role shifted dramatically in the 1930s, and certainly after 1955, because of a larger ideational change in the United States about the proper role of the judiciary relative to the other two branches of government. Perhaps a contrary shift is occurring again today. Similarly, in investigating questions of foreign policy or world politics, you might not find cases that occurred during the Cold War to be comparable to those between 1990 and 2001, or after September 11, 2001. Those historical periods reflect major differences in the structure of the international system, and you might want to keep that factor—the structure—out of your study by holding it constant, that is, picking all your cases from only one of those three periods (Cold War, 1990–2001, post-9/11).

Some kinds of questions lead to the examination of a great many cases, or what political scientists like to call "large N [for number of cases] studies." Large N studies are conducive to performing statistical analysis of the data. If you have easy access to data in numerical form, using many cases helps improve accuracy. (As pollsters' work shows, you do not need to use the universe to obtain useful results, but you need to sample appropriately.) Other questions, however, particularly ones that involve examining historical phenomena, are not going to be evaluated in the same way. Usually researchers choose a small number of cases, but not just one, to evaluate their hypotheses.[12]

Our student Samantha has a research interest that, depending on how she transformed it into a thesis, could lead her to grapple with not only which cases she should study but also which kind of study should she conduct. Her thesis is, "Gender affects how a candidate for national office uses new media." In making that argument, she is building on other media and campaigning literature that makes a similar assertion.[13] She knows from her literature review that some analysts discount the role of gender and instead assert that status (incumbent or challenger) and party affiliation (Republican, Democrat, or other) are really more important in affecting how candidates use media.[14] In performing her research, Samantha is trying to make two contributions: (1) understand how social media are used in campaigning and (2) explore the impact of gender on candidate presentation.

Because social media are such recent phenomena, Samantha knew that she would be looking at the 2010 election, but then she had to ask herself, Which campaigns? She decided on Senate elections because those candidates typically have far more resources than their House counterparts and funding makes a more multifaceted media strategy possible. Second, she also thought that choosing fairly among the candidates for 435 House seats would be a more difficult task than selecting among the competitors for the 34 Senate seats that were up for grabs that year. Because her cases were not the seats themselves, but the campaigns, Samantha had at least 68 campaigns to choose from (assuming all were contested by at least two candidates).[15]

Now, should Sam examine all of these races? In some ways, this is a question about the kind of data or information she would like to gather and the type of study she would like to perform (i.e., other issues on our task list, operationalization and methodology—remember that I said that these decisions were often interconnected?) as well as a question about resources. Samantha decided she was very interested in understanding the visual impressions candidates were trying to make and thought that she should analyze image making both quantitatively and qualitatively. She would evaluate many pictures and make tallies about opportunities to connect, but she would also like to discuss her qualitative impressions of the site.

The desire to examine pictures (and there were thousands of them) and to provide a sense of the web presence meant that Sam would need to sample, but how? With the priority of variation and control, she would have been trying to vary gender while holding party and status constant—because these two were competing explanations. Thus, she would ideally like to compare

| Female | Democrat | Incumbent | with |
| Male | Democrat | Incumbent | |

OR

| Female | Republican | Challenger[16] | with |
| Male | Republican | Challenger | |

She would then expect gender to affect self-presentation of candidates, and she is holding the other factors—party affiliation and status—constant. Her literature review told her that women would likely use images to seek to bolster their professionalism while men would try to stress their human sides. In terms of the linking aspects of the new media, she would expect women to have more opportunities to interact with the public and provide more feedback opportunities because given female socialization, women are purportedly more interested in others' opinions and in pleasing others. Providing opportunities for interaction and feedback would also support the perception that women candidates are more personable, gentler, and warm, characteristics that are often valued by voters.[17] Last, because we tend to associate technological prowess with men and not women, male candidates would be likely to use social media in a more sophisticated way and have more tech-savvy websites in general. So moving from the general insight that women would use media differently, Samantha has generated three specific ones to explore.

In sum, when selecting cases for your study keep in mind the following issues. Seek at least one case for comparison. When you choose cases, you are not trying to *prove* your thesis. In fact, you need to eliminate that word from your vocabulary. You are seeking to give your thesis a fair evaluation, so you want to be careful not to introduce bias into your sampling procedure. Most of the time—because of research constraints, we will choose a sample of cases and not the universe. When we sample fairly, we need to be aware of (and take into consideration) the alternative explanations. Our goal is to pick cases that hold the values of those competing factors constant (provide control) while varying the value of our preferred cause or outcome. We are trying to determine whether our explanation accounts for the results.

In the real world, we find that sometimes our understanding of the literature isn't as clear as it should be when we initially make our case selection decisions. Then, at the analysis and assessment stage, we go out, gather data, start thinking about it, and realize, Oh no! From the perspective of evaluating my thesis, I have not proceeded as I should have. I have not, for instance, controlled adequately for a competing factor or captured enough variation in my variables. If this happens to you, realize that you are not alone. Frequently, case selections are imperfect; then, however, you have to decide (here, often, in consultation with your instructor) how to proceed. If you still have the time to redo data collection, you may have to rethink the case selection and go back to the beginning in finding your information. For semester-long projects, however, students usually don't have this kind of time. In this situation, you would need to discuss—in your Research Design section—the ways in which your design is imperfect but also exactly why someone might still study these cases—they might be particularly important or interesting and they might highlight the role of one key factor (with poor control of others). Later, in the conclusion, you would come back to the problems with case selection and think of how this may have affected the results of the study. You should remember, however, that selecting cases perfectly is typically impossible. So do the best you can to have variation and control, and recognize explicitly the limits and problems with your cases. Then, move on to your next task, returning to think about these weaknesses when you write the conclusion.

CONCEPT DELINEATION AND MEASUREMENT

The second job in the research design is *operationalization*, which means translating your concepts (what we earlier called "variables") into identifiable entities and specifying their values. As we saw back in chapter 5, values may be numbers—such as per capita GDP (GDP PC), voter participation rates, percentage of women elected to a legislature—they may be categories—presidential or parliamentary systems, women or men—or they may be qualities that a researcher describes in more detail—nature of leadership, conservatism, or strength of institutions, for instance.

You have to give operationalization significant thought because knowing exactly what you are looking for and how you are going to conceive of your factors is central to doing a good project. It also forces a precision of thinking that will help you better understand all that you have to consider. For instance, returning again to Boyd's Hobbes thesis—Hobbes is an opponent of liberal associationalism who defends and supports royal rule; therefore, he is not a forefather of liberalism as some have contended[18]—we see that anyone who sought to evaluate that argument should break it down and then consider how to define and conceive of its key concepts, that is, opponent of liberal associationalism, defender and supporter of royal rule, and liberalism.

For absolute clarity, credibility, and replication—the precise repetition of the steps—a researcher needs to explain exactly what each of these terms means, both in the abstract and for the actual research. In this example, then, an analyst should explain what liberal associationalism and liberalism mean and how she is going to know when Hobbes is arguing for or against them. In the research design, the writer thus establishes standards that guide her through her project: they help her be sure that what she is finding is what she knows and not simply what she wants to know or what she thinks. In other words, by setting out clear definitions and steps for evaluating her concepts, the researcher develops a transparent system for determining her assessments. She does not measure or evaluate yet; she simply states her plan in this portion of the paper. Again, following this example, the writer would provide her definitions (for liberal associationalism, royal rule, and liberalism) and the key words or phrases that she will use to note Hobbes' opposition to the first and defense and support of the second. Moreover, her definition of liberalism will be linked to positions on these key concepts (liberal associationalism and absolutist rule), and therefore Hobbes' stance on the first two points will affect his ability to be a source of liberal thought. This is her *plan* for determining the extent to which Hobbes is an opponent of active social groups, a defender of royal rule, and therefore an opponent of liberal ideas. The writer will be well served to explain this final logical connection in her research design too, stating, for instance, "Because of liberalism's belief that a vibrant civil society benefits the life of the polity as a whole and its firm commitment to the equality of all individuals, someone who is opposed to the role and fluidity of groups in society and supports the hierarchy of monarchical rule cannot be a forefather of liberalism." By making an explicit plan and clearly laying out her logic, the writer works to eliminate wishful thinking or other flaws when she actually performs the analysis.

All researchers have to use great care with concept definition and the translation of concepts into actual variables. When we set out our models in chapter 4 we were technically identifying the key concepts that we believed were related to each other. To make them true variables, we transform the theoretical ideas into actual measures. Where does any researcher—whether assessing a thesis or a model—find guides to specifying and measuring concepts? One of the best sources is other authors who have investigated similar questions or concepts; you may use their definitions and measurement strategies as long as you give them credit. The advice here is *not* to take their data or to replicate exactly their studies. I am suggesting that you *base your approach* on other works. To find these *strategies*, go back to the authors you identified in your literature review and look at what they did—which choices did they make when conceiving of their variables? Which kind of methods did they employ to measure them? Pick from among the approaches, and explicitly defend all of the choices that you make by explaining them in your text.

There is often a problem, however, with using existing work as your sole guide to specifying and operationalizing your concepts: established scholars may have access to far more resources (e.g., time, money, research assistance, information) than you do. One of my favorite examples to use for teaching students about research and research paper writing is Robert Putnam's *Making Democracy Work*. Putnam's study, however, took about two decades, involved many research assistants, and required a number of large grants to complete. Thus, he was able to develop measures for variables that used multiple indicators, required the interviews of legions of local officials, and consisted of many statistical sources. If you were interested in probing the importance of culture versus economic development in explaining the efficacy of democracy in different regions of the United States, you might take Putnam's work as an inspiration, but you certainly could not strictly apply his approaches to measuring variables.[19] You would have to modify the strategies to make them doable given your time and research constraints yet still logically sustainable.

Sometimes, if you have consulted purely theoretical articles in your literature review to help you answer your general question, you will be able to write an excellent section on the theoretical debate, but these articles will be a poor guide at the research design stage. In this case, you need to find additional studies, ones that are more applied, dealing with real-world cases and seeking to assess an argument similar to your own. Compare the way concepts are defined and measured, and pick one out of the new set that you find best, while being sure to credit your source. Or if you feel confident that translating the concepts into knowable entities is relatively straightforward, you can advance a plan based on your own logic.

Let's look at some examples of operationalizing concepts for empirical papers to understand this process better. I'd like to compare the two models and hypotheses related to gender and politics that we have seen from Kate (chapter 5) and Samantha here:

Level of   →   Proportion of Women Elected
Economic Development   to National Legislatures

The higher the level of economic development in a state, the higher will be the proportion of women who will be elected to national legislatures.

Gender of   →   Levels of Professionalism
Candidate   and Receptivity Exhibited

Women are more likely than men to have images and interactions that stress their high levels of professionalism as well as their openness to communication, feedback, and ideas.

Starting with the first set, we can identify two key concepts whose values we have to know. These are the level of economic development and proportion of women elected to the legislature. In this case, proportion of women elected is more straightforward. To know its value for any given state for a particular legislative session, a researcher would find or, if this information were not available in some data set, calculate the percentage of legislators who are women. Coming up with a value of economic development might be more challenging because scholars have different understandings of that concept. One view privileges the overall size of the economy and scales that by the population, GDP PC. Another, however, says that this notion does not capture a key essence of development—how well people are living in that society— which is measured in the United Nation's Human Development Index (HDI). If this were your project, you would have to take a stand on the essence of this concept. Both sets of figures are easily available through the World Bank and United Nations, so your decision about which to choose has to be a reasoned one regarding which best captures what you think development means for your project.

The second model and hypothesis pair also contains one easy concept to operationalize and another that is more difficult. The causal factor is relatively easy to determine: is a candidate female or male? The second factor (actually there are two outcomes here—level of professionalism and level of receptivity) is more complex because Samantha has named two effects, and no standard definitions exist for either one. To operationalize, Samantha turned to some scholars of gender and elections who have observed that women still tend to need to build citizen confidence in their ability to handle important issues such as security and the budget. Voters believe that women are inherently more nurturing and more suited to social issues, so to be taken seriously, women tend to overcompensate and show themselves as competent, serious, and tough. Men, on the other hand, often use their advertising to show their human or softer side. Particularly since the end of the Cold War, however, femininity can be seen as a plus, as women are perceived as gentler, warmer, and more compassionate.[20] To get at the level of professionalism, Sam also realized that she had to specify her case selection even further. She wanted to look at photos, but which ones and at which time? She ultimately chose to examine the pictures on the front page of the candidate's website as well as the Facebook profile that were available at the height of campaign season—from Labor Day to election day. She reasoned that these were the most important for impression making, which is her central concern.

Concentrating on assessing professionalism, Sam decided to code three elements in the pictures: attire, with whom the candidate was pictured, and what the candidate was doing. For each candidate, she would calculate an average professionalism score for all the relevant pictures. For level of receptivity, she would also score the number and type of opportunities for interacting with the candidate. Then Sam would compare the averages on professionalism and receptivity for female candidates versus male candidates. If her hypothesis was correct, a difference of means test would tell her whether women scored higher than men and therefore gender mattered in candidate's use of new media.

Sam also sought to understand professionalism and receptivity through a qualitative analysis of the website and the nature of the opportunities to interact with the candidate. She would look at the aesthetics of the pages as well as the ways in which candidates were reaching out. These she thought she would record, describe, and classify using words. She also planned to interview campaign staffers to see what she could learn about the media strategies and whether gender had an impact.

As you can plainly see, regardless of which approach (numeric or word representation of the values) researchers choose, operationalizing involves important decisions for the variables, which can have a huge impact on the study. When translating concepts into variables, be very careful that the measures are both *valid* and *reliable*. Valid means that the strategy for knowing their value provides accurate representations of the concepts (or at least as accurate as possible). In making the choice between GDP PC and HDI, Kate is trying to choose the more valid measure. If she's more concerned about standard of living, then Kate would choose HDI to account for economic development. Some might argue with Samantha that her professionalism scale does not adequately capture the image, but I think that she has done the best that she can here in finding a relatively simple way of understanding that concept numerically.

There's a second issue involved in knowing your value, called *reliability,* the repeated ability to achieve the same measure—regardless of who is doing the measuring. When you're choosing from a list of data, as with determining HDI levels for various countries of the world, all you need to do is read the number off the list. Unless your eye skips incorrectly across the column, the reliability of your value is very high. However, when your measure entails judgment, then it might be more subject to problems. The goal in defining your strategy is to make it easy for others to perform the same task and get the same value. In Samantha's case, her strategy for measuring professionalism is very clear, and someone who wanted to replicate it (given that she also precisely defined her sample) certainly could do it.

If we think of operationalizing as a game of darts, a measure that is both valid and reliable consistently hits the bull's eye. A measure that is valid but unreliable will scatter around the bull's eye unpredictably, while a measure that is reliable but invalid will always land in the same vicinity but never hit the center. Valid means the aim is on target, and reliable means the throw is consistent. The best players (and strategies) are both valid and reliable, helping the research consistently capture the true value of the concept.

IDENTIFYING DATA SOURCES

The third part of the research design is to identify which information you are going to use to know the values of your variables and exactly where you are going to get it. The focus is on finding the data that you need to evaluate your hypothesis. Here is where you seek *primary sources*, bits of unprocessed information, on which you will rely to know the values of the variable. With some data, the primary source material translates directly into the values you need to determine. Kate knows that she can find her GDP PC data from the World Bank. She might not know, initially, how to find the information about the percentage of women in Parliament. A little digging (her literature review sources or some Internet searching should be helpful) would lead her to the Inter-Parliamentary Union for this information.[21] Samantha needs to find Senate candidates and track down their websites and social media sources. She has to do some of this before the election to be sure that she is following the interactive traffic. Thus, for her, not only finding her data but getting them at the right time are very important.

When you are identifying your sources, you should not simply take information from any place that you can find it. You want to be sure that you have the best source, given your constraints. While Internet searches for data are useful, please do not perform a Google search and take information off of any website that you find. In general, reference librarians will tell you that when you come upon a source you need to interrogate it along five dimensions: authority, accuracy, coverage, currency, and objectivity.[22] For the first, you want to ask yourself, Who is providing this information? Is it someone or some organization that you have a reason to believe is credible and respectable? Here, look not only at the individual's name but at his or her title and institutional affiliation to determine whether this person has authority. Second is accuracy. When considering that factor, you have to take the motives of the source into consideration. For instance, during the Cold War, the Soviets provided false statistics about their economy, and students of the USSR used instead CIA estimates of that country's economic activity. While the CIA might have had some propaganda motives for underestimating the Soviet economy, it also was charged with gathering information so that the United States would be prepared for threats. Thus, most scholars thought its data were more valid than those released by the Soviet government. If you have some doubts about your source's accuracy, note it and explain why you still think that this source is the best.

Coverage refers to how broad in scope is the information or the site. Is the scope right for your purposes? If you need information from a particular time period, group of states, or candidates, your sources must have the coverage you require. Currency refers to how recent the information is. For historical projects, currency will often not matter. Samantha, however, needs very current information, and you might too, so be sure to check how recently updated the site or publication is. Finally, you want to consider objectivity. Many organizations have an explicit political agenda. Try to avoid taking data from these groups, but rather look for arguably more objective sources such as government or international agencies or nonpartisan organizations. For instance, you would not want to take all your data about the dangers of smoking from cigarette makers or information about the relevance of class size to student performance from the American Federation of Teachers unless, of course, you were trying to investigate what manufacturers argue about the ill effects of smoking or what union positions are on class size.

You may think consulting your data sources now, when you are only making your plan for your research, is premature, but it is a crucial step in creating the Research Design section. By looking for data at this point, you make sure that what you hoped you could get—as you defined in your first two subsections—is available for the cases you want to study. In effect, then, specifying your data sources here and checking that they actually have what you need ensures that your wonderful plans for evaluating your argument are actually possible. If you can't get access to the information that you need, then you might have to modify your earlier strategy, and it's better to know that now rather than later.

To underline the importance of checking out your information sources at this stage, let's revisit one of our examples. Imagine you were investigating the way in which ideology affected people's attitudes toward the 2010 health care reform bill. You had originally wanted to argue that ideology was the most important indicator of popular attitudes toward the bill, and you assumed that the major polling organizations routinely asked—from January 2009 until March 2010 (when the bill passed)—respondents both about their opinions toward health care reform and about their ideologies. When you actually tracked down the polls, however, you found that these organizations did not ask about ideology. Many times pollsters asked only the question, "Do you support the health care reform package making its way through Congress?" and a few times they also asked respondents to provide their party affiliations as Republican, Democrat, Independent, or other. Now that you know the information you were hoping to use isn't there, you have some choices to make. Are you going to keep the case selection (pollsters' samples of the U.S. population) the same, or are you going to look at a different one? You could decide to change, looking at some local subset at the current point in time only (which would also require you to modify the question slightly since the reform had already passed)—people on campus, people in a nearby community—and design and perform the survey yourself to get at your precise issue. Or you could choose to keep your case selection but introduce a *proxy* variable (or stand-in) such as party affiliation for ideology. Then, you would need to include a discussion of the possible weaknesses of this measure as a proxy. (Is this valid? What are its limitations, or in other words, what do you lose by using party instead of ideology?) If you find that this approximation for your preferred factor is not strong enough, you may decide to go back and change the thesis under investigation (party affiliation → attitudes), noting, "The data made me do it!" As long as you explain what you are doing and why (and these points are logical and accurate), you are safe from criticisms on methodological grounds.

STRATEGIES FOR UNCOVERING AND, AT TIMES, CREATING DATA

After you have operationalized your variables, picked your cases, and found your sources, there may be an additional step. There are times when the operationalization of your concepts means that you have to come up with ways for uncovering and, in a sense, generating data. I hesitate to use the word *create* because I do not want any reader to think that you just make up your information to suit your purposes, but we have seen Samantha develop a scoring system for professionalism and receptivity. Those are efforts at generating data. But while operationalizing often means conceiving (or reconceiving) of your variable as a factor for which data can be easily found (e.g., GDP figures, poll data for a certain time period, election results, or level of military intervention) or even producing some sort of a composite out of indicators, at other times you are going to have to come up with an additional strategy for generating raw information, which you will then have to transform into useable data.

Typically this occurs when the data or information doesn't exist in any central location because you are applying a thesis to a new area or application or you are looking at some very current problem. In those cases, you might need to develop a survey or an interview questionnaire so that you can amass the information that you need. Remember, any time you plan to perform research on human subjects you need to receive permission from your institution's research board. So you will need to design this instrument and submit it to both your professor and your insitution's review board for approval. In writing the survey or interview, you, the author, also face many questions. Two very important ones are (1) Should it be open ended, or should I give respondents answers to choose from? and (2) How long should it be? Other concerns involve the very careful writing of the questions so as not to confuse, mislead, or suggest an answer to any of the participants in the study. Here you must pay close attention to reliability (meaning that neither you nor whoever is administering the instrument is *eliciting* particular answers) as well as validity (the questions you are using to generate information are a good translation of the variables in your model).[23] Later we will see how Sam wrote her survey of campaign media consultants, keeping these concerns at the forefront.

In sum, whenever you need to develop a method for generating information, you must explain exactly what you are doing and how you are doing it. In addition, you must set out the logic behind your approach, justifying every decision that you made as the best one for accomplishing the task at hand given the resource constraints under which you are operating.

METHODOLOGY

As a last part of the planning process, you should have an explicit discussion of how you are going to put all these pieces together, a discussion of what we might call your methodology. What you actually do is very much dependent on the earlier steps. If you have chosen a large N study with quantitative data, you are likely going to perform a statistical analysis. At this point, you should inform your reader that you will be performing a particular kind of test, for instance, a chi-square test or a simple linear regression. Both you and your reader should understand what that means.

Alternatively, your thesis might lend itself to discourse analysis. The Hobbes example earlier in the chapter is a kind of discourse analysis of Hobbes' texts (the primary sources) to determine whether he can be considered a liberal. Other forms of discourse analysis ask you to trace the meanings of concepts in the writings or words of key political actors and which behaviors then follow. As Roxanne Lynn Doty explained in her study of U.S. intervention in newly sovereign Philippines, the words used produce results. In this case, Americans' views of themselves as noble, well-intentioned protectors; of Filipinos as child-like, gullible decision makers; and of the Soviets as evildoing imperialists com-pelled the United States to disregard its earlier commitment to the Philippines' independence to intervene. Doty's method was to analyze primary sources, this time U.S. foreign policy documents, to see exactly which language American decision makers used to portray themselves, Filipinos, and the Soviets to come to her findings. Words and terms were her data, and she searched for the lin-guistic themes, contending that these words then compelled action. Before performing her analysis, Doty set out the types of phrases that she would be looking for and what they would mean for her thesis. Then, she went through the government documents and literally counted the incidence of these themes and was able to show which ones were more prevalent. While she did not per-form a statistical test, Doty summarized her findings in a table and was able to show where the preponderance of the evidence lay. That allowed her to support her claim that because American policymakers saw their motives as altruistic and protective, had very patronizing views of the Filipinos, and held a menacing perspective of the Soviets and communist activists on that archipelago, U.S. intervention became the only sensible policy, despite America's having given the Philippines its sovereignty a few years before.[24]

Both of these approaches are types of qualitative content analysis, and Samantha is going to perform quantitative content analysis. In both efforts, researches seek to understand content, either by characterizing and classifying it by terms (qualita-tive) or counting up certain words, phrases, and behaviors (quantitative).[25]

In addition to discourse analysis, other forms of qualitative analysis ask researchers to trace what has happened to the independent variable over time. Remember even qualitative factors have values. Here again, being clear in the research design about exactly how you will know what the strength of institu-tions and the level of democratic stability will be—in our friend Joe's case—is very important. He spells out in the research design what will indicate institu-tional strength and democratic stability and then uses both figures and words to determine what happened to these factors.

FINISHING TOUCHES ON THE RESEARCH DESIGN

You have now become acquainted with the tasks you need to accomplish in the research design. As you write up this section, remember that it should be able to stand alone as an essay yet be integrated into the rest of the text. Consider this the section in which you explain exactly how you are going to conduct your research and why your research strategy will help you answer your question as accurately as possible. Thus, the section answers the query, How should I proceed for the truest assessment of my thesis? It should be set off from the rest of the text with a heading and include introductory and concluding sections. The body of the essay must accomplish the three tasks identified at the start of this chapter.

To name this section, remember the focus is on communicating what you will do and why. Something like "Planning a Comparative Study of American Polarization" for Latisha or "How to Explore the Impact of Gender and the Use of New Media in American Political Campaigns" for Samantha would work nicely. Again, the heading both sets off this section from the others and informs the reader of its purpose. In the research design, you are performing four or five rather involved tasks—concept definition and operationalization, case selection, data identification, information generation, and a brief discussion of methodology. Because of these many different requirements, you may want to use subheadings here.[26]

To help us see how to handle all of these difficult responsibilities in one section, let's turn to Samantha as she makes her plan for investigating her model, stated above, and these corresponding two hypotheses:

Hypothesis 1: In web-based images, women candidates are more likely to bolster their professionalism, while men in the context of the 2010 election (which was anti-Washington) stress their human side.

Hypothesis 2: In terms of the linking aspects of the new media, women are more receptive to and interested in interactions with citizens than are men.

How to Explore the Impact of Gender on the Use of New Media in American Political Campaigns

The literature suggests that despite all the progress that female candidates have made, gender still exerts an impact on campaigning in the United States. Interestingly, being female or having feminine qualities is not always perceived negatively, and depending on the election cycle, femininity can have its advantages. So in some ways, "you *have* come a long way, baby," as the old cigarette jingle maintains.[a] But how exactly are femininity and masculinity manipulated in web-based and new media communications to create a candidate's image? Moreover, are these campaign strategies truly taking advantage of gender, or are they merely reflections of other relevant markers of identity such as party affiliation or status as a challenger, for instance?[b]

To answer these questions and to explore the insight that gender matters more and therefore women have to stress their professionalism but will take advantage when possible of the perks of femininity (being warm and responsive), I will explore a subset of Senate races in the 2010 election. I chose the 2010 cycle because it was one of the first to occur in the aftermath of the social media revolution in politics. While websites have been around for a "good long time" in the relatively young Internet and politics era, social media have only recently become pervasive and more sophisticated in politics. The focus on Senate races resulted because of my belief that all major Senate contenders (unlike their House counterparts) would have the funds to develop adequately their websites and new media connections. In 2010, thirty-four seats were up for grabs, and prior to election day (and before I perhaps best understood all the factors that should go into my research design), I zeroed in on fourteen candidates because of their national prominence and the contestation of women for these seats. In my examination, I have decided not to control for party—even though some scholars might say that gender and party are indistinguishable[c]—because a few Republican women were so unusual (e.g., Christine O'Donnell). I have, however, seven women and seven men, and they are not necessarily locked in competitions with other members of this sample. Instead, I chose campaigns that received a lot of attention—either because the race itself was so important (a key state, a highly contested competition, or an interesting candidate). Perhaps some will say that therefore my results are biased. I believe, however, that these are the races in which the web would be most relevant and therefore the most important for me to study. Among my seven women, there were three challengers, two incumbents, and two open seats; for the men the status breakdown was the same. I also tried to have a similar party distribution and have three Democrats and four Republicans among the women as well as three Republican and four Democratic men.

Another element of case selection is to discuss just which part of the web and new media to examine. Anyone who has looked at campaign websites knows that some are vast while others are more limited. I will be focusing on the front page and Facebook profile—for first and important impressions—for images and then looking also at the front page to see the ways in which the campaign encourages interaction and the ease with which a viewer can interact with the candidate. Again, this may bias my analysis, but the narrowing is reasonable given the importance of making the right impression on viewers when they first meet online.

In operationalizing my concepts, obviously the independent variable is easy to determine. I can see whether the candidates are female or male. Then, I need to find ways to conceive of professionalism and receptivity. Here I will proceed in a quantitative fashion to determine whether gender has an impact on how candidates behave, scoring each picture on a 0 to 3 scale.

I will calculate an average score for each candidate, and I would expect that female candidates' averages would be higher than those of males. A difference of means test will determine whether there is any significant difference. Regarding receptivity, I will compare the average number of ways that women and men allow voters to connect with them. In addition, I will look at the aesthetics of the site to gain insight on both professionalism and receptivity. Typeface, color schemes, and lighting can provide a sense of both of these factors. I will discuss and describe the aesthetics qualitatively.

In addition, as I look at the websites, I expect big issues such as the economy and health care to be front and center on a female candidate's site as she attempts to underline her knowledge and preparation. To establish professionalism, I would expect women—even in the context of 2010—to be seeking to showcase their competence and men—in a year when Washington and the status quo were greatly disliked—to be more informal, seeking to communicate they were just regular guys. As gender scholars tell us, men can be casual because their competence is not automatically questioned; in fact, they benefit from the assumption of professionalism. Regarding the second dependent variable, receptivity, I am trying to capture the opportunities candidates provided for the public to meet and connect with them (both in person and digitally) as well as to investigate the nature and type of feedback candidates desire. I will measure these both quantitatively as well as qualitatively, looking for the number of opportunities to communicate with the campaign as well as the nature—are these opportunities simply for obtaining yard signs, volunteering, or making a donation, or are they designed to engage the viewer in a conversation or another form of interaction? The literature here would suggest that female candidates' front pages make both more opportunities and more extensive forms of interaction possible.

This strategy for knowing the values of my variables leads me to create a questionnaire with which to evaluate each one. It will include the following:

Candidate: Sex = M or F	Notes/Answers to the Questions
Professionalism	
Image (average score per candidate)	
Attire? suit = 1, other = 0	
With whom? nonfamily = 1, other = 0	
Setting? official function = 1, other = 0	
Total number of pictures examined	
Issues	
Content/which issues?	
Placement/prominence on site?	
Receptivity	
How many opportunities to interact?	
Which kinds of opportunities to interact? (explain)	
How easy to interact?	
Aesthetics	
Typeface	
Color scheme	
Lighting	
Other	

In addition to this information from the websites, I hope to do some interviews of campaign staff to understand what the priorities were for designing the sites. These would be open-ended questions to allow the respondents to reveal elements of the strategy. I want to learn whether and to what extent gender was consciously or unconsciously on the minds of the campaign as well as understand the extent to which staffers thought gender was something they could exploit. The interview data will give richness to the analysis that the evaluation of the media alone would lack.

Candidate: Sex = M or F	Notes/Answers
Staffer's Name:	to the Questions

Image/professionalism

In the design of your web-based materials, what impressions were you trying to convey about your candidate?

    a. Were there any particular strengths that you were trying to highlight?

    b. Were there any perceived weaknesses you were trying to overcome?

Do you believe you succeeded in making the impression that you sought? Why?

How did the campaign make decisions about what would appear on the front page of the website? Which issues were central as you considered materials for the front page?

Connectedness/receptivity

How did your campaign view social media? What were your goals for social media?

How important do you think social media were for your campaign?

What do you think the people who were linked in with your candidate felt about social media?

Final Questions (particularly if these issues have not yet been raised)

What do you think you could have done differently or better with the website and social media to both

    a. create the impression that you wanted for the candidate and

    b. use social media effectively?

Did your candidate's gender have an impact on the design of your site and your social media strategy? Was this conscious or not? How exactly?

Is there anything else you would like to tell me about the key messages the campaign was trying to convey and the nature of the web and social media strategy used?

While I can test to see whether status or party also has an impact on the use of new media, I do not have the breadth in case selection to be able to claim a victory for the importance of gender overall. The study will, however, advance our understanding of the effects of gender and campaigning by extending it to social media activities and give us some hypotheses about gender's effects in 2010 and beyond.

The strategies for knowing professionalism and receptivity appear both valid and reliable. Being perceived as professional in contemporary American culture is synonymous with having a particular look and interacting with certain kinds of people in appropriate settings. It also encompasses having a command of the important issues. Perhaps some would argue that my strategy is still a bit dated, that voters do not think that competent people must wear suits, for instance. Still, I remain committed to the idea that where women are concerned, stereotypes remain, and to be taken seriously, women need the suits. Women have come a long way since 1988, when a woman's crying on the shoulder of her husband—as Pat Schroeder did when she withdrew from the Democratic presidential primary process—undermined the perception of professionalism of a female candidate. Many of the gains in viewing professionalism more broadly—casual dress, interacting with all types of people—have accrued disproportionately to men. Receptivity, too, captures in quantity and quality the idea of being interested in, being connected to, and wanting to hear from people, very feminine traits. My strategy of going to websites and using the questionnaire, as well as asking the same questions to staffers (and not tipping my hand about my interest in gender until the end) helps keep this approach reliable.

NOTES

a. This is a line from the Virginia Slims cigarette ads that were trying to attract young, professional women to smoke this brand. Emphasis added. See http://tobaccodocuments.org/ads_pm/2058500255.html.

b. Kim Fridkin Kahn, "Gender Differences in Campaign Messages: The Political Advertisements of Men and Women Candidates for U.S. Senate," *Political Research Quarterly* 46, no. 3 (1993): 481–502; Kathleen Dolan, "Do Women Candidates Play to Gender Stereotypes? Do Men Candidates Play to Women?" *Political Research Quarterly* 58, no. 1 (2005): 31–44.

c. Dianne G. Bystrom et al., *Gender and Candidate Communication: VideoStyle, WebStyle, NewsStyle* (New York: Routledge, 2004).

Samantha has a good start on her design. Her logic, strategies, and actual practices are spelled out here, although she will likely need to explain more explicitly how she is measuring receptivity and what her qualitative aesthetic analysis will entail. She has also justified her choices as well as recognized that her claims and understandings will not be as general as she might have hoped because of case selection and some data issues. Notice, too, that Samantha lays out her plan, but she doesn't begin to enact it yet. She doesn't tell us what she has found—what she learns about the levels of professionalism and receptivity—from the Internet or interviews. That story is the subject of the analysis and assessment. Still, she needs to be explicit and clear here so that she knows what to do in the next section and so that her work can stand up to the scrutiny of knowledgeable readers. She wants to create a good evaluation plan for her hypothesis, much like the medical researchers try to design an appropriate study for evaluating the impact of vigorous but not daily exercise.

As Sam begins the analysis, she might want to make some adjustments in her strategy. Perhaps some of her criteria aren't specific enough or some other problem or uncertainty arises. What's important is for any researcher—including Samantha—to make small adjustments as experience requires and then come back and rewrite the design section accordingly; however, if you find that major changes are in order, you may realize that the premise and design are seriously flawed. More likely, given the constraints of your class, you will proceed knowing that your study has limitations. Then, you will want to be very careful about determining what you might have done differently to perform a good study and acknowledging these weaknesses in the concluding section.

Let's be optimists, though. With proper care and attention to the complexities involved, all students should be able to design effective studies. Thanks, Sam, for giving everyone confidence that the research design is not too complex to think through or write up. This is a great example!

PRACTICAL SUMMARY

The research design is the section of the paper in which you provide the plan for your research—how to choose cases, define and operationalize concepts, identify information sources, generate data (at times), and explain your methodology. Typically, you cannot define or conduct a true experiment to evaluate your hypothesis, so you have to make well-informed choices about how to proceed. As long as you are aware of the concerns about methods—minimizing bias, controlling for other explanations, choosing cases that maximize variance in either the dependent or the independent variable—you can come up with a good plan. Such a program, however, is likely not to be perfect, so you must be explicit about the possible imperfections and their effects on your research. You will return to consider how the choices that you made about the design affected your analysis in the concluding section of the research paper.

To write the research design, I suggest that you proceed as follows:

1. Develop an introduction that links the plan to what has come before. Typically a focus on the hypotheses and the literature are in order here, as is a mention that the plan and justification follow.

2. Then, decide which cases you are going to study. Be sure that you are choosing a sufficient number to evaluate your argument effectively. Also, you must be concerned with controlling for other possible causes when you pick your instances. If you are performing empirical research and are going to use statistical techniques, you must have more than thirty cases. If you are performing a historical case study, you must find a way to make this analysis comparative. Find another case (either by

dividing your preferred case into periods that differ because of varying outcomes on the dependent variable or by finding another incident that is comparable) to study. When you are not using the universe of cases, beware of introducing bias into your study by sampling. And remember that your goal is not to prove your thesis but to evaluate it. (Again, eliminate the words *proof* and *prove* from your vocabulary, now!)

3. Next, discuss precisely how you will translate your concepts (independent and dependent variables) into knowable entities. This is often a multistep process. For evaluating a contentious statement, you have to provide careful definitions of these terms and specify steps that will show how you will know when the parts of your argument are sustained by the evidence. When analyzing a hypothesis, you might have to find indicators or even proxies for your variables. You may even have to determine how multiple indicators will combine to create your final value. After determining this plan for coming up with an assessment, explicitly address the validity and reliability of your measures and recognize that measures are not necessarily numbers.

4. Identify the data sources that you will use to help you determine the values of your key concepts or variables. Be sure that each of these is reputable. Do not simply use Google to find some information on the Internet. You must be sure that the source of the information and the data themselves are trustworthy; subject them to the five-criteria test. If you cannot get access to the data that you wanted, you need to rethink the decisions that you made in the first and second subsections.

5. If necessary, include a discussion that clearly specifies how you will generate data that do not exist. If you need to design an interview questionnaire or survey, describe your goals for writing it and any concerns you had in developing the instrument, and include a copy of it. Also, fill out the necessary paperwork and submit this questionnaire to your institution's review board for approval for using human subjects in your research.

6. Finally, discuss the methodology that you will use. Perhaps you have already done this because questions of exactly how you are going to evaluate your thesis come up as you think about the cases and operationalization. But if you haven't, think explicitly about the steps you will take to evaluate whether your argument holds.

7. Write a conclusion that specifies the choices that you made, acknowledges potential problems that may result from these choices, and suggests that after you perform the analysis you may have to revisit the significance of these decisions. However, you are now ready—with your plan established—to proceed with the evaluation of your argument.

8. Remember, this section provides only the plan and justifications for your work. The actual evaluation of the variables and the discussion of the relationship occur in the next part of the paper, the Analysis and Assessment section.

SUGGESTED CALENDAR

About halfway through the course, you should begin developing your plan for your study. This step is crucially important for determining a workable and sensible project. Have you chosen appropriate cases? Do you know how you will determine values for your variables? Have you determined whether actual data exist to carry out your design or whether you can generate the information that is essential for your study? Have you justified all your decisions? Too many students do not take this phase seriously, and then at the analysis and assessment stage they realize to their horror that they have not put together a workable proposal or that they really have no plan at all. Please do not think that this planning process is simply a make-work project. See how important Samantha's section is for actually conducting her study? So take the research design seriously, and work through all aspects of it—case selection, operationalization of dependent and independent variables, source searches, data generation, and methodology—by about the halfway point in your project. That way, you will have the time to adjust your plan if necessary and not be left in the last few days before the paper is due with a completely unworkable and nonsensical study.

EXERCISES

1. Determine the cases for assessing either of the following two theses:

   - In the United States, the courts are not as effective an instrument of social change as are legislatures.
   - Women should wield political power at a level comparable to the level at which they exist in a population.

   Explain how your cases will provide an excellent and fair way to evaluate your thesis.

2. Operationalize the concepts for either of the following two theses:

   - In the United States, the courts are not as effective an instrument of social change as are legislatures.
   - Women should wield political power at a level comparable to the level at which they exist in a population.

   Evaluate the validity and reliability of your measures.

3. Identify data sources for any one of the studies you have already begun designing in questions 1 or 2 above.

4. Write a hypothetical Research Design section (complete with a title, introductory paragraph, and conclusion) for one of the theses identified in question 1.

Checklist 6: Research Design

Have you provided a substantive title that focuses on the purposes of this section to plan your research and defend your decisions?   Yes _____ No _____

Have you written an introductory paragraph that reminds the reader of the model, hypothesis, and literature as well as explains that a plan and justification for it will follow in this section?   Yes _____ No _____

Have you explained your case selection?   Yes _____ No _____

Have you explicitly mentioned control and variation?   Yes _____ No _____

Have you explicitly considered and explained in the text the strengths and weaknesses of choosing the cases that you did?   Yes _____ No _____

Have you provided a strategy for operationalizing (transforming concepts into knowable values) all of your variables, independent and dependent?   Yes _____ No _____

Have you explicitly explained why these variables are valid and reliable?   Yes _____ No _____

Have you explicitly considered any questions that might arise about their validity and reliability?   Yes _____ No _____

Have you explained which values of the independent variables (or the indicators that you create to operationalize them) will be associated with which values of the dependent variable?   Yes _____ No _____

Have you looked to see whether and where you can get the information that you need for this project?   Yes _____ No _____

Have you evaluated the sources to make sure they are appropriate and they have what you need?   Yes _____ No _____

If necessary, have you created a questionnaire for creating your data? This is useful as a kind of checklist to evaluate any hypothesis and makes your analysis and assessment much easier. (See Sam's example.)   Yes _____ No _____

If necessary, have you created an interview sheet for obtaining data? Have you done what you need to receive permission at your university to conduct research on human subjects?   Yes _____ No _____   Yes _____ No _____

Have your discussed your methodology and explained   Yes _____ No _____
exactly how you are going to conduct your research?

Have you written a concluding section that is honest   Yes _____ No _____
about any weaknesses but explains why you are
moving forward this way and why these results will
still be valuable?

Note: Remember to consult the Appearance, Format, and Style checklist at the end of chapter 6 as you write your research design.

NOTES

1. To repeat, the research paper–writing process is iterative. In a marathon, you wouldn't go back and run mile 10 again, but in this endeavor, you might rethink a decision you made earlier. However, you need to be aware that (1) a clock is ticking (you usually have a due date for your paper), and (2) you have made important forward progress. Keep thinking and writing, realizing that as you take new steps you may have insights that you need to incorporate or ideas that you need to adjust in older parts of the paper.

2. For detailed and methodologically sensitive discussions of research design see Donald T. Campbell and Julian C. Stanley, *Experimental and Quasi-experimental Designs for Research* (Boston: Houghton Mifflin, 1963); W. Phillips Shively, *The Craft of Political Research*, 5th ed. (Upper Saddle River, NJ: Prentice Hall, 2002), 72–94; W. Laurence Neuman, *Social Research Methods: Qualitative and Quantitative Methods*, 5th ed. (Boston: Allyn & Bacon, 2005), 137–168.

3. Shively, *The Craft of Political Research*, 17.

4. The medical community now generally thinks that daily moderate exercise is better; if I were deciding to proceed with this research (and hoping for external funding), I would have to sh0ow a good reason for thinking that this consensus was flawed. My apologies that I have not selected a medical example that reveals awareness of the cutting edge of current research on cardiovascular disease; I do know something about political science, though, and I recommend that you pursue a hypothesis that you have good reason to believe (because of your literature review and knowledge of politics) could be correct.

5. Of course, people who are in the position to be in this study might not be thrilled about their choices. They might enroll in the research as a last resort, and they might not enjoy the long (in our example, three years!) commitment or what they have to do. Often, individuals drop out, so researchers have to make sure that sample sizes are large to be able to overcome the attrition.

6. As mentioned in an earlier chapter, Gwynn Thomas and Melinda Adams explore this very puzzle in "Breaking the Final Glass Ceiling: The Influence of Gender in the Elections of Ellen Johnson-Sirleaf and Michelle Bachelet," *Journal of Women, Politics & Policy* 31 (2010): 105–131.

7. Thomas and Adams, "Breaking the Final Glass Ceiling," 106–108.

8. Researchers and students alike are often tempted to study on its own the case in which a phenomenon didn't occur. Like Sherlock Holmes, however, we recognize that there could be multiple reasons that the dog didn't bark. Thus, single-case analysis of the absence of a result is particularly problematic and incapable of showing us with any confidence the most important reasons producing the non-outcome.

9. Daniel A. Smith and Caroline J. Tolbert, *Educated by Initiative: The Effects of Direct Democracy on Citizens and Political Organizations in the American States* (Ann Arbor: University of Michigan Press, 2004); Peter Schrag, *Paradise Lost: California's Experience, America's Future* (New York: New Press, 1998).

10. Richard Boyd, "Thomas Hobbes and the Perils of Pluralism," *Journal of Politics* 63 (2001): 392–413.

11. It is not, of course, a perfect one. You need to determine whether your participants are likely voters. In 2008, turnout was around 62 percent, and about 56 percent of Oklahoma voters cast ballots. If you ask a participant directly whether he or she is going to vote, you are likely to get the answer "yes." Most Americans know that they are supposed to vote to be considered good citizens. So to get at likelihood more accurately, you may want to ask, "For whom are you going to vote" first and then ask when was the last time the person voted. For more on the importance of careful case selection, see Arend Lijphart, "How the Cases You Choose Determine the Answers You Get," *Journal of Policy Analysis* 2 (1975): 131–152. Regarding turnout figures for the 2008 elections, see "General Election Turnout Rates," http://elections.gmu.edu/Turnout_2008G.html, accessed January 14, 2011. Also, Shively noted that the *Literary Digest* made a huge sampling error in 1936 when it polled telephone and car owners on their preference for president. Taking those who returned their surveys, the publication predicted a defeat for Franklin Delano Roosevelt, who ultimately won convincingly. W. Phillips Shively, *The Craft of Political Research*, 6th ed. (Upper Saddle River, NJ: Prentice Hall, 2005), 50.

12. They may perform a single case study for other purposes, for instance, considering the plausibility of their thesis (plausibility probe) or as a heuristic case study, to determine how multiple perspectives account for what happened. See Alexander L. George and Andrew Bennett, *Case Studies and Theory Development in the Social Sciences* (Cambridge, MA: MIT Press, 2004).

13. See Dianne G. Bystrom, Mary Christine Banwart, Lynda Lee Kaid, and Terry A. Robertson, *Gender and Candidate Communication: VideoStyle, WebStyle, NewsStyle* (New York: Routledge, 2004); Kim Fridkin Kahn, "Gender Differences in Campaign Messages: The Political Advertisements of Men and Women Candidates for U.S. Senate," *Political Research Quarterly* 46, no. 3 (1993): 481–502.

14. Kathleen Dolan, "Do Women Candidates Play to Gender Stereotypes? Do Men Candidates Play to Women?" *Political Research Quarterly* 58, no. 1 (2005): 31–44.

15. Samantha generally focused on the candidates that observers thought of as serious.

16. There were some open seats that she would have to exclude here with this means of control.

17. In the 2010 election, which was about sweeping away business as usual in Washington, these values would be particularly useful. As Sam's work and the work of others have shown us, when and how more feminine qualities are assets or liabilities depends on the context of the election. See Paul S. Herrnson, J. Celeste Lay, and Atiya Kai Stokes, "Women Running 'as Women': Candidate Gender, Campaign Issues, and Voter-Targeting Strategies," *Journal of Politics* 65, no. 1 (2003): 244–255.

18. Boyd, "Thomas Hobbes and the Perils of Pluralism." A student could decide to evaluate this contention him- or herself, for instance, with a different sample or to replicate Boyd's study, if he or she were skeptical of the finding.

19. Robert D. Putnam, with Robert Leonardi and Raffaella Y. Nanetti, *Making Democracy Work: Civic Traditions in Modern Italy* (Princeton, NJ: Princeton University Press, 1993).

20. Herrnson, Lay, and Stokes, "Women Running 'as Women.'"

21. See Pippa Norris and Ronald Inglehart, "Cultural Obstacles to Equal Representation," *Journal of Democracy* 12, no. 3 (2001): 126–140, for mention of the Inter-Parliamentary Union and then the group itself at http://www.ipu.org/wmn-e/world.htm.

22. Reference librarians have created these particular terms and helpful ways of assessing sources. See "Evaluating Web Sources," First-year Seminar Library Modules, Saint Joseph's University, http://librarytoolkits.sju.edu/content.php?pid=103334&sid=776924.

23. Many research methods textbooks provide excellent advice on designing surveys and performing interviews. See, for example, Janet Buttolph Johnson and H. T. Reynolds, with Jason D. Mycoff, *Political Science Research Methods,* 6th ed. (Washington, DC: Congressional Quarterly Press, 2005), 297–350.

24. Roxanne Lynn Doty, "Foreign Policy as Social Construction: A Post-positivist Analysis of U.S. Counterinsurgency Policy in the Philippines," *International Studies Quarterly* 37, no. 3. (1993): 297–320, www.jstor.com.

25. For more on content or document analysis, see Johnson and Reynolds, 282–295.

26. You may want to use subheadings in other sections too. Typically, the longer a section is, the better a candidate it is for subsections.

Evaluating the Argument: The Analysis and Assessment Section

You're more than halfway through the research paper–writing marathon, and you are feeling pumped because the course is now downhill and there's a wind at your back. The most fun part of the project (in most people's opinion) is about to begin; you are ready to investigate the actual phenomenon in which you are interested, and all the work that you have done so far in your literature review, model and hypothesis, and research design will help guide and protect you during this evaluation. The goal of this section is to *analyze* relevant information to *assess* your thesis.

Briefly, there are two main forms of analysis—*qualitative* and *quantitative*. With qualitative analysis, an investigator assesses evidence in the form of words or images to determine where the weight of it lies—on the side of the thesis or against it. With quantitative analysis, the evaluation of the argument is primarily on the basis of statistics. A researcher rejects a hypothesis if the data show that the relationship posited among the variables is not statistically significant. In other words, the researcher makes a calculation that allows him or her to throw out or accept the thesis.[1] Oftentimes, however, scholars combine qualitative and quantitative forms of analysis in their work, so do not be surprised to see a mixture.

Regardless of which type of analysis you pursue, you need to remember that (1) your thesis or hypothesis allows you to concentrate on what is important and (2) your research design specifies exactly what you need to do. In other words, this section is where you keep a laser-like focus on your argument and your plan for evaluating it. Although you might be enticed to add additional, interesting, yet extraneous information, resist that temptation! That tendency is an old habit developed from your report writing days. Now you are beyond that; you know that a research paper consists of the careful analysis of a thesis, not simply a broad story about some political event, phenomenon, or idea. To put yourself in the proper mindset for this section, think back to the many courtroom dramas you have seen. The Analysis and Assessment section is the trial phase of your research project. You've done the background work, and now you are ready to present your case. What do lawyers do at the trial? They present the logic of their argument and then the evidence that supports their interpretation of events. They do not, for instance, recount all the details of the various interviews they conducted prior to their date in court or bring witnesses to the stand who do not add something substantial to their case. In this section of the paper, like the attorney, you are going to lay out the facts that you have collected that are pertinent to your argument. Unlike the lawyer, however, you should have no vested interest in whether your thesis holds or not; you are not an advocate for a position but an investigator in search of knowledge.

QUALITATIVE ANALYSIS

Political science undergraduates are most likely to be familiar with qualitative analysis. Many of us become interested in political science because we like reading newspaper, magazine, or policy articles that make arguments (predominantly based on logic, values, and historical evidence) about political ideas or phenomena. Most of the readings you have done in your introductory courses and even many of your upper-division classes (especially in political theory; in American politics courses on the presidency, urban politics, the bureaucracy, and the courts; and in many topics in international relations and comparative politics) primarily use qualitative analysis. But what is this as a form of analysis? Isn't it just description and argumentation? Yes, there are descriptions and arguments included in these assessments, but remember that the evaluation is focused, concentrating on the thesis and employing the methods that you set out in your research design.[2]

Let's think back to some of the theses that we have seen before and consider how to assess and analyze them. Because we have already learned a good deal about Joe's and Samantha's papers, these seem like good places to start. Joe claimed, "The stronger the governing institutions, the greater will be the level of democratic stability," while one of Sam's assertions was, "Women will be more likely to bolster their professionalism while men in the context of the 2010 election (which was anti-Washington) will try to stress their human side."

Turning to Joe first, his research design—which we did not see—establishes a comparative case study of Salvadoran politics. He juxtaposes the early postwar period (1992–1997) with the more recent past (2005–2010), believing that this will provide variation on the dependent variable, the level of democratic stability. While Joe will proceed primarily using qualitative methods, he will rely on some numeric information to understand his concepts. In operationalizing stability, Joe will look to Freedom House data (rankings of 1–7) to determine whether it has improved. Developing a strategy for knowing his independent variable was more complicated. He decided that the strength of state institutions would best be captured by understanding the power of the two major political parties to represent citizens, the ability of the military and police to do their redefined jobs, and the capacity of the economy to provide citizens a livelihood. We can call each of these elements of the strength of state institutions *indicators,* and together the indicators combine to produce an understanding of how strong state institutions are. Given his operationalization strategy, Joe will likely not be able to say exactly what the strength of these structures are, but he will know in relative terms whether there has been improvement and how intense any change has been.

When writing his analysis and assessment, Joe then needs to evaluate for each case study the values (and most of the time for his case, these will not be numbers) of indicators for the independent variable and then explain how these come together to create an overall approximation of institutional strength. Determining the independent variable is not enough, of course. Joe then needs to specify the dependent variable's value, too. Ultimately, he wants to see whether his hypothesis—stronger state institutions lead to greater democratic stability—is true. Moreover, Joe would be well served to discuss not only the correlation—that as institutional strength changes, so does democratic stability in the predicted ways—but also the causal connection that he can see. Joe should look for ways in which the changes in the power of the state affect democratic stability. If he can perform such a complete analysis, then Joe will be able to assess fully his hypothesis.

The easiest way for Joe (or anyone else) to proceed is to create a hypothesis and data chart from his research design, fill it out as he collects data, and then think about what the information means. With clarity that comes from the information, Joe will then find that his data chart provides his outline and essential information for his analysis and assessment.

Before we look at Joe's information (see Table 8.1), I need to clarify some of the terms and concepts that he uses. First, Freedom House assesses levels of democracy around the world by scoring countries on how well they provide citizens with political rights and civil liberties. Each state earns either an F for Free, a PF for Partially Free, or an NF for Not Free based on its political rights and civil liberties tallies.[3] The two major political parties in El Salvador are ARENA, which was the rightist party that ran the country during the civil war, and FMLN, the leftist group that fought the government during that time. Regarding economic data, Gross National Income Per Capita gives an estimation of the size of the economy, and GINI measures the levels of inequality. Perfect equality scores 0, while perfect inequality earns 100. Thus, countries with high rich-poor gaps will have higher GINI scores. See Table 8.1 for Joe's data.

Making a data chart helps you understand what you know (and what you don't know). We can literally see that Joe knows a lot here because each of the boxes for his variables across the two cases contains information. As we look more closely, however, we see that Joe might want to find out more about what

Table 8.1 Joe's Data Chart

Hypothesis: The stronger the governing institutions, the greater will be the level of democratic stability.

Variable (or Indicator)	Case 1: 1992–1997	Case 2: 2005–2010
Democratic stability[a]	Partially Free from Freedom House until 1996. Then scoring Free consistently with 2 on Political Rights and 3 on Civil Liberties	Constant Free score, 2 on Political Rights and 3 on Civil Liberties

Strength of state institutions

a. Political parties[b]	FMLN transforms into a democratic force and participates in politics. ARENA continues to dominate by winning more seats in legislative assembly and the presidency. Concerns that while there is overtly competitive politics, the right wing still dominates and might not tolerate transfer of power.	Early in this period some question about whether ARENA would tolerate a big FMLN victory. But by 2009, questions laid to rest. FMLN wins most seats in legislature and the presidency. No reaction; political life goes on. Excellent sign that democracy is more stable now.
b. Security forces	Important reforms put into place. Military loses control over domestic security; civilian police force inaugurated. Both forces—military and police—integrated with government and former rebel fighters. While percentages of FMLN aren't as high as some hoped and leadership remains primarily in government hands, efforts are seen as positive and hopeful. Moreover, citizens no longer live in fear of state- or insurgent-sponsored violence.	No worries about insurrection of the security forces or fighting among the groups within. A new security challenge has emerged, however. Gang activities have led to an increase in violence and murders. El Salvador has become a very dangerous country. Citizens see the initial gains from the peace (in terms of fewer worries about security) being wiped away. State is struggling with how to respond and institutes the *Mano Dura* (strong hand) policy. These measures worry some civil libertarians as they expand the power of the military and the police to use violence and restrict protections of those suspected of being gang members. Still, these steps have strong popular support.
c. Economic conditions	Significant reforms to the banking sector. Some smaller attempts at land reform. Promises of economic development. World Bank Data:[c] 1995, Human Development Index (HDI) was .562	Reforms have transformed the macroeconomic picture. Development improvements too, but not as much as people would like. World Bank Data:[d] HDI shows a gain of 16 places in the rankings since 1980. Still a middle-income country. In 2005 HDI was .635, and then in 2010 HDI was .659.

Table 8.1 *(continued)*

	Poverty headcount ratio in 1995: 50.6 percent	Poverty headcount ratio in 2006: 30.7 percent
	Literacy rate (1992): 74 percent	Literacy rate (2008): 84 percent
	Gross National Income Per Capita (GNI PC) (1992): $1,070; (1994): $1,349	Gross National Income Per Capita (2005): $2,790; (2009): $3,370
	GINI (incomplete World Bank data):	GINI figures:
	1989: 49	2000: 50
	1995: 50	2005: 52
	1997: 51	2007: 47
		Some clear improvements in economic figures although troubling inequality remains. One of the ways that El Salvador has made HDI gains is through remittances, as emigrants go overseas and send money home. This may not be sustainable, particularly in light of the current world economic crisis. Also emigration causes social problems.
Composite: Strength of state institutions	A country moving out of authoritarianism and trying to respond to significant economic problems.	Positive improvements in institutional strength from earlier period. Stronger competition between parties and stability of the political system. Reforms of the security sector have integrated former enemies but concerns that old habits about abusing civil liberties are returning. Also worries about extensive violence. Economic conditions better in some ways, yet troubling inequality and high levels of immigration.

a. Please note that on his real table, Joe had more detail about the exact scores for each year. Freedom House, "Country Ratings and Status, FIW 1973–2010 (Excel)," http://www.freedomhouse.org/template .cfm?page=439.http://www.freedomhouse.org/template.cfm?page=439.

b. Joe had many citations here, and you should be sure to cite fully as you make your table.

c. World Bank, "El Salvador," http://data.worldbank.org/country/el-salvador; GNI data from World Bank, "GNI Per Capita, Atlas Method (Current US$)" http://data.worldbank.org/indicator/NY.GNP.PCAP. CD?page=3; GINI data from World Bank, http://databank.worldbank.org/ddp/html-jsp/QuickViewRe port.jsp?RowAxis=WDI_Ctry~&ColAxis=WDI_Time~&PageAxis=WDI_Series~&PageAxisCaption=Ser ies~&RowAxisCaption=Country~&ColAxisCaption=Time~&NEW_REPORT_SCALE=1&NEW_ REPORT_PRECISION=0&newReport=yes&ROW_COUNT=213&COLUMN_COUNT=30&PAGE_ COUNT=1&COMMA_SEP=true.

d. World Bank, "El Salvador," http://data.worldbank.org/country/el-salvador; GNI data from World Bank, "GNI Per Capita, Atlas Method (Current US$)" http://data.worldbank.org/indicator/NY.GNP.PCAP .CD?page=3; GINI data from World Bank, http://databank.worldbank.org/ddp/html-jsp/QuickView Report.jsp?RowAxis=WDI_Ctry~&ColAxis=WDI_Time~&PageAxis=WDI_Series~&PageAxisCap tion=Series~&RowAxisCaption=Country~&ColAxisCaption=Time~&NEW_REPORT_SCALE= 1&NEW_REPORT_PRECISION=0&newReport=yes&ROW_COUNT=213&COLUMN_ COUNT=30&PAGE_COUNT=1&COMMA_SEP=true.

exactly went on with security-sector reform and how it evolved. He would also be well served to have some hard figures on crime statistics and gang activity in both periods. In addition, Joe wants to say something about emigration's taking pressure off of unemployment and contributing to the improved economy, but he needs to bolster those assertions with some hard data. Joe benefits from realizing what he still needs before he creates the narrative for each case. So he will go back to the data and find more information before writing this up.

Still, this data chart provides Joe with the values he needs to assess his hypothesis. From the looks of the data presented here, Joe appears able to confirm the contention that as institutional strength improves, so does stability, but he will also likely say that those increases have not been as great as some have hoped over the past almost two decades. State strength has improved somewhat, and democratic stability (Freedom House rankings) has increased slightly, too. A nice finishing touch would be for Joe to discuss how state strength affects democratic stability, if he can. Detailing the causal connection would strengthen his theoretical arguments in favor of the Institutionalist perspective. Including a *summary* of his data chart in his Analysis and Assessment section would also make his evaluation clearer. This table would not be detailed like the one shown here but would provide the value of each indicator and variable across the cases in a word or a short phrase.

Note that while Joe uses some statistics, he is not performing quantitative analysis. The numerical information helps him get a read on how institutional strength and democratic stability have developed, but his strategy doesn't provide him with an ultimate number in terms of strength improvement, nor does it allow him to evaluate the statistical relationship between the variables. Still, the figures that he uses are important for giving him the understanding of his concepts so that he can assess what has happened to each of them over his cases.

In sum, this discussion of qualitative analysis shows just how important your thesis/hypothesis and research design are for guiding you in performing your analysis and assessment. You have determined what you think is true (thesis/hypothesis), and you know how you want to assess it (research design). This is the "Nike phase," when you "Just Do It." Use the directions that you established in the planning stage to create a data chart, and then determine the values of your variables and, at times, their subindicators. When you have done that, you should have a read on whether the hypothesis appears to hold (at least as a correlation). Then you will want to consider whether you can see causal connections between the independent and the dependent variable and try to explain how and why you see changes in the cause creating the effect.

Just to be sure of the links between this data chart and the actual writing of the analysis and assessment, let's look at some excerpts from Joe's paper. I will share the section title and introduction, as well as the beginning of the first case study. At the outset of the analysis of the 1992–1997 period, see Joe establishing the value of the dependent variable and then turning to discuss what has happened to the first of his indicators of state strength, the representativeness and legitimacy of political parties and elections.

Making Progress on Stability: Modest Improvements in State Strength in El Salvador, 1992–2010

Citizens and the world greeted the Chapultepec agreement in El Salvador with much hope, as they were all wishing that the terrible violence would stop and life could become "normal," in other words, people would be free from daily fear and able to live decently. In some ways, those aspirations have come true as the former rebels and the government forces have laid down their arms and literally become partners (or at least the loyal opposition). Insurgents have transformed the FMLN into a normal, democratic political party that contests elections and represents voters at all levels in the system, and ARENA has watched the FMLN gain power and reacted, for the most part, respectfully. In the realm of security policy, the military no longer has a domestic policing function, and both it and the police have been integrated with FMLN fighters. The economy too has taken some positive steps forward. Thus, there have been clear improvements in state strength, and we can see these steps being taken in the immediate aftermath of the war in 1992–1997. The gains, however, have not been as impressive as hoped. Probably most remarkable have been the political victories of the FMLN, winning the presidency in 2009 and a majority in the lower house. But in terms of security, a new menace has emerged—gang violence—which threatens citizens every day. In addition, economic gains at the aggregate level have not slowed the emigration from El Salvador and the belief that there is little hope for a better future. Thus, the state is stronger, but the present is not as bright as was hoped back in 1992. The gains for democratic stability—from Partly Free to Free (because of a change from a score of 3 to 2 in political rights)—are small too. Perhaps these reflect the long and difficult path that postconflict stability inevitably takes.

The Early Postwar Period: Important Steps Forward on the Road to State Strength

During the war, Freedom House classified El Salvador as a Partly Free state. It typically received ratings of 3 or 4 in the Political Rights category (with the exception of a 2 in November 1983–November 1984) and a 4 or a 5 in the Civil Liberties column. This gave El Salvador a mixed reading; while it was a country that held elections, these were typically not free and fair as party competition was restricted and citizens did not have their civil liberties protected. After the war, however, there were clear (though small) changes in the Freedom House rankings. From 1993 until 1996, the scores kept El Salvador in the Partly Free category, but they were consistently both 3. This improvement and the consistency showed that something had changed in El Salvador. And in the fifth year (and last of this case), political rights improved to a 2. That upward move placed El Salvador in the Free category for the first time since 1975.[a]

This postwar period was an important time for reform in El Salvador, when the country was seeking to reform and build key state institutions, including political parties, the security forces, and the economy. Establishing legitimate elections and competitors in them was vital. Political scientist Dinorah Azpuru explains that "in contrast to other postconflict societies, where democracy building has often had to start from scratch and founding elections have been organized by international actors, El Salvador already had formal electoral institutions and procedures in place by the time the peace accords were signed in January 1992."[b] While elections were held during the civil war, "Many scholars considered those elections to be less than perfect because in the context of the ongoing civil war, ideological pluralism was limited, and the military retained a lingering amount of power over the elected civilian authorities."[c] The first set of elections after the Chapultepec Accords was held in March 1994. This contest was particularly noteworthy. Aside from the obvious fact that these were the first elections held after the peace accords, "for the first time, the whole range of political forces competed in the race."[d] This aspect bears immense importance. An important characteristic of a legitimate election is, without question, the presence of multiple interests as represented through different parties.

Table 1 Legislative Election Results by Party

Year of Legislative Elections	Seats Won by ARENA	Seats Won by FMLN
1994	39	21
1997	28	27
2006	34	32
2009	32	35

Sources: International Foundation for Electoral Systems, "Election Guide," http://www.electionguide.org/election.php?ID=1428; International Foundation for Electoral Systems, "Election Guide" http://www.electionguide.org/election.php?ID=633.

Table 1 offers a side-by-side comparison of the successes of ARENA and the FMLN in the 1994, 1997, 2006, and 2009 legislative elections. In the 1994 legislative elections, ARENA won the majority of seats in the Legislative Assembly, but not by a particularly impressive number. Of the 84 seats in the Legislative Assembly, ARENA won 39 (less than half of the Assembly). The FMLN took 21 seats, and the Christian Democrats (a relatively centrist party) won 18 seats.

The presidential election that year was noteworthy, as it "took place peacefully in the presence of 3,000 international observers, 900 of them from the United Nations. ARENA nominee Armando Calderon received 49 percent of the vote; Ruben Zamora [backed by the FMLN] obtained 26 percent.... The April runoff election ... gave Calderon 68 percent, Zamora 32 percent."[e]

In 1997, elections for the Legislative Assembly were held again. ARENA held on to its majority, but only barely. As reported by the International Foundation for Electoral Systems, ARENA won only 28 seats while the FMLN took 27. The Christian Democrats won only 7 seats.[f]

These were the only major elections that took place in El Salvador in the first five years after the Chapultepec Accords. While that may not seem like much from which to base analysis, one can draw certain ideas from these results. There are, by and large, several interests being represented among the parties. Even though ARENA did win majorities in both legislative elections, these could hardly be called resounding victories; in 1997, ARENA won by only one seat. In the presidential election, the ARENA candidate did end up winning in a runoff.

Thus, democratic practices and the postwar political parties became consolidated in this early period. These developments showed that the country undertook some of the necessary political reforms and that these changes were becoming habituated. Forming a state with capable institutions would be important for stabilizing and habituating stability in El Salvador.

NOTES

a. See Freedom House, "Country Ratings and Status, FIW 1973–2010 (Excel)," http://www .freedomhouse.org/template.cfm?page=439.
b. Dinorah Azpuru, "The Salience of Ideology: Fifteen Years of Presidential Elections in El Salvador," *Latin American Politics & Society* 52, no. 2 (2010): 108.
c. Ibid.
d. Ibid., 109.
e. Anthony James Joes, *America and Guerrilla Warfare* (Lexington: University Press of Kentucky, 2000), 269–270.
f. International Foundation for Electoral Systems, "Election Guide," http://www.electionguide .org/election.php?ID=633.

In this excerpt, we observe that Joe lays out the broad outlines of his analysis in both the title and the introduction to the section and makes clear whether his hypothesis is supported. Then he creates a subsection, also with a nice heading that puts the focus on the independent variable. Here we see him reminding the reader of the three indicators of strength and discussing what has happened to the state in the area of politics. Thereafter, if we were reading more, we would see Joe discuss the values of his other subfactors, the strength of the security forces and the economy. He would conclude by examining how those indicators help him to understand what the strength of the state is in the first period and to what extent this factor actually enabled El Salvador to create a sound foundation for democratic stability.

This excerpt allows me to stress something very important about Joe's analysis. The central point of this section is to analyze data to assess the thesis. To make that evaluation, Joe explains the values of his variables and whether they correspond to expectations. You will need to do that too. The ultimate argument of this section is to determine the extent to which your contention holds or doesn't. You are looking to identify and highlight the essential information that allows you to make that judgment, the data that let you really know what the values of your variables are. When you have this information, you can evaluate whether what you expected to happen (given your work in your literature review and your hypothesis/thesis) really did. Also remember that if your argument isn't sustained by the data, there is no need to worry. Your goal is not to be correct but to learn something from holding your contention accountable to relevant information. If your process in creating the design was good and your follow-through on finding the information was thorough and accurate, then your instructor will be satisfied, even if you cannot uphold your hypothesis.

QUANTITATIVE ANALYSIS

As you would expect, much of quantitative analysis deals primarily with statistical analysis, which is particularly useful for assessing highly general contentions, ones that can apply to many cases. When you begin contemplating quantitative analysis, you need to (1) identify what kind of data you will be using—continuous or discrete—and (2) be sure you have sufficient cases to make the statistical analysis valid.

Remember the following hypothesis:

> Democrats are more likely than Republicans to favor the 2010 health care reform bill; Independents and nonaffiliated Americans are less likely than Democrats but more likely than Republicans to view the bill favorably.

What type of information is involved here? To evaluate this hypothesis, you would be putting people into categories, reflecting both their party affiliations and their attitudes toward the health care bill. Imagine you decided to evaluate this contention by studying students on your campus. In compiling your data, you were allowed to survey virtually all freshmen in introductory social science classes.[4] You asked them to provide some basic demographic information and then asked them to check off answers to the following:

I consider myself a

Republican   _____
Democrat   _____
Independent/Other   _____

My attitude toward the 2010 health care reform bill is

Favorable   _____
Unfavorable   _____
Don't Know/None   _____

Your results are presented in Table 8.2.

This matrix shows you how party affiliation lined up with attitudes toward health care reform. If partisanship affects attitudes as hypothesized, with Democrats more likely to support the reform and Republicans more likely to oppose, then we would expect the data to reflect a pattern: more supporters in

Table 8.2   Party Affiliation and Support for Health Care Reform

| | | Party Affiliation | | | |
		Democrat	Independent/ Other	Republican	Total
Attitudes toward	Favorable	90	40	40	170
2010 health	Unfavorable	20	10	80	110
care reform	Don't know/none	40	50	30	120
	Total	150	100	150	400

the upper right and very few in the lower left. While we may be able to discern a pattern simply by looking at the results, we can calculate the precise nature of the relationship by using something called the *chi-square statistic* (χ^2). This statistic will tell you the extent to which your observations are different from what you would expect to see if there were no relationship between the independent (party affiliation) and dependent (attitude) variables. Moreover, if the results are significantly different, then the statistic will let you know at what *confidence level* (or *probability level*) you can uphold your hypothesis. In other words, if your statistic holds at the .01 confidence level that means you can be 99 percent sure the results you found could not have occurred by chance. In other words, you can be 99 percent sure that you have found a relationship between your independent and dependent variables.

There are a number of *statistical packages* that will perform this computation for you. (A statistical package is a software tool that comes ready to perform all sorts of functions as long as you supply the data and tell the program exactly what you want it to do.) Below I use SPSS, which is a Windows-based program. There are many other packages that you can use, so feel free to employ one with which you are already familiar or the one that your professor recommends.

In this particular example, the relationship between party affiliation and support for the 2010 health care reform bill is incredibly robust. It is significant at greater than the .001 level, and this means that you can be confident 99.9 percent of the time that party affiliation is an excellent predictor of attitudes toward the 2010 health care reform bill. In this case, the numbers are overwhelmingly good. But imagine that we had a different dispersal of answers from our respondents so that even when looking at the table we could see little difference between the opinions of Democrats, Republicans, and others. If that were true and then we calculated the χ^2 value, we would find that our confidence level was higher than the .100 level. In other words, we would be less than 90 percent sure that there was a relationship between our variables. In that case, we would conclude that the relationship between party and attitude toward health care was not strong enough, and we could not confirm our hypothesis. In general, you need a 90 percent or better confidence level to accept your contention.

The χ^2 is useful in evaluating relationships between sets of discrete data (information that comes in categories), but there are other tools to use when understanding the relationship between continuous or interval data (information that spans a continuum). The last type of quantitative analysis that we will consider is what is called a *simple linear* or *ordinary least squares regression*. Please note that there are other statistical tests that you can use. I am simply demonstrating one that I have found useful for my students. You should consult a reference book and/or ask your professor as you determine precisely which type of statistic you should calculate. Ordinary least squares will evaluate whether your independent variable affects your dependent variable in a predictable way, in a linear relationship. While there are other types of regression that you can perform, we are going to assume that a linear relationship is adequate for many types of research that beginning students will be evaluating.

Remember Kate and her project investigating the hypothesis that the higher the levels of economic development, the higher will be the percentage of female legislators? Recall also that in her literature review, Kate found that culture might be another important explanatory factor. So to test her assertion, she decided to control for culture, picking a subset of states with similar values. Then, Kate began collecting data about economic development, deciding to use GDP per capita values because many studies linking development to democracy use this as a proxy for development.[5] To assess the level of women in politics, Kate also decided to examine the percentage of women in the national legislature. Suppose she gathered her data and found the figures summarized in Table 8.3 (note that I have created these data for illustrative purposes). Kate's job is to make sense of this information. What she would like to determine is whether the level of women in Parliament is a function of economic development. To do that, she ran a linear regression.

Kate ran a regression because she has two continuous (or interval) variables and she wants to see if they are related. What regression analysis does is fit a line through the points, not by connecting the dots but by capturing the trend of the direction and slope of the data. Then, the program computes a statistic called the R-squared, which tells us something about how close the line is to the actual data. When R^2 is 1, then the calculated line fits the data points exactly. The R^2 tells us the amount of variation in our dependent variable that our independent variable explains. As R^2 decreases, it shows our independent variable as less powerful in accounting for the dependent variable. In other words, the closer that R-squared comes to 0, the worse the line fits. For a low R^2, one very close to 0, the points are either scattered throughout the diagram with seemingly no pattern to them or arrayed in a band around a horizontal line (one with zero slope). If we see no pattern, then we can guess intuitively (and see visually) that the independent variable has no effect on the dependent variable. Also intuitively, when our eyes can see a line (assuming we're performing a linear regression), then we are likely to

Table 8.3 Development Levels and Percentage of Women in Parliament

Country	Economic Development Level (GDP per capita, in dollars)	Percentage of Women in National Legislature
1	20,000	15
2	15,000	25
3	25,000	20
4	22,000	22
5	28,000	33
6	29,000	8
7	18,000	11
8	17,000	9
9	24,000	18
10	30,000	32
11	31,000	38
12	13,000	14
13	15,000	15
14	14,000	12
15	19,000	10
16	23,000	21
17	33,000	5
18	31,000	25
19	26,000	20
20	28,000	6
21	21,000	28
22	17,000	10
23	11,000	8
24	13,000	10
25	14,000	12
26	34,000	35
27	37,000	30
28	14,000	15
29	15,000	12
30	13,000	8

find a relationship when we have the package perform the calculation. In the social sciences, an R^2 of .4 (an R of about .63) is decent. If our calculations give us those values, then our cause explains 40 percent of the variance of our effect.

FIGURE 8.1 **Economic Development and Percentage of Women in Parliament**

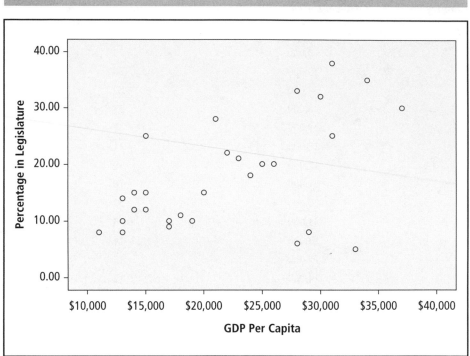

First let's use SPSS to create a *scatterplot* of these data. A scatterplot is simply a graphing of the data. Here, the x-axis is our independent variable—GDP per capita—and the y-axis is our dependent variable—percentage of women in the national legislature. Let's look at our graph (see Figure 8.1).

Just looking at Figure 8.1, we can note a few things. You can probably eyeball an upward-sloping line here, although there are some important outliers (particularly the three data points indicating low levels of women in the legislature when the GDP per capita is between $28,000 and $33,000). Still, looking at the scatterplot tells us there is likely some positive relationship (because the line we can imagine best fitting is upward sloping). Now let's actually compute the line and see what the R statistic tells us.

Using SPSS again, we can run the regression to find the equation for the line as well as the value of R^2.

As you can see, SPSS provides us with a lot of information. What is most important for our purposes is two of these key statistics. The first is the R^2 value. As we can see, R is .551 and R^2 is .303. This means that economic development levels explain 30.3 percent of the variance in the levels of female

Table 8.4   Economic Development and Percentage of Women in Parliament:
Statistical Results

Model Summary

Model	R	R-Square	Adjusted R-Square	Standard. Error of the Estimate
1	.551 [a]	.303	.278	7.99024

a. Predictors = (constant), GDP per capita (in dollars).

ANOVA[a]

Model		Sum of Squares	df	Mean Square	F	Significance
1	Regression	777.734	1	777.734	12.182	.002 [b]
	Residual	1787.632	28	63.844		
	Total	2565.367	29			

a. Dependent variable = percentage in legislature.

b. Predictors = (constant), GDP per capita (in dollars)

Coefficients[a]

Model		Unstandardized Coefficients		Standardized Coefficients	t	Significance
		B	Standard Error	Beta		
1	(Constant)	2.676	4.509		0.594	.558
	GDP per capita (in dollars).	0.001	0.000	.551	3.490	.002

a. Dependent variable = percentage in legislature.

representation in Parliament, leaving 59.7 percent explained by other factors. While there is a relationship between GDP and female representation levels in Parliament, there are other important determinants too.[6] We should note that when using other kinds of data— for instance, survey data—we would be more likely to find lower R-squared values. Individual behavior is much harder to predict than country behavior, as individuals have so many reasons for acting the way they do (as psychologists will remind us).

After you have performed the regression, be sure to look again at the scatterplot to see if you can gain any further insight. Look at the points that are far removed from the trend—this is called "residual analysis." In this case, we might want to look at those three points clustered at low levels of female representation and very high levels of economic development. Perhaps further analysis would show us that these three countries had only recently experienced a huge increase in economic development levels compared to the other wealthy countries in the sample. That might allow us to assert that there may be a lag time between economic development and female electoral success. Or maybe, looking at these countries again, we would conclude that we have been a little too lenient in including them in our sample because they were culturally distinct from the rest of the cases in a few definable ways. That would reinforce our commitment to controlling for culture.[7]

In writing her Analysis and Assessment section, Kate would want to include a table presenting all of her data, as well as the computer-generated results (including the scatterplot). Then she would need to interpret the results for the reader, writing a paragraph or more to explain what these computations mean for her hypothesis. She should also engage in residual analysis and perhaps perform a second regression, excluding the questionable data points. If she does that, she again should show the statistical analysis that her package produces and interpret the meaning of these computations for her hypothesis. Through all this she must remember that not upholding her hypothesis is fine. Kate is graded not on whether she had the correct argument but on whether she performed proper and careful analysis, interpreted her results correctly, and presented them in an effective manner.

In sum, when performing quantitative analysis, you make calculations with the help of computers, but then you must interpret the results for your reader. Moreover, you are well served to collect as many data as you think might be relevant (keeping in mind the alternative arguments that you found in your literature review) to help you better understand the relationships that you are observing and to perform controls.

This brief foray into quantitative analysis shows you that numbers and statistics are highly useful and can be very interesting to political scientists as figures help us better understand (or ask more questions about) political phenomena.

FINISHING THE ANALYSIS AND ASSESSMENT SECTION

The Analysis and Assessment section of the paper is where you have the opportunity to tell the story of the phenomenon that sparked your interest in the first place. In general, the best approach to examining whether your contention holds is to break the thesis or hypothesis down into its parts. If you have only a few comparative cases, you may also want to designate each case as a major section and follow this advice within each section. Divide the analysis and assessment into subsections, each focusing on how you have actually evaluated a particular key concept in your argument. Then determine where the weight of the evidence falls on your thesis. Can you sustain it? If your thesis has multiple parts or concepts, to what extent does the evidence fit each of your contentions? If you are performing empirical analysis of a causal argument, organize the analysis around the determination of the independent variable and the dependent variable and then an assessment of the causal connection. Can you uphold your hypothesis?

As you write up this section, you want to make sure that it can stand alone as an essay that answers the following questions:

1. What is the evidence or data about your thesis?

2. What do the data suggest about the veracity of your argument?

3. Why is this so?

In addition, you want to be sure to come up with an appropriate title for this section and consider using subheadings to divide the section into parts, particularly if you are evaluating different hypotheses or performing residual analysis. Your section should also have introductory and concluding paragraphs. Within the section, be sure to present evidence and information in ways that are clear and easily accessible to the reader. Whether you are using qualitative or quantitative analysis, including a *summary* chart of the evidence is an excellent idea because it focuses the reader's attention on the precise argument as well as the weight of the data. Many students using qualitative analysis will be surprised to learn that they can develop a summary table; it is not simply a technique for numerical information, as Joe's experience shows. So the reader can better follow your narrative, you can make a short-form data chart to capture in a few words the ultimate values of your variables. Also remember that regardless of which type of analysis you choose, your text—your explanation and interpretation of the evidence—is extremely important in walking the reader through the information and discussing what it all means. You must remember to stay closely focused on your argument when you write your narrative. You may feel a pull toward telling the reader everything you know about a particular phenomenon. But the everything-but-the-kitchen-sink approach to analysis and assessment is counterproductive. The reader wants (and needs) to know only the extent to which the evidence supports your preferred argument. Thus, you don't want to lace your assessment with lots of extraneous facts. Note that in this section you will have many footnotes to the sources of your data (where you actually found the raw information—whether it is from texts, statistical handbooks, speeches, or your own surveys and interviews), but the interpretation of it should be all your own. No one has performed this precise analysis before, and you are explaining what it all means.

PRACTICAL SUMMARY

The Analysis and Assessment section of the paper is where you decide whether (and sometimes to what extent) you can sustain your argument. You make this decision based on evidence that you carefully assemble according to the method you set out and the sources you identified in your research design. You should not feel compelled to reach a positive finding. Social and natural scientists are constantly learning by being wrong about what they originally thought. What is important is that you accurately assess your contention using appropriate data. Depending on your research question, the type of information that is available, and the number of cases that make sense to study, you will perform qualitative or quantitative analysis. (Sometimes, you may be able to mix the two.) Regardless of which you employ, you want to amass evidence carefully—looking at all sides of the argument and, where appropriate, assessing the relationship between the variables. Remember not to get distracted by extraneous information. Also, while other experts may have interesting opinions about related subjects, what is most important for you is to develop your own set of evidence and interpret its meaning on your own, without the help of those scholars. In this section, you follow the plan that you set out in the research design to know the values of your variables and to evaluate the nature of their connection. The data are so important here; what you think should happen no longer matters. Analyze the information, and make your assessment of the thesis/hypothesis based on those data.

To write this section of the paper, do the following:

1. Write an introduction that sets out briefly the weight of the evidence for your argument and what this information means for your thesis.

2. If the value of the dependent variable is relatively easy to explain, you may want to establish it at the outset of the section. Otherwise, you can choose whether you want to evaluate the dependent variable here or after you have established the values of the independent variable(s). Your decision should be based on what makes sense to you for writing this section.

3. For qualitative analysis, begin with your first case study, and explain the value of your independent variable.[8] If possible, present the information in a summary chart, and then write a narrative explaining the meaning and significance of these data. You would likely be well served to treat this as a separate subsection with its own title. Once the value of the dependent variable is clear, consider whether the thesis holds. If it is a causal hypothesis, be sure to think carefully about any evidence that supports the idea that the cause creates the effect.

4. If you are performing quantitative analysis, be sure to remind the reader of your hypothesis, explain what you are doing, and show the data that you have used. Then present the outcome of the statistical tests (and any plots that follow). Be sure to explain what these results mean.

5. Throughout the presentation and analysis of your evidence, remember to stay focused only on the thesis and the plan of action you set out in your research design. Do not include information that will distract or confuse the reader. Also remember that your job is not to prove your contention but to evaluate your argument.

6. Write a conclusion that explains what you found and why.

SUGGESTED CALENDAR

Ideally, you should be working on your Analysis and Assessment section throughout the second half of the course. Your goal should be to finish a first draft of this part with sufficient time left (about two weeks) to write your conclusion and introduction and revise and edit (again) your whole paper. Check with your professor regarding his or her precise timing recommendations.

EXERCISES

1. Write the text of an Analysis and Assessment section for Kate's paper that explores the relationship between economic development and female political empowerment. What would you call this section and its subsections (if any)?

2. Consider the hypothesis and the provided data linking party affiliation and attitudes toward the 2010 health care reform. Write up an Analysis and Assessment section for a research paper that explores that hypothesis and has amassed those data. What would you name this section and its subsections (if any)?

CHECKLIST 7: ANALYSIS AND ASSESSMENT

Here is a checklist to consult while you are writing your analysis and assessment. The importance of your data and the centrality of your thesis/hypothesis are obvious. The whole idea is to analyze the relevant information (as defined in your research design) and assess whether your thesis/hypothesis holds. You must uncover the values of your variables and the relationships between them, through either qualitative or quantitative analysis. Particularly when you are performing qualitative analysis, you need to walk the reader through the values of your variables and then show him or her what these particular independent/dependent combinations mean for your thesis. For statistical analysis, the numbers speak loudly, but you want to be sure to interpret them for the reader. Explain what these results mean for your thesis. Also remember that readers need the data to understand you and be convinced, so you often benefit from including charts and tables in this section.

Checklist 7: Analysis and Assessment

Did you create a data chart to uncover the values of your variables?	Yes _____ No _____
Does your data chart provide the *essential* information (as identified in the research design) for evaluating your thesis/hypothesis?	Yes _____ No _____
If you are performing quantitative analysis, did you run your statistical tests?	Yes _____ No _____
Did you add other tests that you didn't originally consider after looking at the results?	Yes _____ No _____
Did you perform residual analysis?	Yes _____ No _____
If you modified your strategy for performing your research, did you revise your Research Design section?	Yes _____ No _____
Did you analyze the data chart or the statistical results carefully (thinking about what they mean for your hypothesis) before writing this section?	Yes _____ No _____
Did you use the data to help you understand what you can say about your hypothesis?	Yes _____ No _____
Have you provided a substantive title that focuses on the goals of this section (analyzing information to assess your thesis/hypothesis) and your argument?	Yes _____ No _____
Have you written an introductory paragraph that summarizes what you learned about the values of your variables and then what these values mean for your thesis/hypothesis?	Yes _____ No _____
As you systemically analyze the data in essay form for the reader, do you present and explain the value(s) of your dependent variable?	Yes _____ No _____
As you systemically analyze the data in essay form for the reader, do you present and explain the value(s) of your independent variable(s)?	Yes _____ No _____
Have you included other data in the form of tables, figures, graphs, or a summary chart to help the reader follow your analysis and assessment?	Yes _____ No _____
Do you use subsections to make your presentation easier to follow?	Yes _____ No _____
Do these subsections have substantive headings that reflect the argument?	Yes _____ No _____

| If you make causal claims earlier in the paper, do you not only examine whether the variables correlate as you expected but also consider the evidence for causation? | Yes _____ No _____ |
| Have you written a concluding paragraph for the section that explains what you found overall and what this means for your thesis/hypothesis? | Yes _____ No _____ |

Note: Remember to consult checklist 5, Appearance, Format, and Style, so your section will look and sound good.

NOTES

1. Note that with statistical analysis, there is always some probability that the relationship that you find to be significant is not. If we accept a hypothesis at the 99 percent confidence level that means there is still a 1 percent chance that the relationship occurred by chance.

2. An excellent resource about a form of qualitative analysis, case studies, is Alexander L. George and Andrew Bennett, *Case Studies and Theory Development in the Social Sciences* (Cambridge, MA: MIT Press, 2004).

3. Freedom House, "Freedom in the World," www.freedomhouse.org.

4. You might choose this sample because it is one to which you could get easy access at your school. In your Research Design section, you would want to discuss the significance of using this sample, of course, and consider what impact it could have on your findings.

5. Seymour Martin Lipset, *Political Man: The Social Bases of Politics* (Baltimore: Johns Hopkins University Press, 1981); Adam Przeworski and Fernando Limongi Neto, "Modernization: Theories and Facts," *World Politics* 49, no. 2 (1997): 155–183.

6. Students with more training and interest in statistics would want to note the following: another useful statistic, the F statistic, evaluates whether the line that we calculated through these points is significant. And here, with a significance level of .002, we can say that yes, our line is significant. And what is this line? To determine the line, we look under the coefficients and see that we have values calculated for the intercept and the slope (a and b, respectively, in the equation $y = a + bx$). The line for this equation would be $y = 2.676 + .001x$. We need to note that our intercept is not significant, while the slope is (at the .02 level, or 98 percent of the time). In addition, after running this regression, a student might want to scale the values for economic development levels, relating thousands of dollars of GDP to percentages. (In other words, for country 1, the economic development level would be 20 instead of 20,000.) After rescaling, the R value would be the same, but the slope would be

calculated as .687. Prior to scaling, the slope was .000687, which got converted to .001 with rounding.

7. If Kate had more data points, she might want to eliminate those outlying cases and recalculate her statistics.

8. Of course, you may have multiple independent variables. If that is the case, then you need to look at the values for all of them and their connection to the dependent variable.

Bringing the Paper Together in Three Essential Ways: The Conclusion, Introduction, and Title

When you have performed your analysis and written all of the substantive parts of your paper, you are at the equivalent of the home stretch of a race; the crowds are cheering, but you have hit the wall. You feel that you can't run any more. Like the marathoner in the last few miles, the research paper writer who has finished all of his or her paper except the first and last sections is also very tired at this point. Still, you—whether runner or writer—want to end strong as you finish these crucial and related parts of the paper—the conclusion, introduction, and title.

You might be surprised that I am mentioning them in the reverse order from how readers will encounter these sections. The reason for this seemingly backward approach is that to write the introduction well you need information from the conclusion, and the best titles reflect the introduction. So bear with me as we proceed in an opposite but sensible sequence.

These kindred parts of the paper help you sum up what the research has been all about as well as point you forward to potential additional work, create positive initial and final impressions, and entice someone to pick up and read your paper. The conclusion reminds readers of what you argued and why, as well as what you learned. In addition, it steps back and makes sense of your results, interpreting them in light of any methodological challenges that you had, and suggests further research, showing your vast understanding of the area of inquiry in which you have been engaged. The introduction, though separated from the conclusion by many pages, performs related functions. First, however, it must both introduce the reader to your question and convince that person to keep reading. Typically, you can accomplish those goals by explaining why your topic and query are important and interesting to multiple audiences, stating your thesis, and providing an overview of the whole paper. When the introduction is drafted you can turn to perfecting the title. You have put forward earlier working titles, but for the last version, you want to expend some serious brainpower on coming up with a great name for the paper. Why? The title captures, to the best of your ability, the argument and cases of your paper, and it creates that very first impression on the reader. The title, then, is the equivalent of a firm handshake, while the introduction compares with appropriate and engaging initial conversation with a new acquaintance and the conclusion is a satisfying end to your meeting that creates confidence in you, underlines the initial positive first impression, and makes your interlocutor want to see or hear from you again.

CONSIDERING THE SIGNIFICANCE AND LIMITATIONS OF YOUR FINDINGS: THE CONCLUSION

Your conclusion accomplishes several tasks. First, it ties the whole paper together by restating your thesis and where the weight of the evidence came down. Second, the conclusion discusses why the argument and the particular findings (across your cases) are important and what your results mean for various audiences. Third, it assesses the versatility of your thesis, considering the extent to which you can apply your argument to other cases or, conversely, whether you need to limit its applicability. Fourth, the conclusion is a critical assessment of what you accomplished. Here, you return to those best decisions that you made in the Research Design section and consider what impact they had on your findings. What, if anything, would you do differently if you could do this study over? Last, the conclusion is a jumping-off point for the future, for you or other researchers who might like to pick up where you left off. This is where you can set out questions to pursue to continue this line of research in a fruitful manner.

As you know by now, the research paper consists of several sections that appear prior to the conclusion. When you first started writing this paper, you probably could not adequately conceive of how these parts were related to each other and what the logical flow between them would be. At this point, you have, I hope, mastered the interrelationship between the segments and through your section introductions and conclusions have helped to provide smooth transitions between the different parts of the paper. The conclusion also helps you accomplish this task by tying the paper together one last time: briefly reminding the reader of your question, why it was important, what you thought the best answer to it was, how you were going to evaluate this contention, and what the assessment of the evidence showed. The concluding section briefly walks the reader through the significance of the research, the argument, and the evidence.

A vital part of this discussion is to remind the reader why anyone should care about what you found. Why was your research question so important?

Why are the instances that you studied significant? Remember, you want to answer these questions from the perspective of several audiences. For the social scientific community, your findings say something about a theoretical debate in the field. Remind your reader of the scholarly controversies and what you have learned about the merits of a particular line of reasoning. In addition, your results also have significance for the interpretation of a particular set of cases. For practitioners, your findings might provide advice about appropriate behavior when dealing with comparable situations, and for citizens, your work might be important for understanding the world or being better members of a local, national, or global community. Normative work provides the added benefit of enlightening us about what ought to be and how we ought to behave.

Your conclusion likely engenders feelings of both pride and humility. As you consider what you did and what you found, you should think about the extent to which your findings provide insight into other cases. Take pride if your results help you understand any other political phenomena. But perhaps you need to scale back your earlier claims, finding that your thesis only partially applies or is relevant to a smaller subset of cases. Consider whether some of the limitations may have resulted from faulty decisions you made at earlier stages in the research (literature review or research design), from which you could never recover.

Thus, while the conclusion requires that you wrap this paper "package," you should not feel that the tying has to be neat and that once tied you are done with your discussion. In fact, research is often quite messy, and despite our best efforts to find uncomplicated support for our original contentions, we often cannot reach such a nice conclusion. Turning back to our discussion of medical research, you do not have to confirm your assertions to do well; you simply need to evaluate them honestly. This section is where you come back to the compromises and the lines of logic you pursued—whether you found support for your thesis or not—to consider whether your choices had both a significant and possibly a detrimental impact on your study. In the conclusion, you might want to suggest that a different school of thought appears stronger now or that you would alter the plan for conducting the study (whether in selecting cases, operationalizing the variables, choosing sources, and/or generating information) in certain ways. Of course, you should explain why you want to make these changes as well as assert why you think these modifications would lead to a better design and outcome.

Finally, regardless of how tired you are of this paper, the concepts involved, and the cases, you should discuss how you would proceed if you had the resources (and stamina) to continue. In doing this, you reinforce to the reader that you understand the significance of your findings for this area of scholarship. Moreover, you indicate what you would do differently or which new paths you would pursue to enhance the field's understanding of this debate and these sets of cases (or even related instances). By charting a hypothetical next course, you impress the reader with your enthusiasm and command of the discipline, and you help yourself on any future research paper assignments. Next time, you won't have to agonize about your research question. It will be set out for you in the conclusion of your last paper!

For an example of a conclusion, let's turn again to Joe's paper about post–civil war El Salvador. Remember, he argued that to create democratic stability after an internal conflict, state institutions need significant power to do good for citizens. The stronger institutions are, the more stable the country will be. First, notice Joe's title. It captures the purpose ("Concluding") and argument (the portion after the colon) of the section. Then, as you read, look how systematically Joe accomplishes each of the requirements for this section, reminding the reader of his question, the literature, his hypothesis, and the outlines of his research design. At the outset, he walks through the values of his dependent variable, and later, he mentions the indicators that help him know the value of his cause. Joe also faces head-on some of his weaknesses, and we see him grappling with something many students face: the realization that conceiving of a variable differently would have been helpful. Thereafter, he makes suggestions about how to carry on the research, discusses realistically the progress that El Salvador has made, and assesses the value of his research to scholars, practitioners, and observers. Joe has done a fantastic job racing, not whimpering, to the finish line and turning in an excellent performance.

Drawing Conclusions: State Strength (Better Yet, Responsiveness) Promotes Stability

By 1992, both the Salvadoran government and the FMLN had petitioned the United Nations to intervene in the country and help end their bloody conflict. The Chapultepec Accords, signed by both groups, laid the foundation for a cessation of violence. In many respects, the agreement has been a great success, and some observers hold El Salvador up as a model for other postconflict societies.[a] Former deadly military enemies have become political adversaries interacting civilly in a competitive democratic system.[b] For many, the laying down of weapons and the general freedom in society are great indicators of democratic stability.

What precisely has brought about this transformation? Scholars most convincingly assert that the strength of the institutions created after war is essential to the creation of stability. Other arguments are problematic. The Separate and Balance school, which calls for dividing former domestic enemies into distinct territories and balancing power between them to prevent recurrence, was neither workable nor desirable in this case. Reconciliationist solutions of focusing on societal healing seem too backward looking as well as incomplete. Since El Salvador had fundamentally flawed political and security institutions, as well as an economy that could not meet the basic needs of a majority of its people, political and economic reforms were far more pressing than finding the truth and hoping for some vaunted reconciliation process to magically transform people. Political Populism in some ways had led to the conflict. Many citizens were mobilized, but against each other and the rival institutions—those of the state or the guerrillas. A better solution seemed to be to make government more responsive to popular concerns and create economic opportunity for individuals. This responsiveness would actually encourage citizens to demobilize and allow them to be less angry about politics as well as to be linked socially and not simply for defensive purposes.

To investigate whether stronger domestic institutions have a positive impact on democratic stability, I focused on the roles of the two key political parties, the security organs, and the national economy. I sought to understand what had happened to the strength of these institutions, expecting them to have become more powerful in 2005–2010 than in the early postwar period of 1992–1997. Regarding the major parties, each of them has maintained and solidified its presence in elections and politics. In the legislative competitions, ARENA and the FMLN won a substantial amount of support. The year 2009, however, was huge for the FMLN, the former guerrilla force, when it scored two big victories—control of the most seats in the Legislative Assembly as well as the presidency. This peaceful, legitimate transfer of power to a different party bodes well for the future of Salvadoran politics in general. Moreover, the continuing existence of ARENA as the loyal opposition indicates that these democratic parties and practices have become stronger throughout the postconflict period. No longer are worries taken seriously that the FMLN will invoke a Marxist revolution if elected or ARENA will declare a state of emergency if challenged.

Turning to a second set of important institutions, Salvadoran military and police forces appear to be stronger as democratic institutions. In the "bad old days," the security forces wielded enormous power, both at the behest of the undemocratic government and in response to their own sense that state security was threatened. They were responsible for the death and destruction of tens of thousands of lives as well as much property. Today's achievements include the state's taming of these institutions and using them to further democratic goals. Violence, however, is still a problem in El Salvador, although it now tends to present itself as the result of gang efforts. The challenges of responding to gang violence have given broad-based popular support to a return to very violent retaliatory tactics, as well as opportunities for police corruption. While some observers fear that *Mano Dura* (strong hand) policies threaten democratic achievements by empowering the security forces to see gang members and other violent criminals as guilty before proven innocent (in ways reminiscent of the old methods of equating peasants with insurgents), many citizens, suffering from the terrible violence, support tough tactics. Thus, evaluating the strength of the security organs as state institutions is a bit difficult. They have been reformed and are clearly under civilian authority, but the civilian leadership seems to be supporting old-style policies for dealing with the crime problem, and incidentally, these solutions are not working well. Thus, while the initial transformation of the security and police forces shows considerable gains in that the military recognizes civilian authority and its role in providing for security from external threats, the challenge of coping with crime has reversed some of that initial positive progress toward viewing citizens as people who tend to be law abiding and in need of protection.

Last, to understand state strength, I sought to examine the economy, not assert-ing that the government should run an economy but in recognition that government policies establish a foundation on which an economy is built. Sound policies lead to the potential of economic possibility and improvement. In the years immediately before and after the peace accords were signed, the government privatized El Salvador's financial institutions, an effort that provided almost instant payoffs. This liberalization freed up credit lines, encouraged confidence in Salvadoran banks, and created a stable environment for financial competition, even inviting foreign financial institutions to participate. In typical neoliberal fashion, however, these financial-sector reforms were not accompanied by improvements in social service provision, so the monetary disci-pline has been hard medicine for the poor. El Salvador still faces a huge rich-poor gap, and many believe these disparities have contributed to civil unrest and the rise of gangs. Thus, economic improvements have not been as widespread and distributed in ways that would benefit all sectors of the population. These achievements do little to enhance the foundation for stability.

Regrettably, this paper suffers from a number of limitations. For one, finding data was difficult. For example, the exact number of gang members operating in El Salvador would be impossible to determine. In addition, my limited knowledge of Spanish as well as some concerns about the legitimacy of some sources affected my information gathering. Additionally, finding popular responses to shifts in Salvadoran monetary and fiscal policy proved difficult. As every level of society is affected by any change in policy, this information would have been very useful. Most important, however, I real-ize that conceiving of the independent variable as strength of governing institutions was not the best idea. After performing the analysis, I see that I am really trying to capture the idea of how well these institutions respond to citizens' needs and demands so that people do not look to outside actors (such as insurgent groups or gangs) to represent them, fight their battles, protect them from harm, or feed their children. If I were to start again, I would point instead to the responsiveness of state institutions, and that would affect my operationalization strategy in numerous ways. I am confi-dent, however, that my results would be similar.

Still, the results confirm that in El Salvador, governmental institutions affect demo-cratic stability. El Salvador has seen great progress in the area of party development and responsibility, important yet modest improvements in security-sector reform, and still further limited progress in the economy. These add up to enhanced governmental institutions, although the progress is ultimately not as significant as observers of and participants in the 1992 peace likely hoped. Why are the gains so small, and what might be done to fortify them? A new research trajectory would entail exploring more carefully the key governmental institutions and learning about the impact of their responsiveness. For instance, to what extent do the political parties ARENA and the FMLN propagate old battles, and are citizens looking for ideological and/or organiza-tional alternatives to them? Second, with respect to the role of security institutions in promoting stability, examining whether gang violence is politically motivated would be important. If gangs are a manifestation of opposition, then contemporary violence between them and the police sounds reminiscent of the civil war. How can legitimate security institutions become more responsive to citizens' and the state's concerns? Third, the actions of Salvadoran financial institutions have been very closely scrutinized, yet few positive economic changes that transform the prospects for ordinary Salvadorans have emerged. Emigration is still prevalent. With the recent global economic crisis, is Salvadoran stability coming under greater pressure as the economy hasn't provided jobs and opportunity for citizens and possibilities (and remittances) from overseas have dwindled? A fourth, and a significantly different, track would be to study El Salvador in comparative terms, juxtaposing its progress with another, similar state, perhaps Guatemala. Researchers often expect difficult processes to unfold too quickly, and eighteen years might be just the beginning of El Salvador's transformation. Where does Guatemala stand with respect to stability? Does a comparison with this country also highlight the importance of state institutions and give more perspective on the complexity of both creating responsive and capable structures and consolidating democratic stability? Does the Guatemala comparison, on the other hand, stress the importance of putting in place viable reconciliation processes as well as focusing on institutional change?

In 2009, Mauricio Funes of the FMLN was elected to the presidency. That he was the first FMLN candidate who was not a former guerrilla is probably no coincidence. These results demonstrate that El Salvador is capable of transferring power from one party to another with little to no violence. Given where this country was more than twenty years ago, that feat is remarkable. To continue on a positive path toward democracy and stability, this research suggests that El Salvador's governing institutions need more capacity and responsiveness to citizens to craft sound policies that ensure political participation, reduce the violence throughout the country, and decrease the gap between rich and poor.

For scholars, this research reinforces the idea that good institutions are the best guarantor of a democratically stable state. Policymakers can see that efforts—international, national, and grassroots—to strengthen and make more responsible key state structures are essential for stability. Institution building appears to be even more important than efforts to heal societies, and therefore any assistance should be targeted toward making the state more capable of meeting people's needs. The lesson of El Salvador for interested observers is that civil violence can be overcome, but the process is a slow one and requires the transformation of the structures of previously war-torn states. Such a solution is not the one ordinary people often see as essential or even interesting—watching dramatic interventions or truth commissions is much more riveting—but it appears to bring real and substantial results. Thus, as scholars, policymakers, and citizens reflect on contemporary postconflict challenges that dominate the news—in Iraq and Afghanistan, for instance—El Salvador can be instructive. Its experience underlines the complexity and long-term nature of the stabilization process while also stressing the importance of creating capable and responsive political, security, and economic institutions that meet the needs of the people.

NOTES

a. David Holiday, "El Salvador's Model Democracy," *Current History* 104, no. 279 (2005): 77. www.proquest.com.
b. Freedom House has rated El Salvador as Free (scoring a 2 on Political Rights and a 3 on Civil Liberties) since 1996. Freedom House, "Country Ratings and Status, FIW 1973–2010 (Excel)," http://www.freedomhouse.org/template.cfm?page=439.

WRITING A GOOD INTRODUCTION

With the conclusion completed, you can turn to the introduction. Although the introduction comes first in the paper, one of its most important functions (and one that many students overlook) is to provide an overview of the whole work. Thus, writing this piece at the end—when you have written all of the sections, logic, arguments, evidence, and conclusions—makes sense. Very basically and obviously, your introduction introduces the reader to your research paper.

What most students know about the introduction is that it should grab a reader's attention; it should entice the reader into wanting to continue. In attracting the reader, you can be most effective if you not only tell something about your topic but also communicate your question and then explain why this query is interesting and important to multiple audiences (scholars, policymakers, and citizens). Does this sound familiar? It should because you thought through these issues at the beginning of the process. Your checklist from the question development and annotated bibliography phase will come in handy here.

After enticing the reader, the introduction provides that overview of the paper so the reader knows what you are arguing and why, how you are performing the study, what you actually found, and what is the significance of these results. In other words, you provide a kind of road map to the paper. Some students chafe at the idea of the overview because they think it is repetitive. True, you should avoid needless redundancy in a paper, and you should never cut and paste your own words from section to section. Still, in discussing complex issues, reminders and reinforcement are good. They help the reader understand better. So don't be a mystery writer—holding your thesis and key evidence until the end—when writing research papers or essays. Give your reader the necessary previews to enhance his or her understanding and your paper's clarity.

You have already had experience writing a good introduction that includes an overview. In chapter 4, we explicitly discussed how to write this part of the literature review, and the job here is analogous. Again, you want to communicate your query (here it is your research question; in the literature review it is how scholars have answered your research question and which response is most compelling). Moving forward to the road map part of the introduction, you want to do something like you did in the conclusion, recapping the essential elements of your paper. In other words, you want to summarize what you have done in each of the subsequent sections of the paper in a way that links each element of this larger process smoothly and logically.

An important metaphor to think about when you write the introduction is that of a contract between you and your readers, and you want to write it to your advantage. You start by attracting readers to your paper (so they will sign on the dotted line and keep reading), and you keep that attention because, in the overview, you promise only what you deliver. You are careful not to mention extraneous information or overstate what you have accomplished because otherwise readers will wonder where those ideas or assertions are. Also, like a contract, you want to lay everything out clearly. Neither you nor readers want surprises, so everything of consequence that follows in the paper is mentioned in the introduction.

Again, let's see how Joe handled this task. We will pay special attention to the ways in which his introduction is similar to and different from his conclusion as well as make sure that Joe has not literally repeated himself, using the same phrases or sentences.

The Challenge of Creating a Stable Government in El Salvador

In March 2009, Mauricio Funes was elected president of El Salvador, narrowly defeating Rodrigo Ávila by just under 3 percent of the popular vote.[a] His victory was notable for two main reasons. First, this win marked the ruling party's (the Nationalist Republican Alliance, known by its Spanish abbreviation, ARENA) initial loss in a presidential contest. Second, Funes was the first of his party's leaders not to have been a combatant in the Salvadoran civil war.[b] The candidate's lack of participation in the conflict is particularly noteworthy because his party, the Farabundo Martí National Liberation Front, or FMLN, was created during that war as a rebel group trying to unseat the government. In fact, in the lead-up to the elections, Ávila tried to depict Funes as a typical FMLN candidate; television commercials attacking Funes even used footage of "street chaos and camouflaged soldiers" to underscore his "ties" to socialism and civic unrest.[c] In the days before the polls opened, this tactic seemed to be able to sway a number of voters away from Funes, who was originally projected to win in a landslide.[d]

That this link seemed to resonate with so many voters is symbolic of the long-lasting effects of the Salvadoran civil war. In the late 1970s, frustration over failed social and agrarian reforms led to the formation of the FMLN, a communist insurgent group. For the next decade, the FMLN engaged in violent rebellion against the Salvadoran government, which responded in turn with violence against guerrillas, suspected rebels, and sympathizers. By the time representatives from the government and the FMLN signed peace accords in Chapultepec Castle, Mexico, an estimated 75,000 lives were lost, and about one-fourth of the country's entire population was displaced.[e]

While some analysts see the achievements since 1992 as remarkable, having "set the country on the path to a stable and lasting peace,"[f] such a conclusion is too positive. Yes, there has been progress, but the nation suffers still from gang violence and economic underdevelopment. Thus, the question remains regarding how far El Salvador has come and what accounts for its level of progress so far.

Four broad theories emerged to explain how countries build stability after sustained conflict. A first contends that the violence in civil wars, especially ethnic ones, makes living together again impossible. Instead, the best solution is to separate the formerly warring parties and balance power between these territories so that neither party will think that future conflict can pay.[g] Another suggests that the country cannot truly progress without recognizing the injustices of the civil war, meting out responsibility for them, and then creating a means of atonement.[h] A third theory holds that on a grassroots level, every strata of Salvadoran society must find some way to be involved in the nation's politics, and successful peace-building efforts must grow from the bottom up, enlist citizen efforts, and take advantage of the linkages between people.[i] Finally, the fourth approach holds that for the nation to make better progress, the mechanisms of the state need to be established and adjusted to address key political and socioeconomic problems. This fourth school seems to be the most sound, given that the citizens of El Salvador can interact with the government through these various institutions, and furthermore these institutions can provide the widest scope of governance.[j]

Thus, the key to building peace or, better yet, democratic stability seems to be developing strong state institutions. When these institutions can do their jobs, then they provide the foundation for stability, as citizens trust the government and can focus on living their lives instead of combating or petitioning the state. To evaluate the role of state institutions in promoting stability in El Salvador, I will compare their strength across two time periods, 1992–1997 and 2005–2010, expecting that in the early postwar years the institutions were less capable and therefore their support for stability was weaker. More recently, these institutions should be stronger—as a result of the reforms instituted—and therefore stability should be enhanced as a result. To conceptualize the strength of institutions, I will focus on political parties, the military and police forces, and the financial sector, key players in shaping the postconflict political and socioeconomic environments in El Salvador. Because ARENA and the FMLN both surfaced in the early years of the Salvadoran civil war, their presence and activities can provide an effective outlet for popular political expression. The military and police forces have seen their duties shift toward eradicating gang warfare and civil unrest, harmful roadblocks that can discourage political expression. El Salvador's government also took steps to stabilize and improve its economy. Banking and financial-sector reforms were to serve as the foundation for macroeconomic stability and make the country attractive to investors. Declines in severe inequality, which fueled the earlier conflict, were supposed to follow.

The analysis shows that stability has improved, but the transformation is not complete. While people do not fear the outbreak of violence between the previous warring factions and El Salvador is characterized by outsiders as a democratic regime, the progress hasn't been as vast as many in El Salvador would like. That partial advancement is linked to the less-than-hoped-for development of those essential institutions. El Salvador has made the most progress in strengthening its party organizations. It has also made strides transforming the military, incorporating former FMLN fighters and creating a police force made up of both the right and the left wing. However, old ideas about how to deal with opponents don't die easily. Recent challenges suggest that violence first and protecting rights later is the preferred approach. In addition, economic policies have transformed the financial sector, but poverty remains endemic, and people find that fleeing for jobs in the United States is their best economic opportunity. Thus, the modest strength of security and economic institutions has not been enough to bring about a greater transformation in democratic stability.

While this study underlines the link between capable and responsive institutions and stability, it also raises other questions. Why have gangs emerged as such a force in El Salvador, and does their emergence suggest something less positive about the progress in the security sector? Will El Salvador be able to hang on to its achievements in the face of the world economic crisis as the full effects of the recent worldwide Great Recession become better understood? Finally, this research suggests that scholars, policymakers, and citizens need a better appreciation for the time involved in building peace. Perhaps El Salvador's progress since 1992 is remarkable given the complexity of this process. Comparing El Salvador's achievement with that of a similar state, for instance, Guatemala, could be instructive.

Concerns about the peace process in El Salvador are interesting not only in their own right but because they suggest much about the challenges of transforming war-torn societies into stable, democratic ones. In academic and policy circles, as well as around kitchen tables, how to create stability after internal conflict is an important question, particularly because of the enormous U.S. resource commitment to Afghanistan and Iraq today. Scholars have been debating why war-torn countries and their populations can't more easily change. This research underlines the importance of institutions and suggests that not only strength—as in how powerfully these organizations can act on their own—but also responsiveness to citizens' concerns is important. Students of the state (Seth Jones) and democracy (Robert Putnam) suggest that insurgencies are dampened and states work better when they are responsive to citizens' concerns and people are linked to the state and each other. This responsiveness obviates the role alternative organizations—such as organized crime families, gangs, and insurgent groups—play in meeting citizens' basic needs for physical and economic security.[k]

Policymakers, too, are concerned about how to respond to the challenges of postwar societies and how to prevent these conflicts from flaring up again. When violence reignites, not only does more suffering result within the state borders, but there are usually refugees and other spillovers. In addition, in these days of dwindling foreign aid sources, finding better ways to transform violence instead of having to deal with its continual reemergence is important. Finally, citizens typically hope for stability around the world, and the El Salvador case helps explain why transforming postconflict societies is so complex and time consuming.

NOTES

a.   "Left-winger Wins El Salvador Poll," *BBC News* (March 16, 2009), http://news.bbc.co.uk/2/ hi/americas/7944899.stm.

b.   Ibid.

c.   Elisabeth Malkin, "Elections in El Salvador Invoke Rivalries of Civil War Years," *New York Times* (March 12, 2009), http://www.nytimes.com/2009/03/12/world/americas/12salvador .html?_r=1&partner=rss&emc=rss.

d.   Ibid.

e.   Roland Paris, "Peacebuilding in Central America: Reproducing the Sources of Conflict?" *International Peacekeeping* 9, no. 4 (2002), 49.

f.   Ibid., 51.

g.   This argument is most closely associated with Chaim Kaufmann, although other realist scholars have made similar arguments. See his "Possible and Impossible Solutions to Ethnic Civil Wars," *International Security* 20, no. 4 (Spring 1996): 136–175.

h.   See Priscilla B. Hayner, *Unspeakable Truths: Transitional Justice and the Challenge of Truth Commissions*, 2nd ed. (New York: Routledge, 2010); Daniel Philpott, ed., *The Politics of Past Evil* (Notre Dame, IN: University of Notre Dame Press, 2006); Tristan Anne Borer, ed., *Telling the Truths: Truth Telling and Peace Building in Post-conflict Societies* (Notre Dame, IN: University of Notre Dame Press, 2006).

i.   Paula M. Pickering, *Peacebuilding in the Balkans: The View from the Ground Floor* (Ithaca, NY: Cornell University Press, 2007).

j.   As we will see, this is the dominant school in postconflict transformation today. Some of its leading scholars (and their essential works) include Roland Paris, *At War's End: Building Peace after Civil Conflict* (New York: Cambridge University Press, 2004); Roland Paris, "Bringing the Leviathan Back In: Classical versus Contemporary Studies of the Liberal Peace," *International Studies Review* 8 (2006): 425–440; Charles T. Call and E. M. Cousens, "Ending Wars and Building Peace: International Responses to War-torn Societies," *International Studies Perspectives* 9, no. 1 (2008): 1–2; Roland Paris and Timothy D. Sisk, eds., *The Dilemmas of Statebuilding: Confronting the Contradictions of Postwar Peace Operations* (New York: Routledge, 2009).

k.   Seth G. Jones, *In the Graveyard of Empires: America's War in Afghanistan* (New York: Norton, 2009); Robert D. Putnam, with Robert Leonardi and Raffaella Y. Nanetti, *Making Democracy Work: Civic Traditions in Modern Italy* (Princeton, NJ: Princeton University Press, 1993), see especially chapter 6, "Social Capital and Institutional Success."

As you would expect—given what I've told you about the introduction and the conclusion—a good deal of the information included in the two sections is similar, and this kind of positive reinforcement helps them to serve as attractive bookends to the material in the paper. The introduction has a title that stresses the overall purpose and argument of this section. Moreover, it spends more time enticing the reader by talking a bit about the past as well as the situation under study. In addition to laying out what is to follow in each section (and notice that the discussion proceeds in the order that the reader will meet this information), the introduction explains why different audiences would find this research interesting and important—again part of its effort to sustain attention. Joe has done another fine job, as each section of the paper is carefully represented, including the conclusion, and while the whole section is similar to the conclusion, the language does not mirror it. Also notice that in both cases, these sections consist of several paragraphs. You have too much to accomplish in each to adequately wrap up and point to new directions for research (conclusion) and entice and preview (introduction) in one or even two paragraphs. Joe has understood the requirements well and has struck the right balance here. Excellent!

A LAST ELEMENT IN ATTRACTING READERS: DEVELOPING AN APPEALING TITLE

Joe has one more job to do before his draft is complete: he needs to come up with a title for the paper. Your title should do three things: communicate your question or puzzle, identify your cases or the specifics of your study, and summarize your argument or thesis. Yet you have a limited number of words—if the introduction is the paper in brief, the title is the microscopic view. Because you're trying to accomplish so much in so few words, you'll often need to use a colon to separate the ideas. Successful titles, in addition, express the question, cases, and argument in a clever way. Be careful, though, that your attempts at cleverness don't introduce confusion. The title's main goal is to communicate the basics of the paper. From the title, readers should understand in a nutshell what you have learned and how.

Taking a careful look at some great titles from published works can help you see how to strike that balance of finding something creative that accomplishes these goals.

Chester A. Crocker, Fen Osler Hampson, and Pamela Aall, eds., *Leashing the Dogs of War: Conflict Management in a Divided World* (Washington, DC: USIP Press, 2007).

Victoria A. Farrar-Myers and Diana Dwyre, *Limits and Loopholes: The Quest for Money, Free Speech, and Fair Elections* (Washington, DC: CQ Press, 2007).

Sarah E. Kreps, *Coalitions of Convenience: United States Military Interventions after the Cold War* (New York: Oxford University Press, 2010).

Ronald Rappaport and Walter J. Stone, *Three's a Crowd: The Dynamics of Third Parties, Ross Perot and Republican Resurgence* (Ann Arbor: University of Michigan Press, 2005).

Larry Sabato, ed., *The Sixth Year Itch: The Rise and Fall of the George W. Bush Presidency* (New York: Pearson Longman, 2008).

Darrell M. West, *Brain Gain: Rethinking U.S. Immigration Policy* (Washington, DC: Brookings Institution Press, 2010).

These titles succeed because they communicate key information in an attractive way. Notice how an author uses his or her imagination most on the first part of the title, and that is no accident since this phrase makes the initial impression. When the title is shortened, the second half—after the colon—is dropped, so you want your opening to be clever. Looking more carefully at the first title, you see it evoking a frightening picture. The second two contain alliterations that make them sound good and increase their appeal. After the colon, these authors tend to communicate the more prosaic information about the subject matter and cases. The last three titles repeat or play with phrases that we all know—typically from popular culture, such as movies, songs, and literature. In sum, by finding a beginning that is evocative, alliterative, suggestive of another famous work, or even surprising or provocative you will be on track to writing a successful title, as it will likely jump out at the reader, attracting him or her to the work. Then, finish up by providing more information so the reader can be clear about your argument. Of course, not all authors succeed in communicating the argument and focus instead on case and subject, but you should strive to be catchy, clever, and clear about your contention.

When his paper was at a draft stage (before he wrote his introduction and conclusion), Joe titled the work "Reforming El Salvador: The Mechanisms of a Peaceable State." That's OK as a start because it communicates his country case and some elements of the argument—something about state mechanisms and peace—but given what a great writer Joe is and that his argument is a bit more complex, I think he can do better. First, he needs to be precise about his fundamental contention. Joe himself tells us later in his text that he is going to study not peace but democratic stability, so he very well should have his key concept identified correctly in the title. Second, his interest is less in reform (although reform is part of the process of creating better institutions) and more in creating stability. In fact, Joe would be best served to find a way to bring his two variables (strength of state institutions and democratic stability) front and center. Now, while also mentioning his case, is there a way to do this in an interesting fashion? Perhaps "Beyond War and Peace: How Strong Institutions Contribute to Democratic Stability in Postwar El Salvador" works? That title provides a literary allusion at the outset while also suggesting that Joe is talking about neither war nor peace but the link between institutions and stability in El Salvador. Another possibility is "Build Good Institutions to Combat War: The Progress of Reforms and the Enhancement of Democratic Stability in El Salvador." That second one originally started as a play on the Vietnam-era phrase, "Make love, not war," but was modified to fit Joe's argument. It might not be as catchy or evocative as the first one, but it does accomplish what a good title should.

ARE YOU DONE? THE JOY (AND CONTINUED RESPONSIBILITIES) OF FINALIZING YOUR DRAFT

If you have proceeded in writing this paper as I have recommended, after you write the conclusion, introduction, and title, you have completed a first draft. That is an accomplishment to celebrate. While I know this is easy for me to say, try to finish your draft in time to get some space from it because as we know from chapter 6, "it ain't over 'til it's over!" Revising and editing gives you that polished *final* product. Again, assuming that you've been writing the paper in sections and have been rethinking and rewriting as you've gone along (e.g., always consulting checklist 5, Appearance, Format, and Style, and integrating your own and your readers' comments into your revisions and edits), then this end-stage task won't be too hard, and it is very important for both the overall quality of the paper and your satisfaction with the process.

In our marathon analogy, it's mile 25. Your feet are hurting, and your legs are aching, but you feel excited because you have a whole paper. As numerous authors have noted, writing a complete version of a paper is hard, and a full draft is a great accomplishment. Take some time, celebrate, and stop thinking about this work for a little while (preferably a few days or at least several hours, not just a few minutes) so you will be in a better position to finish your research paper. Your mind should be fresh when you revise and edit for the last time.

Even if you've been revising as you go, the first completed full draft is seldom perfect. In fact, this version can often be quite awkward and problematic in places.[1] Therefore, you have a little more work to do (maybe another mile to run) before you can cross the finish line. Still, working with a complete draft—particularly one that has already been revised and edited in places—is much easier than starting from scratch. But you can always make it better. Because you have been pushed throughout this book to write often before you felt ready, you now have many pages of text to consider for their overall coherence and methodological soundness as well as basic grammatical and usage problems. In other words, you need both to revise and to edit your paper with the goal of producing a final draft of which you can feel enormously proud.

So go back to chapter 6 to remind yourself of what you need to do to make the rhetorical and logical flow of the paper the best you can. Also be concerned with the formatting and appearance of the paper. Don't put your fabulous ideas in a substandard package! Follow the guidelines there and, at the very last, when you are truly satisfied, print out your work. Feel proud as you hand it in; your accomplishment in writing the research paper has been great. And see— you have completed a task that seemed so formidable. As the tortoise—moving slowly, steadily, and wisely I might add—you have run a great race and written your research paper. Hooray!

PRACTICAL SUMMARY

The last jobs of your paper involve writing some very important elements: the conclusion, introduction, and title. The concluding and introductory sections are not short if your paper is long, and you need to give them significant attention. Although they are bookends for the material that comes within your paper, they are not identical. Be sure to avoid reusing exact phrases or sentences in these sections. When these are complete, turn to the title. It is short, but a good one is creative and attracts readers to the paper. Careful thinking about what best expresses the essence of your argument and accomplishments and phrases the title in an interesting way is essential.

Your conclusion accomplishes five tasks. It

1. ties the paper together by repeating the argument and reporting the findings,

2. reminds the reader why this argument is important to different audiences,

3. assesses the extent to which your thesis can be extended or must be limited,

4. returns to the choices or compromises that you made and evaluates their impact on your work, and

5. establishes a productive path for future research.

While the conclusion leaves the reader satisfied, the introduction and title entice someone to read the paper and prepare that person for what is ahead. Surprises are not welcome in research papers, so as part of your good first impression and your contract, you want to use these opening statements to preview your whole paper. Your introduction should

1. communicate your research question and answer (thesis),

2. indicate the cases you are studying, and

3. provide a road map to your paper.

Your title seeks to convey these same first elements (question, answer, and cases) as briefly and memorably as possible. Typically, your title will have two parts to it, separated by a colon, and the clever phrase will come first.

SUGGESTED CALENDAR

As the due date for your paper looms near (no less than a week before you need to turn it in), you should seek to write your conclusion, introduction, and ultimately your title.[2] You need to complete them early because even when these sections are done, you still have some work to do. You need to revise and edit the paper. And you'll have an easier time with these tasks if you can put the paper down and clear your mind for a little while. So follow the advice here, and write those three interrelated sections that each in its own way seeks to capture the whole of the project. When they are done, then you undertake the revising and editing process for one last time. You should now feel a great rush; you are almost done. You can see the finish line ahead, and when you have printed the paper and filled out your last checklist, you can celebrate. Congratulations!

EXERCISES

1. Thinking about Kate's project and the results you saw in chapter 8, draft a conclusion to her paper. Advance two memorable titles for Kate's paper.

2. Given what you know of Latisha's research project, draft an introduction to her paper. (You may assert what you think to be true about what Latisha found.) Advance two memorable titles for Latisha's paper.

3. Develop another clever title for Joe's paper.

CHECKLIST 8: CONCLUSION, INTRODUCTION, AND TITLE

Here is a last rubric to guide you through the final stages of the process. Please take the revising and editing tasks very seriously; even the best writers need to spend a good deal of time working on the logical flow and wording of their work. Again, presentation is very important too. Especially at this stage, good first and last impressions (as well as everything in between) are essential, so consult again the previous rubrics to be sure that each of your sections is in good shape.

Checklist 8: Conclusion, Introduction, and Title

CONCLUSION

Does your conclusion tie the paper together for readers by reminding them of the topic, literature, thesis, methods, and where the weight of the evidence fell (i.e., to what extent your thesis is upheld)?	Yes _____ No _____
Does your conclusion consider whether the choices you made in your research design (selecting cases and operationalizing data sources, survey instruments, or other elements) had an effect on your findings? If you had frustrating results, do you discuss how to do things differently?	Yes _____ No _____
Does your conclusion discuss fruitful avenues for future research?	Yes _____ No _____
Does your conclusion explain why your argument and findings are important and interesting to different audiences (scholars, policymakers, and citizens)?	Yes _____ No _____

(Continued)

Checklist 8: *(Continued)*

Does your conclusion consider whether you can apply your findings to other cases (e.g., from other time periods, to other countries, to other individuals)?	Yes _____ No _____
If you can extend your findings, do you say what your findings would mean for other prominent cases today?	Yes _____ No _____

Introduction

Does your introduction have an appropriate title that communicates the purpose of the section?	Yes _____ No _____
Does your introduction provide some historical or policy background to entice readers, making them want to keep reading because they understand why the topic is important and interesting to multiple audiences?	Yes _____ No _____
Have you included a complete overview of each section of your paper in your introduction?	Yes _____ No _____
Is your thesis clearly stated in your introduction?	Yes _____ No _____
Have you been careful not to copy and paste material from your conclusion (or other parts of the paper) into your introduction?	Yes _____ No _____

Title

Does your title communicate your question, cases, and argument clearly and in as memorable a way as possible?	Yes _____ No _____
Is your title clever or interesting? Would you look at something with that title and say enthusiastically, "I'd like to read this!"	Yes _____ No _____

Revisions

Have you responded to all the previous comments on your earlier drafts?	Yes _____ No _____
Have you checked, by going back to the chapter summaries and earlier checklists, that each of your sections accomplishes what it needs to?	Yes _____ No _____

Have you developed smooth transitions between sections of your paper?   Yes _____ No _____

Have you given the sections of your paper interesting and appropriate titles?   Yes _____ No _____

Have you been sure that any new ideas have been worked through the whole draft?   Yes _____ No _____

Edits

Have you properly cited the sources of your ideas and kept direct quotes to a minimum?   Yes _____ No _____

Have you avoided plagiarism?   Yes _____ No _____

Have you checked for your personal writing concerns?   Yes _____ No _____

Recognizing the limits of spelling and grammar check, have you edited your paper?   Yes _____ No _____

Have you checked for how the paper will look before you print it, being sure there are no orphans or widows?   Yes _____ No _____

Did you ask an outsider to read your paper? Did you take that person's advice in editing/revising?   Yes _____ No _____

Appearance and Format

Have you numbered your pages, but not the title page?   Yes _____ No _____

Does your paper have a title page, with the appropriate information?   Yes _____ No _____

If you have used a long quote, have you indented it and not included quotation marks unless you have a quote within a quote? (See a style manual for how to handle long quotes.)   Yes _____ No _____

Did you include a bibliography or source list that conforms to the style format your professor chose?   Yes _____ No _____

Are your citations done properly?   Yes _____ No _____

NOTES

1. Eviatar Zerubavel, *The Clockwork Muse: A Practical Guide to Writing Theses, Dissertations, and Books* (Cambridge, MA: Harvard University Press, 1999) provides many quotes from famous authors who discuss the inadequacies of their first drafts. Please note, however, that Zerubavel does not advocate revising carefully throughout the process as I have.
2. For a thesis, your goal is to finish with a significant amount of time before the due date. Typically, you will need to spend a good deal of time rethinking and revising such a significant work. For instance, I tell my honors-thesis writers, students who spend a year on their projects, that they should have completed drafts at least a month before the papers are due. Consult your mentor for this timeline.

Glossary

Academic Search Premier—an online database excellent for searching for information from scholarly journals, newsmagazines, and newspapers.

American politics—a subfield in the discipline of political science, where the focus is the U.S. government and the American political process.

Analysis and Assessment—a section of your research paper, also called the Data Analysis or Case Study section. In this part of the paper, you evaluate your hypothesis or thesis based on the plan that you have established for yourself in your research design. You tell the story of the relationship between the variables or key factors in your argument in this section.

Annotated bibliography—a list of sources cited in appropriate bibliographic form that also includes a paragraph summary of the argument and the most important information from each one. To prepare for the literature review, you can group these sources into common schools of thought and give them labels, although not all annotated bibliographies will be done in this manner.

Anthology—an edited book that contains a collection of articles.

Argument—also called a thesis or hypothesis. This is your best-guess answer in response to your research question. In your paper, you determine whether you can sustain your argument based on logic, normative claims (for normative papers), and evidence (for empirical research).

Case—one incident of the phenomenon that you are studying. If you're interested in voting behavior, for instance, you could conceive of each voter as a case.

Case study—in qualitative research, an in-depth analysis of one particular incident. For instance, if you were studying the causes of intervention in the post–Cold War era, one case study would be an analysis of the American intervention in Haiti. Case studies may be part of the Analysis and Assessment portion of the paper, and the hypothesis always guides them.

Causation (causal relationship)—an instance when at least one factor (cause) brings about an effect. Adjustments in one factor necessarily occur with changes in the other.

Colloquialisms—informal language or ways of communicating. The research paper is a formal form of communication, so you should avoid colloquialisms unless, of course, you are communicating and analyzing colloquialisms as data from interviews, documents, or surveys. Otherwise, avoid slang, second person pronouns, and other informal language.

Comparative politics—one of the subfields in political science in which students examine why politics is the way it is in different states around the world. The focus here is on using the comparative method and developing general understandings of political institutions, processes, and cultures as well as appreciating the differences between regions and polities.

Conceptual research—research in which the inquiry typically explores the meaning of key ideas or terms in politics by looking at the works of important political philosophers or theorists and evaluating their logic.

Conclusion—the last section of your research paper. It accomplishes five tasks: reminds the reader of the thesis and where the weight of the evidence came down, discusses why the argument and the particular findings are important and what they mean to various audiences, assesses the versatility and limits of your thesis, critically evaluates your accomplishments, and serves as a jumping-off point for future research.

Content analysis—a form of data analysis in which the researcher evaluates texts to determine the numerical incidences of (quantitative) or the general disposition toward (qualitative) particular words, phrases, or themes.

Continuous variable—a variable that will hold values that range along a continuum. It can also be referred to as an interval variable.

Control—the attempt to minimize the impact of other factors on your study. In selecting cases, you try to hold other factors constant to eliminate or reduce the possible effects of other variables on your subject.

Correlation—instances when two or more factors change together. Adjustments in one factor necessarily occur with changes in the other, but changes in one factor do not necessarily cause changes in the other.

Data—pieces of information to be used to evaluate your argument, thesis, or hypothesis. Data can be either qualitative or quantitative.

Database—an online resource of information. Often this consists of multiple years of many journals, newspapers, or other media sources. It can also consist of information collected by a particular organization, such as the UN Human Development statistics. Typically, you must access this information through a library; it is not available freely on the Internet.

Dependent variable—the effect or phenomenon under investigation. It depends on some other factors (the causes or independent variables). It is a variable because depending on which value the cause takes on, the effect will change.

Dummy variable—in regression analysis, a variable that measures the presence or absence of a characteristic. For instance, we might be looking at female or not (i.e., male), Caucasian or not, or Catholic or not.

Edit—the process of fixing grammatical, punctuation, or word choice errors.

Empirical—observable, the part of a research paper that examines the evidence. Within the discipline, there are three kinds of empirical research, theory-advancing research, public policy analysis, and conceptual research. Theory-advancing and public policy work is also based on a correlation or causal relationship, while conceptual research explores meanings. Still, to assess the arguments for any of these three types, researchers must turn to evidence.

Evidence—data or information relevant to your thesis, which helps you determine the extent to which the argument is sustainable.

Fragment—an incomplete sentence.

Google—an extremely powerful search engine for the Internet. While most students immediately think that they should Google a topic when they want information about it, in this book you learn that you often should check databases for scholarly information first. For all kinds of information, you should always use the Internet with care, picking only sites whose veracity you can trust.

Grammar check—a word-processing function that finds grammatical errors.

Heading—a title for a section of your paper. Research papers should be written in sections, and each of the sections should have a heading. Headings are not substitutes for transitions, but they mark a change in emphasis. Be sure to consult your style manual because each form can treat capitalization and placement of headings differently.

Hypothesis—your preferred answer to your research question, often synonymous with *argument* and *thesis* in common usage. In an empirical paper the hypothesis takes the form, "The more of X (independent variable), the more of Y (dependent variable)," for a positive relationship of continuous variables or, "If X is A, then Y is B, but if X is C, then Y is D," for a category variable.

Independent variable—the cause of the effect or phenomenon under investigation. Changes in the independent variable necessarily cause changes in the effect or dependent variable.

Indicator—in transforming a concept into a variable (operationalizing), indicators are the factors that you will look at to come up with the value of your variable. In our example in the text, the strength of state institutions was a function of three indicators: (1) competitiveness of political parties, (2) the nature of security forces, and (3) the economic conditions in the polity.

International relations—a subfield in political science (sometimes also called "international politics"). It examines the interactions and external behaviors of states, international organizations, and other international nongovernmental organizations as well as the norms and identities that develop among these actors over time.

Interval data—one of three types of data. Interval data are pieces of information that can be expressed in numeric form (e.g., spending, dollars, votes). If both your independent and dependent variable can be measured with interval data, then you should use regression analysis to evaluate your hypothesis.

Introduction—the first section of your research paper. It is a very important section because it makes that vital first impression on your reader. A type of contract between you and the reader, the introduction establishes the parameters of your work. In general, your introduction will begin by stating your specific research question (preferably not in question form), continue by explaining why this question is interesting and important to different audiences (political scientists, policymakers, and citizens), and provide a road map to the rest of the paper, introducing the reader very briefly to your schools of thought, your argument, your cases, and your findings.

Journal of opinion—a magazine that has a clear ideological leaning. Excellent ones include, among others, the *Weekly Standard* (conservative) and the *American Prospect* (liberal/progressive). These sources are excellent places to find controversial issues for study.

Journal Storage: The Scholarly Archive (JSTOR)—an online database that you can search to find articles from the premier journals in the social sciences, humanities, and natural sciences.

LexisNexis—an online database for searching legal sources (Lexis) and news sources (Nexis) from around the world.

Literature—for academics, this term means the key scholarly articles and books on a particular topic.

Literature Review—the second section of your paper, following the introduction. The literature review is an analysis of the scholarly debate on your research question in its general and specific forms. The literature review uncovers the multiple answers that scholars studying the same general question have given and groups these answers into schools of thought. In this section, you give each school a label, which can be standards in the field or specific, new ones that you have developed.

Measurement strategy—also called operationalization. It is your plan for transforming the concepts that you have identified in your hypothesis into knowable entities. A measurement need not be numeric, but it must help you determine a value for your variable.

Methodology—the approaches that you are going to use to evaluate your hypothesis, all spelled out in your Research Design section.

Model—a pictorial representation of the variables in the most-preferred school of thought that was identified in the literature review, typically presented in the X (independent variable) → Y (dependent variable) form. In empirical papers, it is found in the Model and Hypothesis section.

Model and Hypothesis—a brief but important section of an empirical paper, coming after the literature review. In it, you clearly identify the independent and dependent variables and present them in X → Y form (the model). While the model helps you zero in on the cause and effect, the hypothesis explains precisely how the variables are linked to each other. The hypothesis is written in sentence form, usually in the structure, "The more of X, the more of Y" (for positive relationships of continuous variables), or, "If X is A, then Y is B" (for category variables).

Monograph—a scholarly work published as a book on a specialized topic.

Negative relationship—a relationship that occurs if the increase in the causal factor (independent variable) leads to a decrease in the effect (dependent variable). If the relationship were charted, the curve would be downward sloping and therefore the slope would be negative.

Nonempirical—relying not on data or facts but rather on equations, logic, or values.

Normative—explicitly concerned with values and what ought to or should be. In political science, research often is both normative and empirical, although for research papers as conceived of here, the emphasis is on the empirical.

Observed value—information that you collected or observed. This terminology is typically used in quantitative analysis.

Operationalization—the process of transforming the concepts that you have identified in your hypothesis into knowable entities (variables). Also called a measurement strategy. You accomplish this important task in your research design.

Ordinal measure—information that comes in category form, but the categories can be rank ordered on some criteria (e.g., along an ideological spectrum). You cannot, however, specify the exact distance between the categories. (If you could specify that distance, then this information would be interval, not ordinal.)

Orphan—a bit of text (e.g., the first line of a paragraph or a chart) that appears as a single line at the bottom of a page. Before you turn in a final draft, you should unite all orphans with at least part of their "families" by moving the page break.

Page break—at the end of a typed page, where the text stops. Sometimes, when including charts, graphs, or new section headings, you may have to force a page break so that these graphics or headings and text can appear together.

Paraphrase—to rewrite the sense of another author's text. Paraphrases are always footnoted, but they are significantly different from the original text. To paraphrase appropriately, you typically have to close the book or file and work to distill the sense of a much larger text into a smaller one.

Passive construction—a type of sentence structure in which the subject is not performing the action of the verb. Examples of passive construction include, "It was Pakistan that was the first Muslim country to develop a nuclear bomb," or, "Nuclear weapons in the Muslim world were first developed by Pakistan." The preferred construction is called **active,** and the active voice can communicate the above ideas as, "Pakistan was the first Muslim state to develop nuclear weapons."

Peer review—the policy of having peers read and evaluate a text. With respect to journals, peer-reviewed ones send out any piece that comes in for consideration to other experts to review and approve. This is the type of source you need to consult for a literature review.

Political theory—the subfield in political science that examines the foundations of politics and political ideas, typically by examining the works of key political philosophers. Sometimes this body of work is called "the canon." This subfield is also referred to as "political thought" or "political philosophy."

Positive relationship—a relationship that occurs between two variables if the increase in the causal factor (independent variable) would lead to an increase in the effect (dependent variable). If the relationship were charted, the curve would be upward sloping and therefore the slope would be positive.

Project MUSE—an online database that you can search to find articles in prestigious journals in the humanities and social sciences.

ProQuest—an online database, excellent for searching for information from scholarly journals, newsmagazines, and newspapers.

Prove—to show something to be true. In the social sciences, we are seeking not to prove our hypotheses but to evaluate whether they hold true in certain instances or not. If you're interested in proofs, become a mathematician!

Proxy variable—a variable that will stand in for another. At times we can't actually calculate our desired concept, such as the probability of war, so we develop a suitable substitute (proxy) for it.

Public policy research—the investigation of contemporary problems and their solutions to see what can be done to fix them and how well solutions are working. This is a form of empirical research.

Puzzle—in political science, an intellectual dilemma typically regarding an event or development that lacks obvious answers or whose obvious answers appear to be incorrect. Puzzles are excellent inspirations for a research question, and if you've found one, your puzzle should figure prominently in your paper's introduction.

Qualitative analysis—a form of analysis in which the evidence is in the form of words.

Quantitative analysis—a form of analysis in which the evidence is numeric and the ultimate assessment depends on statistics.

Reify—to think of an abstract concept as real. When operationalizing concepts and coming up with quantitative measures, be sure to avoid reifying. For example, the balance of power is a concept that is useful in political science, but it is not an existing reality.

Reliability—the repeated ability to arrive at the same value of your concept, regardless of who is doing the measuring. Reliable measures mean that investigator bias is minimized, and the goal in operationalization is to have measures that are both reliable and valid.

Report—a traditional paper (i.e., one that you would write prior to reading this book) in which you describe everything you can find out about a political phenomenon or process. A report is typically organized by chronology. In this book, a report contrasts with a research paper, and after learning how to write a research paper, you will never write reports for your political science classes again!

Research Design—the section in the research paper that follows the Model and Hypothesis section, in which you present your plan for carrying out your research and your justification for this approach. Typically, it consists of five subsections: selection of cases, operationalization of concepts, identification of sources, methods for generating information (surveys, questionnaires, etc.), and methodological discussion.

Research question—the specific question that your paper seeks to answer. For empirical papers it usually begins with "Why," "How," "To what extent," "Under what conditions," or "What is the significance of concept X," and for normative ones it usually starts with "Ought," "Should," "What ought" or "How Should."

Revise—the process of making macro-level changes to your text so that each section of the paper accomplishes its necessary tasks and the logic is consistent throughout. At times, revising requires changing, deleting, moving, or adding major ideas and sections to your paper.

Road map—also called an overview. A part of your introduction, it is a basic sketch or outline of your whole paper written in paragraph or sentence form. In the road map, you provide a short summary of each of the other sections of the paper (Literature Review, Model and Hypothesis, Research Design, Analysis and Assessment, and Conclusion).

Sample—a subset of the universe of cases. You must choose your sample very carefully to minimize bias and to achieve both control and variation.

Scatterplot—a graphing of the data, with the independent variable along the x-axis and the dependent variable along the y-axis.

Scholar—a professor (working at a university or college) or a person employed by a think tank, public policy institute, or governmental institute. These people tend to publish their work in what are called peer-reviewed outlets, publications with a policy of sending out any piece that comes in for consideration to other experts to review and approve.

Scholarly source—a source in which scholars publish, such as a peer-reviewed journal or a book published by a university press or other publishing house that uses other academic experts to review works before deciding to publish them.

School of thought—in your literature review, the multiple, scholarly answers to the research question that you identify. Each answer typically posits a different causal variable to account for the same effect (dependent variable). Each school of thought should have a label and at least one academic associated with it.

Secondary source—a source of information that has been "processed," that is, interpreted by someone else. Be careful in using secondary sources in your Analysis and Assessment section because some other student of your research question (the author of your source) has already interpreted the data to reach his or her conclusion.

Spelling check—a word-processing function that finds spelling errors.

Subfield—an area of inquiry in an academic discipline. In American political science, there are at least six: American politics, political theory, comparative politics, international relations, public policy, and methodology.

Test a hypothesis—to determine whether the data are consistent with your best guess. This is the purpose of the Analysis and Assessment section of your paper. Please note that your goal is not to prove your hypothesis but to evaluate it. You are not an advocate for your hypothesis.

Theory-advancing research—empirical research that is basic in nature; that is, it seeks to uncover truths about politics instead of solving a practical problem. This type of research typically answers a "why" or "how is it possible" question.

Thesaurus—a reference or word-processing function that allows you to find synonyms and antonyms, especially useful in varying word choice so that you are not constantly using the same word or phrase. Have your thesaurus handy during the editing stage.

Thesis—a contentious statement, that is, a declaration or description with which reasonable people could disagree. A thesis can be either a normative claim or an empirically verifiable contention. This term is often used as a synonym for *argument* or *hypothesis*.

Title—the name of your paper and another important way (along with your introduction) to make an excellent first impression. A good title communicates your research question or puzzle, cases, and findings in a provocative, evocative, alliterative, or otherwise appealing way.

Topic—an area of inquiry that typically can be described. In writing a research paper, you need to transform your topic into a research question so that you can explain or illustrate an argument.

Universe of cases—all the possible events of the phenomenon under study. For instance, if you were studying American presidential elections, the universe of cases would be all the elections for president from George Washington's first election to the most recent contest.

Validity—when a measure accurately captures the essence of your concept. Part of the challenge in operationalization is to find ways to conceive of and the corresponding data that reflect your precise concept. The best operationalization strategies will create measures that are both valid and reliable.

Variable—anything that can vary, that is, change in value.

Widow—a bit of text (e.g., the last line of a paragraph or a chart) that appears alone at the beginning of a new page. Before you turn in a final draft, you should bring all widows back with at least part of their "families" (their sections or text) by moving the page break.

Word choice—the language that you use. When editing, readers may note word choice problems, which typically means that you have used improper language or you are overusing certain terms.

Bibliography

Abramowitz, Alan I. *The Disappearing Center: Engaged Citizens, Polarization, and American Democracy.* New Haven, CT: Yale University Press, 2010.

Appleby, R. Scott. *Ambivalence of the Sacred: Religion, Violence and Reconciliation.* Lanham, MD: Rowman & Littlefield, 1999.

Azpuru, Dinorah. "The Salience of Ideology: Fifteen Years of Presidential Elections in El Salvador." *Latin American Politics & Society* 52, no. 2 (2010): 103–138.

Baumer, Donald C., and Howard J. Gold. *Parties, Polarization and Democracy in the United States.* Boulder, CO: Paradigm, 2010.

Borer, Tristan Anne, ed. *Telling the Truths: Truth Telling and Peace Building in Post-conflict Societies.* Notre Dame, IN: University of Notre Dame Press, 2006.

Boyd, Richard. "Thomas Hobbes and the Perils of Pluralism." *Journal of Politics* 63 (2001): 392–413.

Breuning, Marijke, Paul Parker, and John T. Ishiyama. "The Last Laugh: Skill Building through a Liberal Arts Political Science Curriculum." *PS: Political Science and Politics* 34, no. 3 (2001): 657–661.

Bystrom, Dianne G., Mary Christine Banwart, Lynda Lee Kaid, and Terry A. Robertson. *Gender and Candidate Communication: VideoStyle, WebStyle, NewsStyle.* New York: Routledge, 2004.

Call, Charles T. "Democratisation, War and State-building: Constructing the Rule of Law in El Salvador." *Journal of Latin American Studies* 35, no. 4 (2003): 827–862. www.jstor.com.

Call, Charles T., and E. M. Cousens. "Ending Wars and Building Peace: International Responses to War-torn Societies." *International Studies Perspectives* 9, no. 1 (2008): 1–21. www.ebscohost.com.

Call, Charles T., and Vanessa Hawkins Wyeth, eds. *Building States to Build Peace.* Boulder, CO: Lynne Reinner, 2008.

Campbell, Donald T., and Julian C. Stanley. *Experimental and Quasi-experimental Designs for Research.* Boston: Houghton Mifflin, 1963.

Crocker, Chester A., Fen Osler Hampson, and Pamela Aall, eds. *Leashing the Dogs of War: Conflict Management in a Divided World.* Washington, DC: USIP Press, 2007.

Deans, Thomas. *Writing and Community Action: A Service-Learning Rhetoric with Readings.* New York: Longman, 2003.

Dolan, Kathleen. "Do Women Candidates Play to Gender Stereotypes? Do Men Candidates Play to Women?" *Political Research Quarterly* 58, no. 1 (2005): 31–44.

Doty, Roxanne Lynn. "Foreign Policy as Social Construction: A Post-positivist Analysis of U.S. Counterinsurgency Policy in the Philippines." *International Studies Quarterly* 37, no. 3 (September 1993): 297–320. www.jstor.com.

"Evaluating Web Sources." First-year Seminar Library Modules, Saint Joseph's University. http://librarytoolkits.sju.edu/content.php?pid=103334&sid=776924.

Farrar-Myers, Victoria A., and Diana Dwyre. *Limits and Loopholes: The Quest for Money, Free Speech, and Fair Elections.* Washington, DC: CQ Press, 2007.

Fiorina, Morris P., with Samuel J. Abrams. *Disconnect: The Breakdown of Representation in American Politics.* Norman: University of Oklahoma Press, 2009.

Fiorina, Morris P., with Samuel J. Abrams and Jeremy C. Pope. *Culture War? The Myth of a Polarized America.* 3rd ed. New York: Pearson Longman, 2006.

Freedom House. "Country Ratings and Status, FIW 1973–2010 (Excel)." http://www.freedomhouse.org/template.cfm?page=439.

Gaddis, John Lewis. *We Now Know: Rethinking Cold War History.* New York: Oxford University Press, 1997.

"General Election Turnout Rates." http://elections.gmu.edu/Turnout_2008G.html.

George, Alexander L., and Andrew Bennett. *Case Studies and Theory Development in the Social Sciences.* Cambridge, MA: MIT Press, 2004.

Hacker, Diana. *A Pocket Manual of Style.* 5th ed. Boston: Bedford/St. Martin's, 2009.

Hayner, Priscilla B. *Unspeakable Truths: Transitional Justice and the Challenge of Truth Commissions.* 2nd ed. New York: Routledge, 2010.

Herrnson, Paul S., J. Celeste Lay, and Atiya Kai Stokes. "Women Running 'as Women': Candidate Gender, Campaign Issues, and Voter-targeting Strategies." *Journal of Politics* 65, no. 1 (2003): 244–255.

Holiday, David. "El Salvador's Model Democracy." *Current History* 104, no. 279 (2005): 77–82. www.proquest.com.

International Foundation for Electoral Systems. "Election Guide." http://www.election-guide.org/election.php?ID=633.

Joes, Anthony James. *America and Guerrilla Warfare.* Lexington: University Press of Kentucky, 2000.

Johnson, Janet Buttolph, and Richard A. Joslyn. *Political Science Research Methods.* 3rd ed. Washington, DC: Congressional Quarterly, 1995.

Johnson, Janet Buttolph, and H. T. Reynolds, with Jason D. Mycoff. *Political Science Research Methods.* 6th ed. Washington, DC: Congressional Quarterly, 2008.

Jones, Seth G. *In the Graveyard of Empires: America's War in Afghanistan.* New York: Norton, 2009.

Kahn, Kim Fridkin. "Gender Differences in Campaign Messages: The Political Advertisements of Men and Women Candidates for U.S. Senate." *Political Research Quarterly* 46, no. 3 (1993): 481–502.

Katznelson, Ira, and Helen V. Milner, eds. *Political Science: State of the Discipline.* Centennial ed. *New York: Norton, 2005.*

Kaufmann, Chaim. "Possible and Impossible Solutions to Ethnic Civil Wars." *International Security* 29, no. 4 (1996): 136–174. www.jstor.com.

Klare, Michael T. "Redefining Security: The New Global Schisms." *Current History* 95, no. 206 (November 1996): 353–358. www.ebscohost.com.

Kreps, Sarah E. *Coalitions of Convenience: United States Military Interventions after the Cold War.* New York: Oxford University Press, 2010.

Lederach, John Paul. *Building Peace: Sustainable Reconciliation in Divided Societies.* Washington, DC: USIP Press, 1998.

"Left-winger Wins El Salvador Poll." *BBC News*, March 16, 2009. http://news.bbc.co.uk/2/hi/americas/7944899.stm.

Lijphart, Arend. "Comparative Politics and the Comparative Method." *American Political Science Review* 65 (1971): 682–693.

———. "How the Cases You Choose Determine the Answers You Get." *Journal of Policy Analysis* 2 (1975): 131–152.

Linz, Juan J. "The Perils of Presidentialism." *Journal of Democracy* 1, no. 1 (1990): 51–69.

Linz, Juan J., and Arturo Valenzuela, eds. *The Limits of Presidential Democracy*. Vol. 1. Baltimore: Johns Hopkins University Press, 1994.

Lipset, Seymour Martin. *Political Man: The Social Bases of Politics*. Baltimore: Johns Hopkins University Press, 1981.

———. "Some Social Requisites of Democracy: Economic Development and Political Legitimacy." *American Political Science Review* 53, no. 1 (1959): 69–105.

Lowi, Theodore J. "American Business, Public Policy, Case Studies and Political Theory." *World Politics* 16 (1964): 677–715.

———. *The End of Liberalism: The Second Republic of the United States*. 2nd ed. New York: Norton, 1979.

Malkin, Elisabeth. "Elections in El Salvador Invoke Rivalries of Civil War Years." *New York Times*, March 12, 2009. http://www.nytimes.com/2009/03/12/world/ameri cas/12salvador.html?_r=1&partner=rss&emc=rss.

Mansfield, Edward D., and Jack Snyder. "Democratic Transitions, Institutional Strength, and War." *International Organization* 56, no. 2 (2002): 297–337. http://muse.jhu .edu.

McCann, Michael. *Rights at Work: Pay Equity and the Politics of Legal Mobilization*. Chicago: University of Chicago Press, 1994.

Mearsheimer, John J., and Stephen Van Evera. "When Peace Means War." *New Republic* 213, no. 25 (December 18, 1995): 16–21. www.ebscohost.com.

Merton, Robert K. *Social Theory and Social Structure*. Enlarged ed. New York: Free Press, 1968.

Morgenthau, Hans, and Kenneth W. Thompson. *Politics among Nations: The Struggle for Power and Peace*. 6th ed. New York: Knopf, 1985.

Mutz, Diana C. *Hearing the Other Side: Deliberative versus Participatory Democracy*. New York: Cambridge University Press, 2006.

National Commission on Writing in America's Schools and Colleges. *The Neglected R: The Need for a Writing Revolution*. New York: College Entrance Examination Board, 2003. http://www.collegeboard.com/prod_downloads/writingcom/neglectedr.pdf.

Norris, Pippa, and Ronald Inglehart. "Cultural Obstacles to Equal Representation." *Journal of Democracy* 12, no. 3 (2001): 126–140.

Paris, Roland. *At War's End: Building Peace after Civil Conflict*. New York: Cambridge University Press, 2004.

———. "Bringing the Leviathan Back In: Classical versus Contemporary Studies of the Liberal Peace." *International Studies Review* 8, no. 3 (2006): 425–440. www.jstor .com.

———. "Peacebuilding in Central America: Reproducing the Sources of Conflict?" *International Peacekeeping* 9, no. 4 (2002): 39–68.

Paris, Roland, and Timothy D. Sisk. "Introduction: Understanding the Contradictions of Postwar Statebuilding." In *The Dilemmas of Statebuilding: Confronting the Contradictions of Postwar Peace Operations*, edited by Roland Paris and Timothy D. Sisk, 1–20. New York: Routledge, 2009.

Paris, Roland, and Timothy D. Sisk, eds. *The Dilemmas of Statebuilding: Confronting the Contradictions of Postwar Peace Operations*. New York: Routledge, 2009.

Philpott, Daniel. *The Politics of Past Evil: Religion, Reconciliation and Transitional Justice*. Notre Dame, IN: University of Notre Dame Press, 2006.

Pickering, Paula M. *Peacebuilding in the Balkans: The View from the Ground Floor*. Ithaca, NY: Cornell University Press, 2007.

Przeworski, Adam, and Fernando Limongi Neto. "Modernization: Theories and Facts." *World Politics* 49 (1997): 155–183.

Putnam, Robert D. "Bowling Alone." *Journal of Democracy* 6, no. 1 (1995): 65–78.

———. *Bowling Alone: The Collapse and Revival of American Community.* New York: Simon & Schuster, 2000.

Putnam, Robert D., with Robert Leonardi and Raffaella Y. Nanetti. *Making Democracy Work: Civic Traditions in Modern Italy.* Princeton, NJ: Princeton University Press, 1993.

Rabinow, Paul, and William M. Sullivan, eds. *Interpretive Social Science: A Reader.* Berkeley: University of California Press, 1979.

Rappaport, Ronald, and Walter J. Stone. *Three's a Crowd: The Dynamics of Third Parties, Ross Perot and Republican Resurgence.* Ann Arbor: University of Michigan Press, 2005.

Richmond, Oliver P. "Critical Research Agendas for Peace: The Missing Link in the Study of International Relations." *Alternatives* 32, no. 2 (2007): 247–274.

Robinson, Michael, and Susan Ellis. "Purple America." *Weekly Standard* 9, no. 46 (2004): 27–29.

Rosenberg, Gerald. *The Hollow Hope: Can Courts Bring About Social Change?* Chicago: University of Chicago Press, 1991.

Sabato, Larry, ed. *The Sixth Year Itch: The Rise and Fall of the George W. Bush Presidency.* New York: Pearson Longman, 2008.

Schrag, Peter. *Paradise Lost: California's Experience, America's Future.* New York: New Press, 1998.

Shively, W. Phillips. *The Craft of Political Research.* 5th ed. Upper Saddle River, NJ: Prentice Hall, 2002.

———. *The Craft of Political Research.* 6th ed. Upper Saddle River, NJ: Prentice Hall, 2005.

Smith, Daniel A., and Caroline J. Tolbert. *Educated by Initiative: The Effects of Direct Democracy on Citizens and Political Organizations in the American States.* Ann Arbor: University of Michigan Press, 2004.

Taylor, Charles. "Interpretation and the Sciences of Man." In *Interpretive Social Science: A Reader,* edited by Paul Rabinow and William M. Sullivan, 25–71. Berkeley: University of California Press, 1979.

Thomas, Gwynn, and Melinda Adams. "Breaking the Final Glass Ceiling: The Influence of Gender in the Elections of Ellen Johnson-Sirleaf and Michelle Bachelet." *Journal of Women, Politics & Policy* 31 (2010): 105–131.

West, Darrell M. *Brain Gain: Rethinking U.S. Immigration Policy.* Washington, DC: Brookings Institution Press, 2010.

World Bank. "El Salvador." http://data.worldbank.org/country/el-salvador.

———. "GNI Per Capita, Atlas Method (Current US$)." http://data.worldbank.org/indicator/NY.GNP.PCAP.CD?page=3.

Yglesias, Matthew. "The Great Divider." *American Prospect* 18, no. 4 (2007): 47–49.

Zerubavel, Eviatar. *The Clockwork Muse: A Practical Guide to Writing Theses, Dissertations, and Books.* Cambridge, MA: Harvard University Press, 1999.

Index